The Audubon Society Master Guide to Birding

A Chanticleer Press Edition

Consultants
Davis W. Finch
Paul Lehman
J. V. Remsen, Jr.

Peter D. Vickery
Richard Webster
Claudia Wilds

Authors
Henry T. Armistead
Larry R. Ballard
George F. Barrowclough
Louis R. Bevier
Peter F. Cannell
David F. DeSante
Kim R. Eckert
John Farrand, Jr.
Davis W. Finch
Kimball L. Garrett
Daniel D. Gibson
Richard E. Johnson
Kenn Kaufman
Ben King
Wesley E. Lanyon
Paul Lehman
Dennis J. Martin
Harold F. Mayfield
Kenneth C. Parkes
Roger F. Pasquier
Wayne R. Petersen
H. Douglas Pratt
J. V. Remsen, Jr.
David Stirling
Paul W. Sykes, Jr.
Scott B. Terrill
Theodore G. Tobish Jr.
Jack Van Benthuysen

The Audubon Society Master Guide to Birding

3 Warblers to Sparrows

John Farrand, Jr.,
Editor

 Alfred A. Knopf, New York

This is a Borzoi Book
Published by Alfred A. Knopf, Inc.

Prepared and produced by
Chanticleer Press, Inc., New York.

Color reproductions by Nievergelt Repro AG, Zurich, Switzerland.
Type set in Century Expanded by Dix Type Inc., Syracuse,
New York. Printed and bound by Dai Nippon Printing Co., Ltd.,
Tokyo, Japan.

First Printing
Library of Congress Catalog Number: 83-47945
ISBN: 0-394-53383-6

Contents

6

Acknowledgments

This book was written not only for the birders of North America but by them. While preparing these guides even my non-birding associates at Chanticleer Press became converts. I was gratified when an enthusiastic group turned out recently in the early morning for a staff bird walk in Central Park. I wish to celebrate the spirit of my colleagues and to thank them for their good will and their professional help.

I am deeply grateful to the authors of the species accounts, both for their expert prose and for suggestions on what photographs and artwork were necessary to accompany their text, and for numerous suggestions and advice. Without their enthusiastic and industrious cooperation, this book would not have been possible. I am equally thankful to the authors of the special text sections, whose contributions have expanded the scope of the book.

Davis W. Finch, Paul Lehman, and J. V. Remsen served as consultants and read all or some of the species accounts. Their careful perusal of the text resulted in many improvements, and the authors and editors are indebted to them.

In addition to the authors and consultants, thanks are due to many other birders and ornithologists for suggestions, advice, encouragement, and additional tangible assistance in the preparation of this series. I would like to make special mention of John Bull of the American Museum of Natural History for his frequent advice on nomenclature and distribution. Others who have assisted the authors and editors are Dennis J. Abbott, Paul Adamus, C. Wesley Biggs, Paul A. Buckley, William S. Clark, Elaine Cook, Betty Darling Cotrille, Robert H. Day, Joseph DiCostanzo, Matthew P. Drennan, Jon Dunn, R. Michael Erwin, Norm Famous, Frank B. Gill, Sharon Goldwasser, Delphine Haley, John P. Hubbard, George L. Hunt, Jr., Ned K. Johnson, Lars Jonsson, Ivy Kuspit, Mary LeCroy, Lori Leonardi, Trevor Lloyd-Evans, Fred E. Lohrer, Frederick C. Mish, Burt L. Monroe, Jr., Gale Monson, Joe Morlan, J. P. Myers, John P. O'Neill, Dennis R. Paulson, Roger Tory Peterson, William C. Russell, Lawrence A. Ryel, Gary D. Schnell, Fred C. Sibley, Kenneth K. Tate, Michael H. Tove, Guy A. Tudor, Barbara Vickery, Peter Warshall, Bret Whitney, Janet Witzeman, and Alan Wormington.

I am deeply indebted to Arnold Small, Kenneth Fink, Herbert Clarke, and the 203 other photographers whose work forms the bulk of the color illustrations in these volumes. I would like to thank Thomas H. Davis, who helped to identify the difficult plumages of gulls, and Stephen A. Bailey for his assistance in selecting photographs of western *Empidonax* flycatchers. I appreciate the help of Robert Cardillo, Martine Culbertson, Alec Forbes-Watson, and Mark Robbins of VIREO, the growing library of bird photographs at the Academy of Natural Sciences in Philadelphia, for their hospitality and willingness to make their files available to me; to Charles Walcott and David Blanton of the Laboratory of Ornithology at Cornell University for permitting us to use their photograph collection for this project; and to Helen Kittinger of the Alabama Ornithological Society for generously sharing the photograph collections of that organization.

Of the many fine bird artists whose work so enhances this book, I am especially indebted to art editor Al Gilbert, who took on the task of assigning the paintings and drawings, coordinated the efforts of the team of artists he assembled, and executed many fine paintings himself, and to art consultant Guy A. Tudor, whose valuable advice was frequently sought and generously given. The other artists who have contributed their work to this book are James E. Coe, Michael DiGiorgio, Georges Dremeaux, Robert

Gillmor, H. Jon Janosik, Michel Kleinbaum, Lawrence B. McQueen, John P. O'Neill, John C. Yrizarry, and Dale A. Zimmerman. All of these artists have been inspired by the late George M. Sutton, and many have benefited from his direct tutelage in the art of bird painting. "Doc" Sutton would surely have been proud of the illustrations herein—of their lifelike quality and the careful attention to proper habitat. The artists would like to dedicate their work in these volumes to the memory of George M. Sutton—ornithologist, teacher, friend, and one of America's greatest painters of bird life.

Special thanks are due to the authorities of several museums for making specimens available to the artists and authors: Lester L. Short and his staff at the American Museum of Natural History; Ralph W. Schreiber and Kimball L. Garrett of the Los Angeles County Museum of Natural History; J. V. Remsen and John P. O'Neill of the Louisiana State University Museum of Zoology; and Stephen M. Russell of the Department of Ecology and Evolutionary Biology at the University of Arizona.

To Les Line, Editor-in-Chief of Audubon magazine, I am indebted for his early endorsement of the idea of this work, and for his constant encouragement during its preparation.

I am very grateful to Massimo Vignelli, who translated the concept of the book into an effective and workable design.

At Chanticleer Press, I owe a debt of gratitude to Paul Steiner for his energetic and wholehearted enthusiasm for the project since its earliest stages; to Gudrun Buettner for the original conception of the book and for her spirited assistance in solving editorial and graphic problems during the preparation of the series; to Susan Costello, whose encouragement and problem-solving abilities have done much to make this book what it is; to Ann Whitman for her assistance in editing and coordinating the manuscript in its various stages and her seemingly tireless attention to editorial details; to Mary Beth Brewer for her invaluable help in editing the special essays and organizing the material to enable us to meet our deadlines; to Carol Nehring, for the knowledge and expertise she brought to bear on the layouts, and her assistants Laurie Baker, Ayn Svoboda, and Karen Wollman; to Helga Lose and Amy Roche, for their expert efforts in ensuring the accuracy of color reproductions and shepherding the project through its intricate production stages; to Edward Douglas for his assistance in gathering and selecting the tens of thousands of photographs that were reviewed during the preparation of this book; and to Karel Birnbaum, Katherine Booz, Lori Renn, and Susan Van Pelt for their assistance in editorial matters.

At Alfred A. Knopf, Inc., I wish to extend my appreciation to Robert Gottlieb and Anthony M. Schulte, whose sponsorship of the project and confidence in it made this ambitious work possible; to Charles Elliott for his unwavering support and help in shaping the editorial content of the work; to Angus Cameron for his far-ranging knowledge of natural history; and to Barbara Bristol, who should be commended for her competent stewardship of the guides.

John Farrand, Jr.

The Audubon Society

The National Audubon Society is among the oldest and largest
private conservation organizations in the world. With over 500,000
members and more than 480 local chapters across the country,
the Society works in behalf of our natural heritage through
environmental education and conservation action. It protects wildlife
in more than 70 sanctuaries from coast to coast. It also operates
outdoor education centers and ecology workshops and publishes the
prizewinning *Audubon* magazine, *American Birds* magazine,
newsletters, films, and other educational materials. For further
information regarding membership in the Society, write to the
National Audubon Society, 950 Third Avenue, New York, New
York 10022.

Preface

For years the birding community has been waiting for an advanced field guide, one that would include the increasingly sophisticated and subtle clues to bird identification discovered in recent decades. These have been brought to light by birders whose expertise may lie with a particular group of birds, the birds of a specific habitat or region, or a single species. The new information resulting from these field studies has validated our assumption that it is impossible for an individual birder to know everything about all the species on our continent.

For this reason we have tried to prepare the most complete, up-to-date, and useful field identification guide ever devised. We began by assembling a distinguished panel of expert authors from all parts of the continent, from Florida to Alaska and California to Maine. The 61 authors contributed 835 species accounts in their areas of concentration or wrote special essays; consultants with a special understanding of both the eastern and the western regions reviewed the text. In addition, we asked the authors to advise us on photographs required to illustrate each species. In some instances a single photograph was sufficient; in others up to six pictures were required. We invited the most accomplished bird photographers to submit their work. From the tens of thousands of transparencies that we reviewed, we selected those that best show the diagnostic field marks of each bird. To illustrate those rare or elusive species that are infrequently photographed, we commissioned nine well-known artists to paint portraits of the birds in their habitats. Artists also provided the hundreds of black-and-white drawings, many of them flight diagrams, to supplement the field marks shown in the color photographs and paintings.

While these guides have been designed to satisfy the demands of advanced birders, we have also supplied beginners with what they need to know to start an absorbing hobby that can last a lifetime. To provide the vital information required during the few seconds a bird may be visible, we list key field marks for each color illustration. For further clarification, those features that can be easily seen are shown with arrows and numbers on the illustration. Maps illustrate the range descriptions are also given. Of interest to birders of all levels are the special essays that expand the scope of the guide by explaining how to find and identify birds and the many ways you can study birds after you have learned to identify them. Rather than present all of this material in a single massive volume, we decided to divide it into three volumes, each of which may be conveniently carried into the field. We have arranged the species according to the latest classification of North American birds adopted by the American Ornithologists' Union in 1982. Accidental species are placed in an appendix of the volume that covers birds related to it.

We hope these guides, with their contributions from many experts, will be what they are intended to be: a master guide to birding.

Part One

Introduction

Bird identification has today almost become a science. Using color, pattern, shape, size, voice, habitat, and behavior, birders are continually finding new ways to distinguish similar species. The journals *American Birds* and *Birding* frequently publish articles on field identification, while at the annual meetings of the American Birding Association, birders attend seminars on how to identify such puzzling groups as storm-petrels, immature gulls, the small sandpipers known as "peeps," and diurnal birds of prey. Birders have spent long hours in the field working out subtle but useful distinctions, such as the differences in the head shapes of gulls, in the wing- and tail-flicking of *Empidonax* flycatchers, and the flight characteristics of storm-petrels. There are now specialists in the identification of shorebirds, gulls, storm-petrels, shearwaters, and hawks. Clues are being found that allow us to differentiate birds that have long been considered indistinguishable.

Birding has come a long way during its history, and the term "birder" itself, in the evolution of its meaning, reflects the change in our attitude toward birds. For centuries a birder was someone who killed birds, usually for sport or for food; Shakespeare used the term in this sense. The modern meaning of the term arose in the 1940s, as birding became an increasingly popular pastime. Today's birders, armed with binoculars, telescopes, and cameras, and aided by the great collections made by the bird students of the 19th century, are vastly more sophisticated than their counterparts of decades ago.

Ludlow Griscom

Born in New York City in 1890, Ludlow Griscom may justly be called the father of modern field identification. He began attending meetings of the Linnaean Society of New York at an early age. Entirely on his own, he set out to learn the birds of the northeastern United States. Later in his life he wrote:

"At a meeting of the Linnaean Society of New York when a school boy, I reported having seen Bicknell's Thrush [a form of the Gray-cheeked Thrush], my identification being based on the erroneous supposition that its call-note was diagnostic. The resultant storm of criticism rendered me practically speechless. Then and there I planned to become a reliable observer and to investigate the scientific possibilities of sight identification."

The results of this determination were not long in coming. Although his prowess in field identification was doubted by many of his colleagues, Griscom developed an ability to identify birds in the field better than anyone else in his time. To prove his point, he finally took one of his friends, a doubting Thomas, into the field. When Griscom identified a small bird high in the trees overhead as a female Cape May Warbler, his friend was skeptical but prepared. Having brought along his shotgun, he collected the bird. When the specimen was retrieved from the ground, they found it was, as Griscom had said, a female Cape May Warbler. After a few more incidents of this kind, the idea that birds were identifiable while still alive and in the field began to gain ground.

The 19th Century

The practice of shooting birds rather than just looking at them was standard among serious ornithologists in North America before Griscom's time. The main method of study for men like Alexander Wilson, John James Audubon, and Thomas Nuttall was to shoot the birds they encountered and then identify them in the hand.

Most birders were men of leisure or professional collectors, and their attention was devoted to discovering new species of birds and documenting, with specimens, the ranges of these species. Although these pioneering ornithologists learned much about the habits of birds, as an examination of Wilson's nine-volume *American Ornithology* or Audubon's five-volume *Ornithological Biography* will attest, there was only one way to enter the field of ornithology— armed with a shotgun.

Gaining a knowledge of birds in the first half of the 19th century was a long and arduous task, the work of a lifetime. North American birds were still poorly understood; many species had not yet been discovered, and males and females of a single bird were sometimes considered separate species. Throughout much of the 19th century, for instance, there were thought to be three species of waterthrushes, rather than two. Moreover, the differences between species that had been discovered were sometimes unappreciated; it was not until 1811, for example, that Alexander Wilson established that the Common Nighthawk and the Whip-poor-will, two abundant eastern birds, are two separate species. A student of birds during this period faced enormous difficulties; communication between ornithologists was poor, and there was no reliable book on the bird life of North America until 1808, when the first volume of Wilson's *American Ornithology* appeared.

A major ornithological work in its day was Elliott Coues' two-volume *Key to North American Birds*, published in 1872 and still in print in the early 20th century. This monumental book began with a 58-page section entitled "Field Ornithology: being a manual for the collecting, preparing, and preserving of birds." In counseling beginning ornithologists, Coues stated: "The Double-barrelled Shot Gun is your main reliance."

The only bird records that were accepted were those accompanied by a specimen. This attitude is succinctly stated in an expression common among ornithologists of the day: "What's hit is history; what's missed is mystery." Private collectors assembled large cabinets of bird specimens, just as entomologists do today. These specimens eventually found their way into public institutions and now form the core of the collections of many museums.

Toward the end of the 19th century, the shotgun began to give way to binoculars and telescopes. By then nearly all North American bird species had been discovered and their ranges established with collected specimens; the sequence of their molts and plumages was generally understood. This gradual change came about partly because ornithologists were turning their attention to the study of living birds in the field and partly, perhaps, because of the growing public distaste for killing birds that were not game birds or species thought to be harmful to crops and livestock. Books began to appear in which field identification was stressed. Foremost among these were Frank M. Chapman's *Handbook of Birds of Eastern North America*, published in 1895, and Florence Merriam Bailey's *Handbook of Birds of Western North America*, which appeared in 1902. Both of these books were less cumbersome than earlier bird books had been, and had briefer descriptions. But even Chapman's book included complicated "keys" intended for identification in the hand, and Chapman considered a shotgun an important piece of equipment in bird study.

Birding Today

The development of field identification techniques was gradual. As late as 1922 Ludlow Griscom himself had certain reservations that seem amusing today. He wrote, for example, that it was "practically impossible" to distinguish immature Forster's, Arctic, and Common terns, the two species of scaups, male Cooper's and female Sharp-shinned hawks, and immature Blackpoll and Bay-breasted warblers. He considered it "very difficult" to tell apart adult Great and Double-crested cormorants, female Common and Red-breasted mergansers, Snowy Egrets and immature Little Blue Herons,

Greater and Lesser yellowlegs, and Herring and Ring-billed gulls. Yet through the efforts of Griscom and the younger men he influenced, among them Allan D. Cruickshank, Joseph J. Hickey, and Roger Tory Peterson, field identification became respectable. At the same time on the West Coast, Ralph Hoffmann was writing *Birds of the Pacific States;* this ground-breaking book appeared in 1927 and was the first to use the term "field mark"—a term familiar to all birders today. Hoffmann italicized his field marks, just as present-day field guides do, and his descriptions were brief, concentrating on the points of distinction between species.

It was Roger Tory Peterson, a disciple of Griscom but like him largely self-taught, who put field identification on firm footing. His *Field Guide to the Birds* was published in 1934 and his *Field Guide to Western Birds* in 1941, and both have appeared in several editions. These were the first truly compact field guides, and with Peterson's own paintings, they resolved the distinctions between the "impossible" or "very difficult" species that Griscom had listed just a few years earlier. The guides gave field marks for all the species then known to occur regularly in North America. Bird identification was now within the reach of anyone willing to learn about it. No mention was made of shotguns; binoculars and telescopes were standard equipment for birders.

Today only a small number of museum ornithologists still require a specimen to verify an unusual sighting, and specimens have become very difficult to obtain. Federal and state permits are usually issued only to professional ornithologists and stipulate which species and how many specimens may be collected. Moreover, rarities usually turn up in parks, wildlife refuges, and bird sanctuaries—places where collecting is impossible. Birders today often document rarities with a camera and recognize them by using the many new field marks that have been found since Ludlow Griscom first made field identification an exacting and respected pursuit. Griscom once said that the secret to identifying birds in the field was to have as clear a mental image as possible of each species. The mental images of the modern birder are growing clearer every year.

John Farrand, Jr.

Parts of a Bird

Head
1. *Malar streak/*
   Mustache
2. *Throat*
3. *Chin*
4. *Lower mandible*
5. *Upper mandible*
6. *Lores*
7. *Forehead*
8. *Median crown stripe*
9. *Crown*
10. *Eyebrow*
11. *Eye-ring*
12. *Nape*
13. *Ear coverts*

Body
1. *Breast*
2. *Lesser wing coverts/*
   Shoulder
3. *Median wing coverts*
4. *Greater wing coverts*
5. *Belly*
6. *Flanks*
7. *Back*
8. *Scapulars*
9. *Wing bars*
10. *Tertials*
11. *Rump*
12. *Secondaries*
13. *Uppertail coverts*
14. *Outer tail feathers*
15. *Undertail coverts*
16. *Primaries*
17. *Leg/Tarsus*

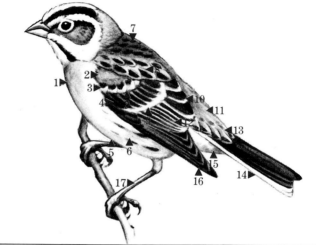

Upperwing Surface
1. *Primaries*
2. *Primary coverts*
3. *Alula*
4. *Wrist*
5. *Lesser wing coverts*
6. *Median wing coverts*
7. *Scapulars*
8. *Greater wing coverts*
9. *Tertials*
10. *Secondaries*

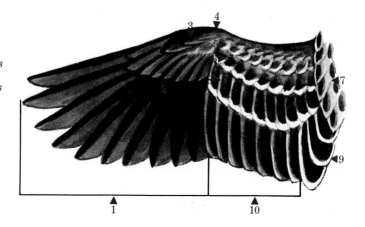

How to Use This Guide

Experienced birders will already know how to use this guide. In each volume the families and species are arranged according to the latest classification of the American Ornithologists' Union, adopted in 1982; this new sequence is followed by professional ornithologists. In all, the three volumes treat 68 families and 835 species. All but the rarest birds—116 accidental or casual species that have been recorded in North America only a few times—are treated in full; these rare birds are discussed in an appendix of the volume that contains their close relatives. If you are familiar with the new A.O.U. sequence, you can quickly refer to the proper volume and page. You can also locate a particular species by consulting the index; each volume has an index to its contents, and Volume III has a comprehensive index to all three volumes.

If you are a beginning birder, take some time to familiarize yourself with the birds covered in these guides. Examine the color plates, and note the kinds of field marks that are useful in identifying a species and in distinguishing it from similar species. Read the family descriptions, which summarize the general appearance of the birds in each family. Note that many species occur in more than one plumage, depending on the season or on the age, sex, or geographical origin of the bird. Take a moment to see how a range map illustrates the range statement for each species; the map should tell you at a glance which species are likely to occur in your area.

Illustrations

In this guide, the color illustrations and text face each other for speedy reference. Each species may have from one to six color illustrations, arranged in an order that facilitates comparison with similar plumages of other species. Next to each color illustration is a small "plate key," that is, a black-and-white reproduction of the color plate. Superimposed on this plate key are numbered red arrows, corresponding to a numbered list of field marks. Beneath this list of numbered features, other field marks such as size, shape, behavior, voice, and habitat are given. Numerous black-and-white drawings, often bearing numbered arrows as well, supplement the color plates. These drawings generally depict the same plumage as that shown in the color plates; a drawing that illustrates a different plumage is accompanied by a label.

Each family of birds begins with a general description of the family and a list of all of the members of the family found in North America. Accidental species, which are treated in an appendix, appear in light-face type in this list.

Each text entry begins with the English and scientific names of the species. A typical species account goes on to discuss the bird's habitat, its behavioral characteristics, and other useful identification information, followed by the following sections:

Description

The description begins with the approximate length of the bird both in inches and in centimeters. The bird's shape, color, and pattern are described, and where necessary, several different plumages are discussed, along with other features that vary in importance, depending on the bird. (For example, bill color may clinch identification of one species, but be of only very minor interest in another.) Geographical forms that were once considered distinct species are included; many of these forms have widely used English names of their own; where these names are mentioned, they are given in quotation marks.

Voice

The voice is described for all species in which it is useful for identification. In general, only diagnostic songs and calls are given.

Similar Species

This section refers the reader to those species with which the bird is most likely to be confused; in many cases, a brief comparative description gives the most important differences between the two. In a few instances, a bird is so distinctive that no section on similar species is included. Accidental species are indicated by an asterisk.

Range

Breeding range

Winter range

Permanent range

The breeding range of a species is generally given first, followed by the winter range. Where only one range is outlined, it may be assumed that the bird is sedentary. A brief indication of the ranges of birds outside of North America is also given. Range maps accompany the range statements. The breeding range is indicated on the map by diagonal hatching. Where there is overlap between the breeding and winter ranges, or wherever a species occurs year-round, both ranges are superimposed. For consistency, the ranges are cut off at the Mexican border, even though the ranges of many species extend into Mexico or beyond. In the case of very rare species that occur in North America infrequently as well as those that have a very limited distribution, no range map is provided.

Other Features

This guide includes a number of features of interest to both beginning and advanced birders. In the front of each book, the orders of birds covered in that volume are described briefly. Drawings have been provided to show the parts of a bird, and special essays on How to Identify Birds and How to Find Birds have also been included. In the back of each volume, a glossary defines technical terms used in the text. Also in the back of each volume is a section that discusses the accidental species that fall within the scope of that volume. The section on accidentals includes brief descriptions and an indication of where these very rare species have occurred. While the guide follows the A.O.U. sequence and nomenclature, the accidentals included are those recognized in the *A.B.A. Checklist: Birds of Continental United States and Canada*, second edition, published in 1982 by the American Birding Association. Finally, an essay discusses the many ways you can study birds after you have learned to identify them.

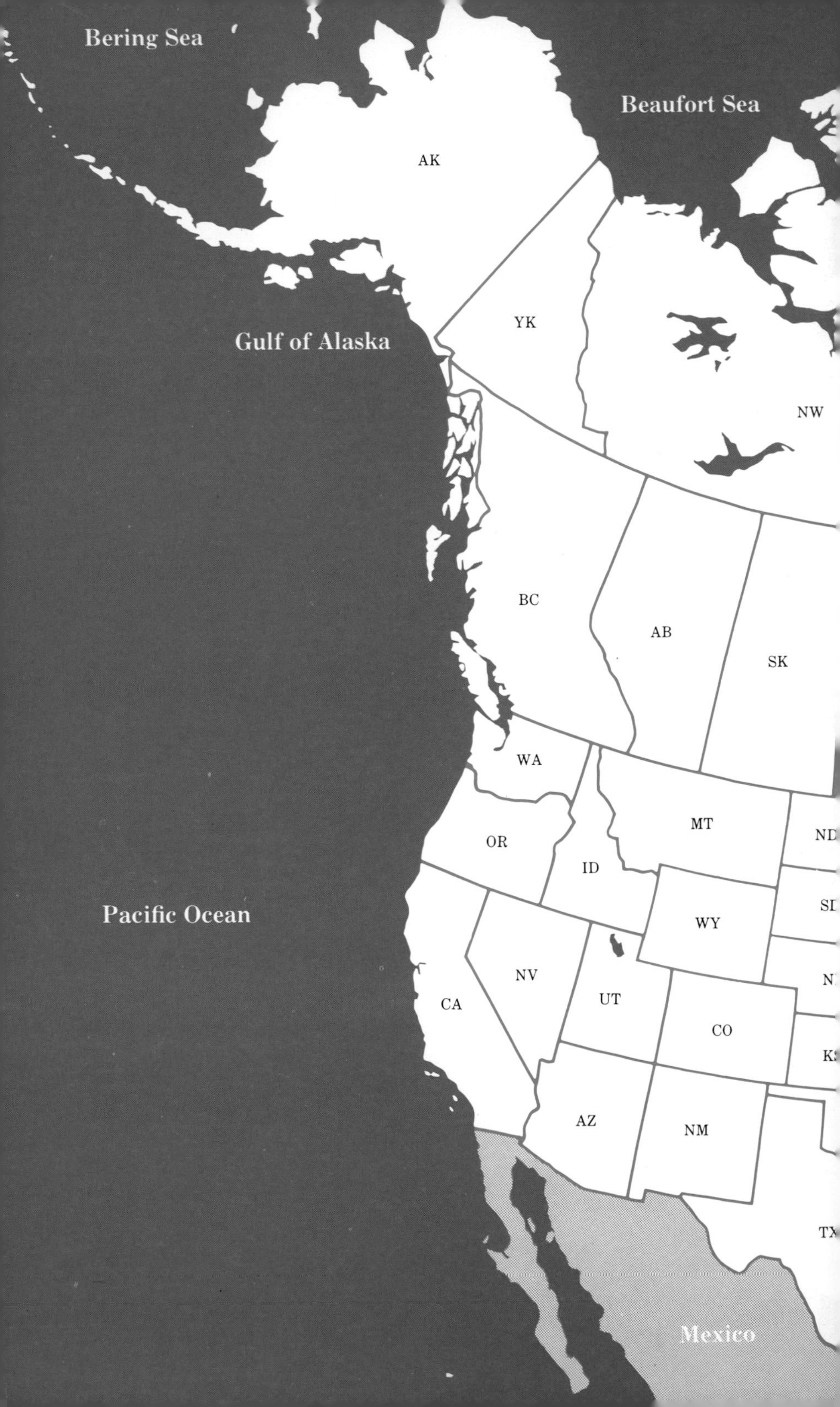
Bering Sea
Beaufort Sea
AK
YK
NW
Gulf of Alaska
BC
AB
SK
WA
MT
ND
OR
ID
WY
Pacific Ocean
NV
UT
CA
CO
AZ
NM
Mexico

Greenland

Baffin Bay

Hudson Bay

B

ON

QU

NF

PEI

NB

NS

ME

MN

VT

WI

NY

NH

MA

MI

CT

RI

IA

PA

NJ

IL

IN

OH

MD

DE

MO

WV

VA

KY

Atlantic Ocean

AR

TN

NC

MS

AL

GA

SC

LA

FL

Gulf of Mexico

How to Identify Birds

Beginning birders usually identify species by comparing birds they
see with illustrations or descriptions. To identify birds correctly,
novices normally must examine them slowly in detail under
favorable conditions. Experts, on the other hand, do not have to
look so carefully; they have a mental picture that is far more
detailed than any illustration. Their identifications are based on a
variety of clues, considered singly or in combination. Here are some
of the most important ones.

Size
The size of a bird, although it may be difficult to determine when the
bird is far away or by itself, is a useful clue in identifying it. As you
learn to recognize birds, you will quickly become familiar with their
size relative to other species. Select a series of common and
widespread birds of different sizes, such as the House Sparrow,
American Robin, Rock Dove, American Crow, Canada Goose, and
Great Blue Heron, and use these to gauge the size of other birds you
see. You will soon be able to judge whether an unfamiliar bird is
smaller than a House Sparrow, about the size of an American Robin,
or somewhat larger than a Rock Dove. Very often in a flock of
shorebirds or waterfowl, a single bird will stand out because it is
larger or smaller than the others. If you already know that the other
members of the flock are Sanderlings, for example, you will have a
head start in identifying the single, unfamiliar bird. In cases where
you cannot judge the size of a bird, its shape is the next feature to
consider.

Shape
Shape is one of the most readily observed characteristics of a bird
and one of the most important in identification. Your impression of a
bird's shape will be influenced by several features. The body may be
compact and stocky, like that of a European Starling or a member of
the auk family, or it may be slender, like a Yellow-billed Cuckoo's or
Red-breasted Merganser's. The neck may be very long, as in herons
and the Anhinga, or very short, as in many small sandpipers. The
legs, too, may be very long, as in most herons, or very short, as in
terns. The bill may be conical, like that of a House Sparrow; slender
and pointed, like that of a warbler or kinglet; heavy and pointed,
like that of a Belted Kingfisher or a heron; decurved, like that of a
curlew or Long-billed Thrasher; or hooked, like the bill of the
American Kestrel and Red-tailed Hawk. The wings may be long and
pointed, like those of terns, swifts, and swallows, or distinctly
rounded, like those of quails. Tails vary greatly in shape. Some
birds, like European Starlings and nuthatches, have short tails,
while others, like gnatcatchers, thrashers, and wagtails, have very
long tails. A bird's tail may be squared at the tip, like a Cliff
Swallow's; notched, like that of a House Finch or Tropical Kingbird;
deeply forked, like the tail of a Common Tern or Barn Swallow;
rounded, like a Blue Jay's; or pointed, like a Mourning Dove's.
Posture is often an important aspect of a bird's shape. Plovers tend
to stand in a more upright position, with the head held higher, than
sandpipers of similar size. Flycatchers usually perch with the body
held almost vertically, rather than in the horizontal posture of
warblers, vireos, and kinglets. Even among closely related species,
there may be differences in posture: Yellow-crowned Night-Herons
often stand in a more upright posture than do Black-crowned Night-
Herons, and Rough-legged Hawks often perch in a more horizontal
posture than Red-tailed Hawks.
Many species can be identified by shape alone. For example,
virtually all North American ducks have a distinctive head shape;
when seen in profile, they can often be identified by this feature.

Stocky build

Slender build

Long legs

Similarly, veteran hawk watchers routinely identify birds at ranges so great that the hawks appear as mere specks in the sky; birders do this on the basis of the wing-to-tail ratio. Even in as large a group as the shorebirds, almost every North American species has a unique outline formed by a combination of body size, length and shape of bill, and length of wings and legs. Of all a bird's characteristics, its silhouette is the least subject to change. If you really know a species' shape, you are unlikely to be misled by unfamiliar aspects of its plumage.

Black-and-white wing pattern

Color and Pattern
Color and pattern are important, too. The brilliant red of a male Northern Cardinal is often one's first clue to the identity of this bird, visible before its conical bill can be seen and before one is familiar with its distinctive, tail-pumping flight. The solid blue of male Indigo Buntings and Mountain Bluebirds at once sets these birds apart from all others. In much of the continent, a flash of bright orange and black in the treetops can instantly be called a Northern Oriole. Before a beginning birder learns the distinctive shape and manner of flight of an American Kestrel, its colors—bluish-gray and rufous in the male, rufous-brown in the female—enable him to identify this small falcon. If you note that a distant goose is white with black wing tips, you have narrowed the possibilities to only two species, the Snow Goose and Ross' Goose. Among the spotted thrushes, a bird in which only the tail is rust-colored is a Hermit Thrush; one with rust on the head and back is a Wood Thrush; a bird whose upperparts are wholly tawny is a Veery; while a bird with no rust or tawny in the upperparts is either a Gray-cheeked or Swainson's thrush.

White outer tail feathers

Carefully noting the color and pattern of a bird is essential in identifying it. Watch for wing bars; vireos, for example, can be sorted into two groups, those with wing bars and those without. Other wing patterns can be helpful, too, especially if the bird is in flight. The black-and-white wing pattern of a flying Willet is diagnostic, as are the red shoulders of Red-winged and Tricolored blackbirds, and the flashes of white in the wings of White-winged Doves, Red-headed Woodpeckers, Northern Mockingbirds, shrikes, and male Phainopeplas. Watch for rump and tail patterns. A departing Northern Flicker can be identified at a glance by its white rump; the pale buff rump of a Cliff Swallow or Cave Swallow quickly eliminates all other swallows. A yellowish or greenish warbler with large yellow tail patches must be a Yellow Warbler, while one with large white tail patches and a yellow rump is likely to be a Magnolia. White outer tail feathers mark the juncos and a variety of open-country birds: meadowlarks, pipits, Horned Larks, and Vesper Sparrows. A large flycatcher with a white tail tip must be an Eastern Kingbird, while in the West, a kingbird with white outer tail feathers must be a Western.

Look carefully at the pattern of the head. Watch for eyebrows, eye-rings, eyelines, mustaches, or throat patches; note the color of the crown, ear coverts, and lores. Take special note of any unusual color pattern: the red head and yellow body of a male Western Tanager, the golden-buff nape of a male Bobolink, the white sides on the rump of a Violet-green Swallow, and the rufous rump of the gray Lucy's Warbler are all diagnostic. The pattern of many species makes them easy to identify. Flying waterfowl and many warblers usually can be recognized by pattern alone. When other features are all but invisible, particularly in poor light or at great distances, a bird's distinctive pattern can often be discerned.

White wing patches

Behavior
Many birds walk, swim, or fly in so characteristic a manner that behavior by itself can permit identification. Given an unlabeled

specimen of a Water Pipit, most birders are not likely to recognize it at once, yet they can identify the living bird from hundreds of yards away by its bounding, stuttering flight or its habit of emphatically pumping its tail when on the ground. Some behavioral clues are obvious, like the big, splashy dives of Northern Gannets and Ospreys, the constant nodding of a yellowlegs, the head-bobbing motion of a swimming coot, the zigzag flight of a Common Snipe when it is flushed from a wet meadow, or the mothlike flight of a Common Poorwill. Others are subtle, such as the flight mannerisms of kittiwakes and the wing- and tail-flicks of flycatchers. Behavioral clues are almost unfailingly reliable and can help in identifying birds under a variety of circumstances. The differing flight styles of hawks, for example, or the various feeding postures of shorebirds can be used to identify them almost at the limit of visibility.

Conical bill

Vocal Clues
In many situations, it is easier to hear birds than to see them. Whether you are in the rain forest of the Northwest, the warbler-filled woods of New England, or the cypress swamps of the Carolinas, you are certain to hear many more birds than you see. The vocalizations of birds may be divided into two rough categories: songs and calls. Songs are usually given by adult males on territory during the nesting season, but may also be heard during migration and, in some species, during the winter as well. In certain species, such as the Rose-breasted Grosbeak and Northern Mockingbird, females as well as males may produce songs. Many songs are rather complex, like those of the Winter Wren and most wood warblers, but some are very simple, like the short, metallic *tslit* of Henslow's Sparrow. Calls, or call notes, are generally more simple, and are often given throughout the year under a variety of situations to express alarm, to maintain contact with other members of a flock, or during interactions with a mate or young.

Slender, pointed bill

Knowing the songs and calls of a region's birds will enable you to identify a far higher percentage than you could with binoculars alone. Identification by voice is almost always reliable. The shorebirds, for example, have flight calls, given at all times of the year, that are absolutely distinctive. Every shorebird native to North America, as well as vagrant species from the Old World, can be identified by these notes alone. Thus, if you are familiar with shorebird voices, you can identify the birds with certainty anywhere at any time of year, whether they are breeding in the Arctic, migrating through our latitudes, or wintering in South America. You can identify them even in darkness, and up to the limits of audibility. All North American songbirds, as well, have distinctive voices; in many cases, even their minor calls—lisps or chips—are recognizable. For example, of the large New World subfamily of wood warblers, about 50 fairly closely related species breed in North America. All have songs that can be learned readily; in fact, their songs differ more markedly than their plumages. Each song can be distinguished and mentally catalogued according to a variety of characteristics: pitch, cadence, duration, loudness, frequency of utterance, and quality. Although the song structure of a species may vary slightly from region to region, the quality of the song will almost always remain recognizable.

Heavy, pointed bill

Habitat and Range
Most people know that ducks and gulls are water birds and that thrushes are birds of the forest, but few beginning birders are aware of how specific most species are in their habitat requirements. Although these requirements may vary somewhat according to region and season, they are still quite rigid; experienced bird watchers expect to see certain birds in certain habitats. Warblers are as selective as any group: Tennessees breed in tamarack,

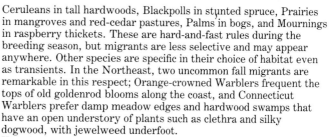

Ceruleans in tall hardwoods, Blackpolls in stunted spruce, Prairies in mangroves and red-cedar pastures, Palms in bogs, and Mournings in raspberry thickets. These are hard-and-fast rules during the breeding season, but migrants are less selective and may appear anywhere. Other species are specific in their choice of habitat even as transients. In the Northeast, two uncommon fall migrants are remarkable in this respect; Orange-crowned Warblers frequent the tops of old goldenrod blooms along the coast, and Connecticut Warblers prefer damp meadow edges and hardwood swamps that have an open understory of plants such as clethra and silky dogwood, with jewelweed underfoot.

Knowing habitat preferences greatly increases the chances of finding particular birds; it can also limit what we expect to find. In many cases, habitat by itself helps us to identify species. For example, even if they can barely be seen or heard, blackbirds in northern bogs are almost certain to be Rusties. Finally, the range of most birds is determined in large part by the availability of a specific habitat. Although the ranges of most species are continuously expanding or contracting, they can nonetheless be geographically defined or mapped. Knowledge of range enters into virtually every identification, usually as a subconscious first consideration. So too does an awareness of the average arrival and departure dates of migratory species.

Pointed tail

Becoming an Expert

To the uninitiated, the identifications made by experienced birders often seem to approach wizardry. Experts, rather than comparing the bird they have seen with illustrations in a field guide, weigh a number of attributes that together give the species a distinctive personality. The better you know a species, the more ways you have to identify it. Many North American birds have three or even more identifiable plumages, which can be bewildering at first, until one realizes how many factors are invariable: shape, voice, behavior, and range.

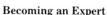

Notched tail

Looking at Birds

There is no secret to becoming skilled in identifying birds: Just look and listen. Observation may seem simple at first, but you will progress faster if you look attentively and repeatedly, even at common species. For many beginners, examination stops and binoculars come down the moment the bird is identified. In fact, this is the time to start looking. Make the effort. Imagine, for example, that this is the last Downy Woodpecker you will see for a long time, or that you will soon be asked to describe or even draw it. If you have difficulty getting a firm grasp on a bird's appearance, first look at its eye, and to force yourself to look closely, try to ascertain the color of the iris. Then study the size and shape of the bill and its length in relation to the distance separating its base from the center of the eye. Next, extend your study of the bird's proportions to the length of its legs and to the position of the folded wing tips in relation to the tip of the tail. From these observations, proceed to an examination of the bird's coloring and patterns. This deliberate approach might seem tedious, but birds lend themselves to careful observation, and you will almost certainly find it engrossing and rewarding. You will soon discover that you can memorize birds in much the same way you memorize human faces. It is possible to acquire a permanent familiarity with a seemingly limitless number of bird species, but to do so you must look carefully. Most expert bird watchers spend much time simply studying the appearance of birds, even familiar ones. This enjoyable exercise results in a far more detailed acquaintance than is required for simple identification, but it also makes one aware of the differences between species that superficially appear to be similar. Bear in mind that you can know

Forked tail

what a bird looks like only by *looking* at it. This sort of bird study demands fairly close-range and leisurely observation, but do not pass up a chance to watch a distant bird—you may be surprised at how much you can see. With good light and good binoculars, you can identify distinctively patterned birds as small as warblers, in flight, even overhead, at a great distance, but you will not know this until you try it.

Rounded wings

Looking at museum specimens or, better yet, at live birds trapped at a banding station, can also be extremely helpful. Side-by-side comparison of similar species can reveal differences that may help you in field identification. Juxtaposing and comparing eight or ten species of warblers, for example, will demonstrate as no field guide can the diversity that exists within this group. You will discover how much these species vary in size, bill shape, wing length, rictal bristles, or any number of small details. Studying specimens or captive birds will also help you to learn about the arrangement of feathers: which ones are involved in the wing bars, for instance, and how the tail feathers are shingled, with the central pair, or "deck feathers," on top and the outermost underneath. These insights will help you to understand what you see in the field.

Listening to Birds

Learning bird songs may seem difficult at first, but we learn them much as we learn melodies, by attentive and repeated listening. You can be more or less energetic in acquiring this familiarity with bird voices, but you will progress faster if you make it a rule to track down every unfamiliar call. This may initially seem overwhelming, but your ear will soon become remarkably good at resolving a tangle of noise into recognizable voices, and a dawn chorus of bird song will become a delightful exercise in auditory discrimination. Try to attach a set of associations to each bird vocalization by describing it to yourself or comparing it with other sounds you know; make your mental description of sounds as detailed as possible. If you can whistle, try to copy the sound you are learning; to imitate it acceptably you will have to listen closely to the model. The more characteristic sounds of most North American birds are available on commercially produced recordings. Although listening to records or tapes removes the learning process one step from direct experience, it will at the very least make you sensitive to aspects of bird song that make the voices of each species distinctive and recognizable. Even the least expensive recording equipment can be helpful, too, since listening to your own tapes allows a comparative or analytical approach to the study of bird song. Moreover, playback of a reasonably good field recording will often attract the singing bird and enable you to observe it more closely.

Long, pointed wings

Conclusion

Bird watching has attracted an ever increasing number of devotees in North America. The science—some would say the art—of bird identification has been considerably advanced and refined in recent years. Field problems have been clarified or resolved, vocalizations studied, behavioral clues detected, and distinguishing characteristics isolated. As a result, bird watchers of today are immeasurably more sophisticated than those of only a few decades ago. Bird identification is now a field in which one can quickly achieve a high degree of competence, with all its attendant satisfactions. And bird watching—need it be said?—is a pursuit with many, many rewards.   *Davis W. Finch*

How to Find Birds

To become a successful birder, you may have to change the habits of a lifetime. The best birders rise before dawn, put on drab clothing, go out in all weathers, and learn to move carefully and quietly, keeping their ears open and their voices soft.

Clothing
Unless you have always been an outdoor person, you will find your wardrobe gradually transformed and your conversation increasingly filled with discussions of boots, rain gear, and long underwear. The most important rule is: Wear dull colors, preferably the natural ones, muted greens, browns, and grays. Steer clear of apparel that squeaks, rustles, or gets snagged easily. In the desert, birders need footgear that is thornproof; elsewhere, choose comfortable shoes that dry quickly or waterproof boots. Boots with rubber feet and leather tops are a widespread favorite, but as you track birds across mud flats and marshes you may want knee or hip boots as well. Since birding often requires standing around in sharp winds and icy temperatures, layers of protection against the cold are essential. However, soundproof ear coverings should be avoided, except perhaps on winter boat trips, one of the coldest of all birding situations.

The Clock
Songbirds are easiest to see during the three hours after dawn, when they feed most actively. The two hours before sunset can also be productive. During the rest of the day, most small birds are relatively sluggish and silent, especially on a warm afternoon. On the other hand, most kinds of water birds are easy to find throughout the day. Vultures, hawks, and eagles are most likely to be seen well after sunup; they hunt when visibility is best and soar on the thermal currents formed by sun-warmed air.
Dusk is the best time to scan winter fields and marshes for Short-eared Owls, cruise back roads for nightjars and displaying Woodcock, and visit summer marshes for spectacular flights of herons and ibis and glimpses of most of the rails.
Birders usually search for rails and owls at night and arm themselves with tape recordings of owl calls and strong flashlights. During spring migration and early in the nesting season, birders in the field at first light are treated to the auditory excitement of the dawn chorus; woodland species in particular join in a crescendo that gradually dies away after sunrise.

Regional Resources
Many states, provinces, and regions now have annotated checklists or bird-finding guides that indicate the time of year that each species is present and most common, as well as the locations and habitats where each might be found. Such a list or guide should be one of your first purchases. If your region has not yet produced this kind of guide, buy one for the area nearest you.
Local bird clubs schedule field trips to visit areas at the times of year that birds are most plentiful there or when seasonal specialties are present. If you cannot join a group expedition, try to visit the site within a week or two of a scheduled outing. Club newsletters or calendars often list other events of interest, like pelagic trips organized especially for viewing seabirds and marine mammals.
In many areas throughout the United States and Canada, recorded telephone messages are available to birders. Updated once or twice a week, they supply information about unusual sightings in the area as well as news of migration, birding sites, and field trips. Call the local Audubon Society chapter for the telephone number, or ask birders you meet in the field for it. These messages often provide

directions to spots where rare birds have been found; these spots
are often fruitful places for a visiting birder to look for common local
species as well.

Weather

Every birder yearns to go afield on a beautiful spring or autumn
day, but wind, rain, and extremes of temperature may keep you
inside when some birds are most visible.

Although strong winds keep small birds out of sight, many water
birds huddle close to the windward shore, in the lee of protecting
banks, dunes, or vegetation. In autumn especially, a day or two
after a cold front has passed through, northerly winds bring the best
conditions for watching raptors migrating down mountain ridges or
along the coasts. Onshore gales accompanying major coastal storms
provide the best opportunities for observing seabirds of all kinds
from land, and the first day after a hurricane many birders rush to
the coast or to bays, rivers, and major lakes within a hundred miles
or so of the sea.

Although bird-watching is virtually impossible in heavy rain, there
is a lot of activity immediately after the rain stops. If you can keep
your binoculars dry, a low ceiling and light drizzle can produce the
best possible conditions for seeing migrating passerines. Songbirds
are often forced down by nasty weather aloft; since they may occupy
whatever cover they can find, you are likely to see a hedgerow, a
clump of trees, or a brushy ravine alive with birds.

The hottest days of summer coincide with the peak migration time
for southbound shorebirds. During the heat shimmer of late morning
and early afternoon, go for a swim or hide in air-conditioned shelter,
but take advantage of the long hours before and after the worst heat
of the day.

Cold winter weather is good for birding snugly from your car,
searching open country for raptors and visiting seedeaters such as
longspurs and Snow Buntings. You may want to comb through
stands of conifers for wintering owls, seek out patches of open water
where waterfowl crowd together, or scan landfills, harbors, and
beaches for rare gulls. If you notice a feeding station, check to see
what species are visiting it.

Effective Behavior

The fundamental skills of birding are looking, listening, moving
carefully, and concentrating on one bird at a time.

On foot, a birder is likely to cover less than one mile an hour. The
point is to hear every chip note or rustle in the foliage and to spot
every movement. Once you have heard a sound or seen a movement,
your goal is to locate, identify, and observe the bird without
frightening it away.

Although sharp eyes are partly a gift, the ability to pick up motion
improves with practice. Always locate and relocate the bird first
without binoculars. Keep your eyes on the motion while you move
your binoculars in front of them. When you acquire a telescope,
study the bird's surroundings through binoculars before you narrow
your field of vision a second time by looking through the more
powerful optical instrument.

Study an unfamiliar bird thoroughly before you turn to a field guide.
If you cannot bear to take notes on its appearance and behavior
before you try to identify it, at least tell yourself exactly what
features you are seeing and hearing before you turn to a guide; if the
bird flies away when your eyes are not on it, you will still have
several features to check. If there are two of you, you can describe
it to each other; one person can keep track of the bird while the
other does the first round of research.

Looking for land birds requires a minimum of conversation and a
maximum of attention to sounds. Speak only when you must, and

then in a soft voice or whisper. Learning to recognize songs takes most of us much longer than visual identification, and learning all the chips, calls, and alarm notes is the task of a lifetime. Begin by tracking down and identifying every invisible singing bird you can. Try to verbalize the pattern you hear, and commit it to memory. Avoid abrupt movements: Shift position only if you have to, and then do so slowly and gently. Learn to refrain from pointing, or to point with your finger only, keeping your hand against your body. Better yet, practice describing where a bird is as economically as possible.

As you stalk a bird, learn to recognize its signs of alarm: a freeze in posture, a cocked head, a half-raising of the wings, and so on. If these clues tell you that you are getting too close, back off a little, or at least stop moving until the bird shows that it is used to your presence.

Try not to loom over a bird. Stay off the skyline if you can; on high ground, crouch or sit. The less conspicuous you are, the more birds you are likely to see.

Imitations of the Eastern Screech-Owl's call in the East or of the Northern Pygmy-Owl's in the West are enormously effective for attracting small birds. If you cannot master the screech-owl's tricky call, use a taped version; it works even better. Anybody can learn to "spish," that is, to make the sound "spshsh, spshsh, spshsh," which can draw quite a crowd of songbirds if you keep at it long enough. One responsive chickadee can pull in dozens of other birds if you keep it fussing at you. Most important, remember that overuse of these techniques quickly turns into harassment, and there is no excuse for seriously upsetting a bird, especially one that may be nesting.   *Claudia Wilds*

Beyond Bird Identification

The greatest pleasures of birding begin once you have learned to identify species and start to study their activities closely. As a result of long evolution, each species fits snugly into a particular environmental niche. The patient observer will see the physical and behavioral traits that reveal how a species has adapted to its niche. Such observation will not only tell you more about the birds, it will also reveal their role in the larger environment we share with them. Ornithology is unusual among the sciences in that many important contributions are still being made by nonprofessionals. Some types of research, in fact, depend almost entirely on the participation of amateurs.

Charting Migrations

The excitement of bird watching is enhanced by the fact that all over North America during much of the year you can see birds on migration, so that you never know precisely what you will find. Unlike the nesting season or the dead of winter, when one can count on seeing many of the same birds day after day, in migration there are always new arrivals and departures. Although birds travel on fairly fixed schedules, they are affected by local conditions, so their movements can never be predicted exactly.

There are several ways you can use information gathered in the field to learn more about migration. Each day make a list of the birds you see. After noting arrival and departure dates for a few seasons, you will learn when to expect each species.

You will quickly discover that the movements of some species are more regular than those of others. Schedules, especially of birds flying long distances, are affected by changes in day length. Local weather conditions play a role as well. Birders hope for the weather to turn suddenly favorable after a period when conditions inhibited migrants from traveling. This situation generally produces a "wave" of birds, in which regular species are extraordinarily common, and rare or displaced ones more likely to be found. By noting the weather conditions in your area and in the region from which birds are traveling, you can determine how weather affects various migrants; some, you will learn, are practically impervious to it, others very sensitive. You will also be able to predict the quality of birding conditions.

Migration Factors

Your daily tallies should estimate the number of each migrant species. This will enable you to consider several questions: Are the birds moving in a steady flow, or are they bunched together? Are they traveling in flocks or as individuals? Do flocks contain more than one species? If the migration is spread out over several weeks, how far ahead is the vanguard and how far behind the stragglers? Are males and females, adults and young birds all on the same schedule? The answers to these questions can be correlated with the ecology of each species. For example, in the spring, males of territorial species often travel north first in order to have a head start on staking a claim to feeding and nesting sites.

Some species migrate during the day, while others travel only at night. If you are out early enough, you may be able to see the nocturnal migrants descend from the sky. In the first few hours of morning do you find them feeding, resting, drinking, or bathing? What are their first requirements after a taxing flight? How, in fact, do they spend their entire day? Do they pause for a few days between flights or leave the next night? It is sometimes possible to determine how long birds stay in an area, as with flocks of geese that monopolize a pond, or smaller birds that remain in the same group of trees.

Among the most spectacular migrants are the hawks and eagles. Especially in fall, they travel along coastlines or the ridges of mountain chains that produce updrafts of warm air enabling the birds to soar without effort. From a good vantage point, you can count and identify nearly all the birds passing by. Hawk watching is so popular today that volunteer observers all over the continent coordinate their tallies, which are compiled and analyzed by the Hawk Migration Association of North America. The results have helped ornithologists determine raptor populations, routes of migration, and the speeds at which different species travel. From late August through November, virtually all hawk lookouts have at least one observer posted throughout the day. Participating in such a project is an excellent way to sharpen your identification skills and to learn more about birds of prey. To find out the location of the nearest good watch station, contact your local bird club.

Local Birds

Birders who have been following the course of the migration all spring often feel some letdown when the last transients have left for their breeding sites. Local species, however, offer many interesting subjects for investigation. The most basic, of course, is to find out which birds breed in your area. Try to determine which ones are common, which are rare or dependent on specialized habitats, how much space they need, and how long they are present. A local bird survey will help you to discover if any types of habitat are vital to birds in your locality, and whether these environments need protection. For example, although many woodland birds have relatively small territories, they will inhabit a forest only if it is so large that their territory is surrounded on all sides by more woods.

Breeding Surveys

There are many ways to conduct a survey of breeding birds. Whatever the method, you should try to find definite proof that the birds observed are indeed nesting—a singing male holding a territory does not necessarily have a mate with which it is breeding. The nesting season varies from species to species. You should not wait until the spring migration is over to begin your survey. Great Horned Owls, for example, are much easier to find in February, when they begin nesting, than when the trees are thickly covered with leaves. Similarly, robin nests are easy to spot when they are being built in April or early May, but it is hard to determine how many families are present in June, when the young have left the nest.

Techniques used in surveys of breeding birds include counting birds seen in a prescribed area, counting birds seen or heard at certain points on a path drawn through a particular habitat, or recording data for all birds found nesting. No method is perfect, but if used consistently over a period of years, any of these techniques will indicate whether the population of each species is stable, increasing, or decreasing.

Winter Surveys

To further your understanding of year-round bird life, you may wish to participate in one of several interesting types of winter surveys. The best known are the Christmas Bird Counts sponsored by the National Audubon Society. During the week before and the week after Christmas, thorough, day-long surveys are conducted in circular areas 15 miles across, with parties combing every accessible spot in the circle, noting all birds seen or heard. The results are compiled and published in the Audubon Society's magazine *American Birds*. In some locales, Christmas counts have been held for decades, while in others they are very new. All such surveys benefit from additional participants, since more thorough coverage guarantees more accurate data. Analysis of the fluctuations in count scores has been one of the most useful ways of tracing the population changes of North American birds.

A single survey taken at the beginning of winter will not reveal how birds cope with the entire season. A series of counts for the same area made from December through March will show which species are "half hardy," leaving when really cold weather sets in; which species come from farther north only when conditions in their normal range are too severe; and which species change their method of foraging according to local conditions. Among the birds most "countable" in winter are waterfowl, which concentrate on large lakes and estuaries where water remains unfrozen.

Birds at Home

Some of the best bird watching can be done right at home, if you have a place to set up one or more feeders. Many books listing which foods various birds prefer are available. Once birds learn to come to your feeder, you will see not only what they eat but also how much and how they consume it. Some species, such as chickadees and goldfinches, are comfortable eating on an elevated tray or a swinging feeder, whereas others, including juncos and most sparrows, prefer food scattered on the ground. There is often a hierarchy of species at a feeder, with larger or more aggressive ones displacing others; a pecking order also frequently exists among individuals of the same species.

By putting out nest boxes, you can follow at first hand the courtship and breeding cycles of many birds. Be sure, however, not to disturb the birds by trailing them too closely or peering into their homes too often. Among the interesting things to note are the dates when various stages of the nesting cycle occur, materials brought in for construction, incubation period, types of food given to the young, feeding rate, age of fledging, and the role of each parent throughout the cycle.

Especially revealing is a comparison between your birdhouse tenants, which will be species that normally nest in tree cavities, and other species in the same area that build their nests in more exposed situations. Because nests in cavities are generally safer than those on the ground or in branches of shrubs or trees, the young in cavity nests usually remain in them longer. The young of small, ground-nesting passerines, for example, usually leave their nest eight to ten days after hatching, hopping after their parents before they can fly. Chickadees, however, nest in cavities, where the young remain until they are 16 days old.

There are, of course, many other differences in the way species, even closely related ones, build their nests and raise their young. It may be worthwhile to take notes on everything you see, since only through regular observation will the patterns become clear. Even if the behavior has already been described and is well known, your powers of observation will be sharpened by recording what you see.

Some of the most stimulating birding projects are group efforts. Your natural history museum, nature center, or bird club may be conducting long-term investigations in which you can participate. Field stations where birds are banded and behavioral or ecological studies are in progress often need volunteers. Under the guidance of experts, you can help gather information; often you can work with equipment that requires special permits and is therefore not normally available to bird watchers. Countless professional ornithologists were first inspired to make birds more than a hobby while working on a project with a club or museum. However far you take your interest in birds—or let the birds take you—identification will be just the first step toward insights into the world around you.

Roger F. Pasquier

The Order Passeriformes

Considerably more than half of the world's bird species belong to the diverse order of perching birds, the Passeriformes. Found worldwide, they form the great bulk of species in most terrestrial bird communities. Their tremendous variety of feeding adaptations makes it difficult to generalize, but all Passeriformes show a "perching foot," consisting of three toes extending forward and one toe extending backward on the same level. In North America, passeriform birds (often called passerines) range in size from that of a wren or a kinglet to that of a raven.

Some passerine families are covered in the second volume of this set. Most of the birds discussed in this volume belong to two large evolutionary radiations, one primarily Old World (the Muscicapidae and related families) and one primarily New World (the Emberizidae). The family Muscicapidae includes the thrushes, kinglets, gnatcatchers, Old World flycatchers (vagrants in North America), and babblers (of which the Wrentit is an isolated North American example). The North American muscicapids are primarily insect-eaters, although many also take fruit. The family Emberizidae includes the wood warblers, tanagers, cardinals, grosbeaks, buntings, and sparrows (called buntings in the Old World), as well as the oriole-blackbird group known as icterids (after the former family name Icteridae). Emberizids range from insectivorous foliage gleaners to fruit eaters and seed crackers.

Other important passeriform families noted in this volume include the mockingbirds and thrashers (family Mimidae), the vireos (family Vireonidae), and the finches (family Fringillidae). Consult the individual family accounts for further characteristics of these and the remaining passeriform families.   *Kimball L. Garrett*

Part Two

Old World Warblers and Thrushes

(Family Muscicapidae)
This is a huge, highly diverse family whose members are found
primarily in the Old World. Many are remarkable for their complex
and beautiful songs. The small contingent occurring in North
America can conveniently be divided into categories. In general, the
Sylviinae are small, drab insectivores with thin little bills. Many lack
any conspicuous plumage markings at all, and closely related
members of some complexes are notoriously difficult to identify. The
kinglets are among the smallest of North American birds; they are
very round and olive-grayish, with very tiny, thin bills; 2 species
occur in our range. The Arctic Warbler is found only in Alaska,
where most of the Old World warblers recorded in our area also
occur. The gnatcatchers are a New World group of tiny, very
slender, mostly grayish birds. Gnatcatchers are very active and
frequently flip their tails about or often hold them straight up. Only
the Blue-gray Gnatcatcher is widespread. The Old World
flycatchers are fairly small birds with flattened bills, conspicuous
rictal bristles, and short legs. Widely distributed in the Eastern
Hemisphere, there are only 3 representatives in our range; these
birds have reached Alaska, primarily as spring vagrants. The
subfamily Turdinae is a worldwide group represented by several
genera in North America. Two members of the Old World genus
Luscinia, the Siberian Rubythroat and the Bluethroat, are found in
extreme western Alaska. Bluebirds (genus *Sialia*) inhabit open
country. The adult males have brilliant blue upperparts; females and
immatures retain similar shades of blue in restricted areas on the
upperparts, but are generally much paler and much more difficult to
distinguish. This subfamily also includes Townsend's Solitaire, a bird
of western montane forests. The genus *Turdus* includes the widely
familiar American Robin, probably the best-known representative;
other members of this genus are casual visitors or vagrants. The
genus *Catharus* includes terrestrial birds with dark brownish, rust-
colored, or olive-green upperparts. The subfamily Timiilinae has but
a single representative in our range, the Wrenit. (World: 1427
species. North America: 34 species.)   *Scott B. Terrill*

Arctic Warbler

Phylloscopus borealis
Breeding in streamside willow thickets of Alaska tundra, this bird is
the only member of its genus to nest in the New World. Two races
reach Alaska; one is browner on the back, the other more green.

Description
4¾″ (12 cm). Breeding adults greenish-brown above, dull whitish
below, with whitish eyebrow, short whitish wing bar, and brown
legs. Bill hooked at tip. Juveniles brighter green above with bright
yellow below, on eyebrow, and on wing bar.

Voice
Song a wrenlike trill on 1 pitch. Call note a clear *zik* or *chik*.

Similar Species
See Orange-crowned and Tennessee warblers.

Range
Breeds in central, western, and northern Alaska; migrates through
Bering Strait. Also in northern Eurasia.   *Daniel D. Gibson*

Middendorff's Grasshopper-Warbler
Wood Warbler
Dusky Warbler
Arctic Warbler
Golden-crowned Kinglet
Ruby-crowned Kinglet
Blue-gray Gnatcatcher
Black-tailed Gnatcatcher
Black-capped Gnatcatcher
Red-breasted Flycatcher
Siberian Flycatcher
Gray-spotted Flycatcher
Siberian Rubythroat
Bluethroat
Northern Wheatear
Eastern Bluebird
Western Bluebird
Mountain Bluebird
Townsend's Solitaire
Veery
Gray-cheeked Thrush
Swainson's Thrush
Hermit Thrush
Wood Thrush
Eye-browed Thrush
Dusky Thrush
Fieldfare
Redwing
Clay-colored Robin
Rufous-backed Robin
American Robin
Varied Thrush
Aztec Thrush
Wrentit

Adult
1. *Whitish eyebrow.*
2. *Greenish back.*
3. *Short whitish wing bar.*
4. *Whitish underparts.*

Wrenlike song.
Alaska only.

Golden-crowned Kinglet

Regulus satrapa
Kinglets are small, short-tailed, olive-colored birds with 2 conspicuous white wing bars. Both the Golden-crowned and Ruby-crowned kinglets often pause to hover briefly in front of twigs and leaves while foraging for insects. The nervous wing-flicking habit, in addition to the high-pitched notes of the Golden-crowned Kinglet, are often more useful for identification of this species than its golden crown and whitish eyebrow stripe. A bird that characteristically breeds in cool coniferous forests, the Golden-crowned Kinglet is gradually expanding its range by colonizing spruce plantations.

Description
3½–4 (9–10 cm). The Golden-crowned Kinglet has a crown that is bright orange in males and yellow in females; in both sexes, the crown is bordered on the sides and forehead with black. The eyebrow is whitish. The upperparts are greenish-olive and marked with 2 white wing bars. The underparts are whitish, tinged with grayish-olive; this color becomes most intense on the sides and flanks.

Voice
Song a high-pitched, ascending series of *see see see see* notes, dropping abruptly at end to chickadeelike chatter. Most common call note a very high *tsee-tsee-tsee;* also more drawn-out single *tseee,* resembling note of Brown Creeper.

Similar Species
Ruby-crowned Kinglet has whitish eye-ring (often incomplete), lacks gold on crown and whitish eyebrow stripe. Warblers larger, longer-tailed, do not flick wings.

Range
Breeds from southern Alaska east to southern Quebec and Newfoundland, south in mountains to southern California and Guatemala, central Minnesota, New England, and in Appalachians to western North Carolina. Withdraws in winter from northernmost breeding range, reaching northern Florida and Gulf Coast.
Wayne R. Petersen

Ruby-crowned Kinglet

Regulus calendula
This tiny, wing-flicking bird is an early spring migrant. It prefers northern evergreen forests and western mountains in summer.

Description
4¼″ (11.5 cm). Like Golden-crowned but has bold white eye-ring; lacks eyebrow and golden crown. Wing bars white, usually with dark area just below. Male's red crown patch usually hidden.

Voice
Song a surprisingly loud, variable *tee tee tee, tew tew tew, teedadee teedadee teedadee.* Note a husky *did-it;* sometimes only 1 note given.

Similar Species
See Hutton's Vireo; warblers larger with larger bill.

Range
Nw. Alaska and Newfoundland south in mountains to Baja California, New Mexico; also Michigan and Nova Scotia. Winters from British Columbia and Maryland south.   *Wayne R. Petersen*

Female
1. *Yellow crown.*
2. *Whitish eyebrow.*
3. *Greenish back.*
4. *Two white wing bars.*

Small size. Flicks wings. Very high-pitched call.

Male
1. *Orange on crown.*

Adult
1. *Broken whitish eye-ring.*
2. *Greenish-olive upperparts.*
3. *Two white wing bars.*
4. *Red crown patch (often concealed).*

Small size.

Blue-gray Gnatcatcher

Tail

Polioptila caerulea
This tiny, slender, bluish-gray bird with a narrow bill and long, thin
tail is unmistakable; throughout much of North America, excluding
the Southwest, the Blue-gray Gnatcatcher is not likely to be
confused with any other species. It forages actively in trees and in
brushy understory and second growth, often making high, thin,
buzzy, insectlike vocalizations. Gnatcatchers commonly carry their
tails cocked at an angle to the body, or held straight down and
slightly fanned; they also frequently flick their tails, showing flashes
of black and white. These birds respond readily to spishing,
squeaking, and owl calls. In the East, the Blue-gray Gnatcatcher is
found in open woods and brushy edges; in the West, it frequents
chaparral, scrub-oak, and piñon-juniper habitats. During the winter,
this species lives primarily in low, brushy thickets.

Description
4½–5" (11.5–12.5 cm). The Blue-gray Gnatcatcher is a tiny, slender
bird with a slim bill, evenly curved underparts and a long, narrow,
slightly rounded tail. The upperparts are bluish-gray, the wings are
darker gray with whitish edgings, and the underparts are pale
grayish to white. The underside of the tail is largely white; above, it
is black with white outer feathers. Both sexes have a thin white
eye-ring. Adult males have a narrow black area on the forehead that
extends back in a thin line bordering the forecrown. Females and
immatures are similar but less bluish above.

Voice
Call a high, thin, buzzy, twangy *psee, tsee,* or *tsseeeit;* notes vary in
duration and temporal frequency, but tone characteristic. Song a
short, thin, insectlike series, often followed by thin, warbled
phrases.

Similar Species
See Black-tailed and Black-capped gnatcatchers.

Range
Breeds from northern California, Nevada, southern Idaho,
southwestern Wyoming, Colorado, eastern Nebraska, southern
Great Lakes region (including southern Ontario, New York, and
Maine) south throughout United States; through Mexico to
Guatemala and Cuba. Winters from southern states south.
Scott B. Terrill

Black-tailed Gnatcatcher

Tail

Polioptila melanura
Similar to the Blue-gray Gnatcatcher in shape and behavior, the
Black-tailed inhabits lower elevations of the Southwest. It is found
in thorny scrub, especially in arroyos and washes, and in riparian
underbrush in desert regions—primarily arid, coastal scrub of
southwestern California. During the winter, Black-taileds can occur
with Blue-gray Gnatcatchers, especially in riparian areas.

Description
4½" (11.5 cm). This tiny, slender bird is gray above and whitish
below, with some brownish coloration and whitish edging on the
wings. The tail is black below on the basal half or more; a little white
on the outer web of the outer tail feathers is visible from above.
From late winter through August, the male has a black cap and a
gray nape. The race from extreme southwestern California, *P. m.
californica,* is dark gray below with almost no white on the
underside of the tail, having only narrow, light edgings on the outer
web and tip that disappear with wear. Its voice is also different.

Female
1. *Thin bill.*
2. *Bluish-gray back.*
3. *Whitish underparts.*
4. *Long black tail with white outer edges.*

Small size.
Slender build.
Thin, buzzy calls.

Male
1. *Narrow black forehead and thin border at side of forecrown.*

Male
1. *Black cap.*
2. *Gray upperparts.*
3. *Whitish underparts.*
4. *Black tail with white tips to outer tail feathers.*

Small size.
Slender build.

Voice
Calls: harsh, scratchy, whining, buzzy *che* notes; also *wheeze, mew;*
all notes highly variable. Also scold note virtually identical to scold
of House Wren. Songs include *chee chee chee* types and light, thin
series of buzzy mumbo jumbo. Some notes sound like imitations,
including call indistinguishable from Verdin's, and *tink* note like that
of Desert Sparrow. *P. m. californica* has notes like Blue-gray's, but
catlike and more prolonged, with distinct downward inflection.

Similar Species
Blue-gray Gnatcatcher has white covering most or all of outer 2 tail
feathers and basal part of third; tail largely white below, including
basal portion; lacks brownish tones in wings. Call a single note, not
series; higher-pitched, thinner. Blue-gray occupies higher elevations
during breeding season. See Black-capped Gnatcatcher.

Range
Resident from southern California, southern Nevada, western and
southern Arizona, southwestern New Mexico, and southern Texas
south into northern Mexico.   *Scott B. Terrill*

Black-capped Gnatcatcher

Tail

◀3

Polioptila nigriceps
A Mexican species, the Black-capped Gnatcatcher has occurred in
southeastern Arizona sporadically since 1971, and its appearances
include 3 nesting records from Sonoita Creek and Chino Canyon. Its
body resembles that of the Black-tailed Gnatcatcher, while its tail is
like the Blue-gray's. This species is probably sometimes overlooked,
and may be more widespread than is currently believed. It inhabits
scrubby riparian areas and dense thorn scrub on hillsides, in washes,
and in canyons.

Description
4½" (11.5 cm). A tiny, slender bird like the Blue-gray and Black-
tailed gnatcatchers, the Black-capped is gray above and whitish
below. Males in breeding plumage have an extensive black cap that
covers the head and most or all of the nape, and extends downward
on each side in a distinctive V shape. The pattern of the tail
resembles that of the Blue-gray Gnatcatcher, with outer 2 tail
feathers and the lower half of the third white, and a great deal of
white on the underside near the base of the tail. The wings, like
those of the Black-tailed, have obvious brownish tones. Some
observers believe that the Black-capped appears longer-billed than
the other 2 gnatcatchers.

Voice
Gives buzzy, whining notes similar to notes of Blue-gray
Gnatcatcher; calls not well known but some experienced birders
may be able to distinguish them.

Similar Species
Black-tailed Gnatcatcher has less white on tail; black cap does not
extend into V shape on sides. Blue-gray Gnatcatcher lacks obvious
brownish or buff on wings, lacks black cap.

Range
Enters North America only in southeastern Arizona (Sonoita Creek,
Chino Canyon). Native to Mexico.   *Scott B. Terrill*

Female

1. *Gray crown and upperparts.*
2. *Whitish underparts.*
3. *Black tail with white tips to outer tail feathers.*

   Small size.
   Slender build.

Female

1. *Gray crown and upperparts.*
2. *Whitish underparts.*
3. *Two outer tail feathers white.*

Breeding male

1. *Extensive black cap.*
2. *Gray upperparts.*
3. *Whitish underparts.*

Siberian Rubythroat

Luscinia calliope
A small, active Asiatic thrush, larger than the related Bluethroat and smaller than a Gray-cheeked Thrush, the Siberian Rubythroat is a rare annual spring and fall migrant through the western Aleutian Islands. There it is a skulker, foraging on the ground in dense cover. When flushed, it flies off quickly, just above or through the vegetation, following the lay of the land, and disappears again into dense cover. This species is often difficult to see well, but the bright red throat of males is diagnostic. The Siberian Rubythroat occurs singly or in small, scattered groups; in Alaska it is almost always silent.

Description
6–6½″ (15–16.5 cm). The male has a bright scarlet throat, white mustache outlined in black, black lores, and white eyebrows. The upperparts from head to tail, the wings, and the flanks are warm cinnamon-brown. A gray band separates the scarlet throat from the buff-white breast and belly. Females, which are seen in Alaska much less frequently than males, are nondescript, but resemble males in behavior, often cocking the tail. Like males, they have cinnamon-brown upperparts, wings, flanks and tail. Unlike males, they have a whitish throat that is separated from the buff-white belly and undertail coverts by a dull gray-brown wash; the eyebrow and mustache are whitish.

Range
In North America, annual migrant through western Aleutian Islands of Alaska. Casual farther east in Aleutians as well as on Alaska islands of Bering Sea. Native to Siberia.
Daniel D. Gibson

Bluethroat

Luscinia svecica
A small, skulking Old World thrush that nests locally in western and northern Alaska, the Bluethroat migrates to and from Asia via the Bering Strait. It breeds in willow thickets along tundra streams, often in hilly country, and occurs along the Alaska coast as a migrant only.

Description
5½″ (14 cm). The adult male is brown above with a whitish eyebrow. The pattern of the underparts is diagnostic: an electric-blue throat and upper breast, with a large, chestnut spot in the blue field. A broad black band and a broad chestnut band separate the blue field from the dirty buff belly and undertail coverts. The female has a similar whitish eyebrow but is quite different below: a whitish throat patch outlined by a broad, U-shaped black border. The juvenile resembles the adult female, but its U-shaped throat border is made up of large spots; the breast and belly are bright buff. In all plumages, the Bluethroat has a diagnostic tail pattern: the basal

Male

1. *Scarlet throat.*
2. *White eyebrow.*
3. *White mustache.*
4. *Cinnamon-brown upperparts.*

Alaska only.

Female

1. *Whitish throat and mustache.*
2. *Whitish eyebrow.*
3. *Cinnamon-brown upperparts.*

Male

. *Bright blue throat and breast with chestnut spot.*
. *Brown upperparts.*
. *Buff belly.*
. *Rufous at base of tail.*

three-fifths of all tail feathers, except the central pair, is bright
rufous, both above and below. The rest of the tail is dark brown.

Voice
Song musical and varied, unlike any other in similar habitat in
Alaska. Call a sharp *tac*.

Range
In North America, breeds in western and northern Alaska, from the
northern Seward Peninsula north and east along northern foothills
of Brooks Range; rare as far east as northern Yukon Territory.
Native to northern Eurasia.   *Daniel D. Gibson*

Northern Wheatear

Oenanthe oenanthe
This small, open-country thrush is a widespread breeding bird
throughout much of Eurasia; in the Old World it winters in Africa,
where it frequents barren fields and short-grass areas. The
Northern Wheatear also breeds in rocky tundra areas of Alaska as
well as in northwestern and northeastern Canada.

Tail

◄5

Description
6" (15 cm). The male Northern Wheatear in spring has black wings
and mask, and a pale gray crown, nape, and back; the rump is white,
and the tail has a diagnostic black-and-white pattern. The spring
female has a similar tail pattern, but is brown above, with brown
wings and no mask. Juveniles resemble the female, but are bright
buff beneath.

Voice
Call note a loud, harsh *chak* or *chak-chak*. Song a musical jumble
that includes harsh call note.

Range
In North America, breeds, in appropriate habitat, in much of
mainland Alaska, eastward into northern Yukon Territory,
Mackenzie District, on Ellesmere and Baffin islands, and Labrador.
Casual but annual vagrant, primarily in fall, to Canada and lower 48
states; most records from East Coast states and provinces; very few
records in central part of continent; a few scattered records from
Pacific states and provinces. Native to Eurasia.
Daniel D. Gibson

Female
1. Whitish eyebrow.
2. Whitish throat with U-shaped black border.
3. Rufous at base of tail.

Breeding male
1. Black mask.
2. Pale gray crown, nape, and back.
3. Black wings.
4. White rump.
5. Bold black-and-white tail pattern.

Female
1. Brown upperparts.
2. Brown wings.

Rump and tail pattern like male's.

Eastern Bluebird

Sialia sialis
Bluebirds are the only thin-billed, medium-size to small birds with
bright blue in the plumage that are likely to be seen in North
America. They perch in a hunched, vertical fashion and feed mostly
as they make short forays to the ground. All bluebirds nest in
cavities. Eastern Bluebirds are found in open woodlands, orchards,
and farmlands. They occur in flocks in the nonbreeding season, often
feeding on berries.

Description
6–6½" (15–16.5 cm). Males are bright blue above, including the
wings and tail, and reddish-brown on the throat, breast, and flanks.
The reddish underparts extend nearly to the chin, which is whitish,
and upward in a partial collar behind the ear coverts. The belly and
undertail coverts are white. Females are similar but duller and
grayer; they too have rather bright blue on the wings and tail.
Females have whitish eye-rings, a white or pale rust throat, a hint
of a dark malar line, and a pale rust partial collar similar in pattern
to the male's. Juveniles are strongly spotted. A race that occurs in
the southwest is slightly paler overall.

Voice
Song a rich warble. Common call a rich *chur-lee*.

Similar Species
Western Bluebird overlaps marginally; male Westerns show some
chestnut on back, bluish throat, and blue-gray belly. Female
Western similar to Eastern, but throat grayish, dark malar streaks
absent, belly and undertail coverts grayish, underparts paler and
duller. Mountain Bluebird overlaps more broadly with Eastern;
lacks rust-colored tones, has somewhat different shape and posture.
Townsend's Solitaire somewhat similar to female Eastern Bluebird
but lacks blue in wings, has longer tail.

Range
Breeds throughout eastern North America north to southern
Canada, as far west as Saskatchewan and Great Plains States (south
locally to eastern New Mexico). Also in mountains and foothills of
southeastern Arizona and adjacent New Mexico. Winters in
southern parts of breeding range. Also from Mexico to Nicaragua.
Kimball L. Garrett

Western Bluebird

Sialia mexicana
This species is the western counterpart of the Eastern Bluebird.
The ranges of the 2 overlap only in the Southwest. The Western's
feeding behavior is like that of the Eastern Bluebird, and it too
perches in an upright, hunched posture and nests in cavities. The
Western Bluebird is found around forest edges, in orchards, and in
open hardwood and conifer forests and woodlands. Except during
the nesting season, Western Bluebirds travel in flocks, feeding on
berries and fruiting shrubs, in addition to the insects they take
throughout the year. In the winter, these flocks may move from
forest and woodland areas into more open country nearby.

Description
6–6½" (15–16.5 cm). The adult male Western Bluebird has deep blue
upperparts, wings, and tail, with a patch of chestnut, variable in
extent, across the back. The throat is blue, never rust or chestnut;
the breast and flanks are chestnut, and the belly is gray-blue.
Females are duller overall than males, with a grayish throat, a

Adult female
1. *Pale rust throat.*
2. *Brownish back.*
3. *Blue wings.*
4. *Pale rust tone on breast and flanks.*
5. *White belly.*

Adult male
1. *Chestnut throat.*
2. *Blue upperparts without chestnut patch.*
3. *Chestnut breast and flanks.*
4. *White belly.*

   Rich chur-lee *call.*

Adult male
1. *Blue throat.*
2. *Blue upperparts with chestnut patch on back.*
3. *Chestnut breast and flanks.*
4. *Gray-blue belly.*

suffusion of brown on the back, and a much paler rust tone on the
breast and flanks; they show blue in the wings and tail. Juveniles of
this species and of other bluebird species are strongly spotted; they
show bluish in the wings and tail.

Voice
Song a warble, similar to that of Eastern Bluebird but somewhat
harsher. Calls include a soft *phew* and a harsh *chuck*, often given in
flight.

Similar Species
Eastern Bluebird overlaps range of Western only marginally; it has
rust or whitish throat in all plumages, rather than blue or gray as in
Western; and has white instead of blue or gray belly. Adult male
Eastern lacks chestnut patch on back. Female Eastern shows partial
pale rust collar (also variable in Eastern males) and often a dark
malar streak—both marks absent in Western Bluebird. Mountain
Bluebird paler blue, without strong rust tones; has longer bill, legs,
and wings; perches in more horizontal posture, rather than in
upright posture of Western and Eastern bluebirds. Townsend's
Solitaire somewhat resembles female Western Bluebird, but is
slimmer, lacks blue in wings, and has longer tail. Male Lazuli
Bunting has conical bill, 2 white wing bars and extensive white on
belly and lower breast; and inhabits open, brushy areas.

Range
Breeds in western North America from southern British Columbia
east to Rockies in central Montana, and south (primarily in
mountains) to southern California and extreme western Texas;
locally to south-central Mexico. Winters at lower elevations
throughout breeding range and in nearby lowlands. Not as
strongly migratory as Eastern and Mountain bluebirds.
Kimball L. Garrett

Mountain Bluebird

Sialia currucoides
A sky-blue bird that frequents open western sagebrush plains,
mountain meadows, and timberline areas, the Mountain Bluebird
differs from other bluebirds not only in its preference for more open
habitats but also in its hovering foraging behavior and its tendency
to gather into large flocks in winter. Its relatively long bill, legs, and
wings and its more horizontal perching posture distinguish it
somewhat from the Eastern and Western bluebirds, with which it
sometimes occurs.

Description
6¼–6¾" (16–17 cm). The unmistakable male is entirely sky-blue,
with the color deepest and brightest on the upperparts, wings, and
tail. The female also shows bright sky-blue on the wings, tail, and
rump, but the head, back, breast, and flanks are uniformly grayish-
brown; the belly and undertail coverts are white, contrasting with
the gray-brown flanks. Females show a white eye-ring. Juveniles
are strongly spotted.

Adult female
1. *Grayish throat.*
2. *Brownish back.*
3. *Blue wings.*
4. *Pale rust tone on breast and flanks.*
5. *Gray belly.*

Juvenile
1. *Spotted underparts.*
2. *Spotted back.*
3. *Blue wings.*

Female
1. *Bright blue wings.*
2. *Bright blue tail.*
3. *Uniformly gray-brown head and back.*
4. *Gray-brown breast and flanks.*

Shows no strong rust tones in plumage.

Voice
Infrequently heard song a short warble. Birds in winter flocks give
unmusical *veer* or *terrr* note.

Similar Species
Eastern and Western bluebirds lack uniform blue of head, back, and
breast; female Mountains in fresh plumage may have tawny wash on
breast, but always have gray-brown flanks and never show strong
rust tones of Easterns and Westerns. Townsend's Solitaire
somewhat resembles female Mountain Bluebird, but lacks blue in
wings and has longer tail.

Range
Breeds in higher plains and mountains of western North America
from east-central Alaska east to southwestern Manitoba and locally
in Dakotas; south to southern California, northern Arizona, and
southern New Mexico. Winters in plains and agricultural areas
through middle and southern portions of breeding range, reaching
south as far as central Mexico. Accidental in eastern states and
provinces.   *Kimball L. Garrett*

Townsend's Solitaire

Myadestes townsendi
The slender, long-tailed Townsend's Solitaire is a thrush that occurs
in small groups in coniferous forests in the mountains of western
North America. Its shape and habits are more like those of a
flycatcher than a thrush, but its warbling, fluty song and the spotted
plumage of young birds reveal this species' true affinity. Townsend's
Solitaires are partially migratory and prone to erratic wandering.

Description
8–9½" (20.5–24 cm). This slender, long-tailed bird often perches
upright with its tail hanging loosely; it has a short, stubby bill. It is
plain gray overall, with paler underparts; there is a thin, white eye-
ring, and the outer tail feathers are white. A tawny or buff wing
patch at the base of the flight feathers is partly concealed when the
bird is at rest. The spread tail shows buff-white on the corners and
outer feathers. Fresh fall plumage may appear slightly brownish,
and a very faint wing bar may be seen. The juvenile's body is
spotted with pale buff; its wings are like those of adults.

Voice
Call a squeaking *cr-eek* or ringing *eeek*. Song a melodious, delightful
rising and falling warble of fluty whistles.

Similar Species
See female bluebirds and Northern Mockingbird.

Range
Breeds from central Alaska to western Alberta, and Black Hills of
South Dakota south to southern California, central New Mexico,
and, skipping some suitable ranges, northern Mexico. Winters
throughout much of breeding range and at lower elevations north to
southern British Columbia. Casual during migration as far east as
Atlantic Coast in Northeast.   *Louis R. Bevier*

Male
1. *Wholly sky-blue plumage, with no rust tones.*

Adult
1. *Gray upperparts.*
2. *White eye-ring.*
3. *Buff wing patch.*

Slender build. Upright posture when perched.

Juvenile
1. *Pale eye-ring.*
2. *Pale buff spots on head and body.*

Veery

Catharus fuscescens
The haunting, flutelike song of the Veery is a characteristic twilight
sound of moist deciduous and mixed woods where this bird breeds.

Description
7¾" (19.5 cm). Tawny brown or olive-rufous above, white below;
sides of throat and breast pale buff with light wedge-shaped spots.
Flanks pale gray; pale, thin eye-ring. Juveniles dark brown above
with tear-shaped tawny olive spots on head and back.

Voice
Song a rolling series of descending, vibrant, breezy notes, *da-vee-ur,
vee-ur, veer, veer.* Call note a soft, down-slurred *wheeu* or *veer.*

Similar Species
Other *Catharus* thrushes and Wood Thrush heavily spotted below.

Range
S. British Columbia to central Newfoundland; in Rockies to Ne.
Arizona; South Dakota; Se. Minnesota; in Alleghenies to Georgia.
Winters in Central and South America.   *Wayne R. Petersen*

Gray-cheeked Thrush

Catharus minimus
This songbird of the north frequents high mountains, cool coniferous
forests, and alder and willow thickets in summer.

Description
8" (20.5 cm). Breast and cheeks grayish; narrow, grayish-white eye-
ring does not create spectacled look. Olive-brown or olive gray
above; whitish below with olive-gray on sides. Juveniles (rare to
south) darker olive above with buff streaks on back.

Voice
Song a nasal, descending *wee-a, wee-o, wee-a, chi-chi-wee;* call note a
pheu; night migrants' call an explosive *spee-a.*

Similar Species
See Veery and Swainson's, Wood, and Hermit thrushes.

Range
Northern Alaska to Newfoundland, south to northern British
Columbia and southeastern New York. Winters in West Indies and
from Central to South America.   *Wayne R. Petersen*

Swainson's Thrush

Catharus ustulatus
Swainson's is a common and widespread thrush that breeds in the
boreal forests of Canada and in mountainous areas of the
northeastern and western United States. Along the Pacific Coast,
there is a russet-backed race that is often mistaken for the Veery.

Description
6½–7¾" (16.5–19.5 cm). The upperparts are dusky olive-brown or
olive-gray in the East, russet in the West; the breast, throat, and
sides of the head are a rich, creamy buff. The eye-ring and lores are
also creamy buff, creating a spectacled appearance. The breast is
washed with buff, and has heavy, rounded black spots that become
wedge-shaped at the sides of the throat. The rest of the underparts
are whitish, suffused with olive-gray on the sides and flanks. A
series of large, pinkish-buff spots on the inner webs of the flight
feathers often looks like a buff stripe in flight, particularly when
seen from below. Juveniles are darker olive above and have buff
streaks on the back.

Adult
1. *Tawny-brown back.*
2. *Buff breast with light spots.*

Distinctive vee-ur, veer, veer *song.*

Adult
1. *Indistinct grayish eye-ring.*
2. *Gray cheeks.*
3. *Breast with heavy spotting.*
4. *Olive-brown or olive-gray upperparts.*

Eastern adult
1. *Buff spectacles.*
2. *Buff breast with heavy spotting.*
3. *Olive-brown upperparts.*

Voice
Song: upward-rolling series of flutelike phrases, like *wip-poor-wil-wil-eez-zee-zee*. Call note a liquid *whit;* night migrants give a sharp, peeping *queep.*

Similar Species
Gray-cheeked Thrush gray on cheeks and breast, lacks spectacled appearance. Hermit thrush has rust-colored tail, streaks on sides of breast and throat; has habit of cocking and slowly dropping tail, often just after landing. Veery less heavily spotted below. See Wood Thrush.

Range
Breeds from central Alaska across Canada to Newfoundland, south to southern California, New Mexico, Arizona, Great Lakes, and in mountains sparingly to West Virginia. Winters from Mexico to South America.   *Wayne R. Petersen*

Hermit Thrush

Catharus guttatus
Found in upland woods and pine barrens in summer, this early spring migrant is the only *Catharus* apt to be seen in winter.

Description
7½" (19 cm). Olive-brown above; tail reddish; face gray-brown with thin whitish eye-ring. Whitish below with pale buff cast; large spots on breast form narrow streaks on sides of throat and flanks.

Voice
Song a series of flutelike phrases on different pitches with short pauses; first note longest and lowest. Scold note a *tuk-tuk-tuk;* also a soft *chuck* and a whiny *wee.*

Similar Species
See Fox Sparrow; Gray-cheeked and Swainson's thrushes; Veery.

Range
Central Alaska to Newfoundland; to S. California, N. New Mexico, central Wisconsin, and Maryland. Winters from southern breeding areas to Florida and Guatemala.   *Wayne R. Petersen*

Wood Thrush

Hylocichla mustelina
The Wood Thrush's flutelike song, robust shape, and habit of nesting in suburban deciduous woodlands of eastern North America make it easy to identify. The Wood Thrush's large round breast spots are darker and more extensive than those of any other North American thrush.

Description
7½–8½" (19–21.5 cm). The upperparts are plain cinnamon-rufous, brightest on the crown and nape, shading to olive-brown on the uppertail coverts and tail. There is a narrow white eye-ring, and the ear coverts are streaked with white and dusky coloring. The cheeks are grayish. The white underparts are extensively and evenly marked on the breast, sides, and flanks with large, roundish, black spots. Juveniles are similar to adults but have tawny-olive or buff spots on the head and upperparts; faint buff spots on the wing coverts often form 1 or 2 indistinct wing bars.

Western adult
1. *Buff spectacles.*
2. *Buff breast with heavy spotting.*
3. *Russet back.*

Adult
1. *Brown upperparts.*
2. *Reddish-brown tail.*
3. *Spotted breast.*

   Cocks and lowers tail.
   Flicks wings.
   Soft tuk *call.*

Adult
1. *Bright cinnamon-rufous head.*
2. *Plainer cinnamon-rufous back.*
3. *White underparts with bold black spots.*

   Flutelike song.

Voice
Song a short, 3-syllable, flutelike *eee-o-lay*. Call note a sharp,
emphatic *pit pit pit;* also a soft, liquid *pip pip pip* and a low *quirt.*

Similar Species
Hermit Thrush has rusty tail and less extensive breast spotting; has
habit of cocking and slowly dropping tail, often just after landing.
Gray-cheeked and Swainson's thrushes olive-brown to olive-gray
above, without rufous on crown and nape. Veery less heavily
spotted below and more evenly colored above.

Range
Breeds from southeastern South Dakota and northern Michigan east
to southern Quebec, northern New Hampshire, and southern Maine,
south to southeastern Texas, Gulf Coast, and northern Florida.
Winters in Mexico and Central America.   *Wayne R. Petersen*

Eye-browed Thrush

Turdus obscurus
This thrush looks like a small, drab American Robin; it is a rare
annual spring migrant through the western Aleutians. It usually
occurs singly; it is often shy and usually silent in Alaska.

Description
9″ (23 cm). Spring male has gray hood with white eyebrow and white
patch from eyelid to chin; upper breast and flanks pastel orange;
center of breast and belly white. Back, wings, rump, and uppertail
coverts pastel olive-brown; tail gray, narrow, with white tips to
outer 2 pairs of feathers. Upper mandible dark gray, lower yellow-
orange. Female similar but duller.

Similar Species
American Robin similar but does not occur in same Alaska range.

Range
In North America, annual in spring in western Aleutian Islands,
Alaska. Casual farther east in Aleutians and on Alaska islands of
Bering Sea. Native to Siberia.   *Daniel D. Gibson*

Clay-colored Robin

Turdus grayi
This tropical bird, an occasional visitor to southern Texas, closely
resembles the American Robin in size and shape, but is completely
redone in shades of brown; it is somewhat more secretive than the
garden-variety American Robin.

Description
9½″ (24 cm). Head, back, wings, and tail dull brown; throat vaguely
streaked with brown and white. Chest dull gray-brown, lower
underparts warmer buff. Bill dull greenish-yellow. Juvenile has
dusky mottling below, faint streaks above.

Voice
Song like that of American Robin, but richer in tone. Call a mellow,
whistled *tooee-wooah*, second part lower; also a thin *tseek.*

Range
Northeastern Mexico to Colombia. Strays rarely to southern Texas;
has nested.   *Kenn Kaufman*

Juvenile
1. *Buff spots on crown and upperparts.*
2. *Faint buff spots on wing coverts.*

Adult male
1. *White eyebrow.*
2. *Orange upper breast and flanks.*
3. *Center of breast and belly white.*
4. *Olive-brown upperparts.*

Adult
1. *Dull brown upperparts.*
2. *Vague streaks on throat.*
3. *Pale buff on lower underparts.*

Rufous-backed Robin

Turdus rufopalliatus
This rare winter visitor to the border states is typically found alone in areas of dense vegetation, often near water and fruiting trees.

Description
9″ (23 cm). Pale dusty gray above; fine streaks on crown and rufous wash on upper back and wings. Throat white; narrow black streaks extend to upper chest; breast, sides, and flanks pale rufous; belly and undertail coverts white. Yellow bill has some black at tip.

Voice
Main winter calls a very thin, high-pitched *sseet* and low, throaty *chgk*. Song weaker than American Robin's, with longer pauses.

Similar Species
See American Robin and, in southern Texas, Clay-colored Robin.

Range
Rare in winter to S. and central Arizona; recorded in W. and S. Texas, S. California. Native to W. Mexico.   *Kenn Kaufman*

American Robin

Turdus migratorius
This widespread bird has flourished in modern, suburban areas; it also frequents forest borders, woodland openings, pastures, orchards, groves, and parks. The Robin was originally a forest species, and where it continues as a woodland breeder it remains much shyer than the familiar suburban bird. In winter, Robins gather in large roosts and feed heavily on fruits and berries. They occasionally become intoxicated by fermented fruits and behave in a somewhat curious fashion. Early risers and early migrants, American Robins are considered the harbingers of spring.

Description
9–11″ (23–28 cm). The adult is dark gray above with a brick-red breast, a white lower belly, and white undertail coverts. Males have black heads, wings, and tails; females are duller. In both sexes, an incomplete, broad white spectacle frames the brown eye. The chin is streaked black and white, and the yellow bill is tipped with black. The outer tail feathers are tipped with white in eastern races, but the white is diminished or absent in the 2 western races. Birds from Newfoundland and Labrador are darker; males have black upper backs. Juveniles have a pale orange breast with large, black spots, a white throat, white stripes on the back, and pale wing bars.

Voice
Loud, rich caroling with short phrases that change pitch: *cheerily-cheery-cheerily-cheery*. Wide variety of call notes: *tut-tut-tut*, also slurred *tyeeep*. In flight, gives a lispy *see-lip*.

Similar Species
Rufous-backed Robin has rufous wash over back and wings, lacks white around eyes, has more extensive throat streaks. Juveniles possibly confused with Fieldfare*, which has gray head, nape, and rump, and chestnut-brown back. See Eye-browed Thrush.

Range
Breeds from northern tree limit in Alaska through Canada to northern Quebec, Labrador, and Newfoundland south to California, Texas, Arkansas, and South Carolina; infrequently along Gulf Coast. Also resident in highlands of Mexico and Guatemala. Winters from British Columbia to Newfoundland, south to California, southern Texas, Florida, and Mexico.   *Peter D. Vickery*

Adult
1. *Pale dusty gray upperparts.*
2. *Rufous wash on back.*
3. *White throat with narrow black streaks.*
4. *Bill nearly all yellow.*

Juvenile
1. *Pale orange breast with black spots.*
2. *Pale wing bars.*

Adult male
1. *Brick-red breast.*
2. *Gray back.*
3. *Yellow bill with black tip.*
4. *White spectacles.*
5. *Black head.*

Eastern birds have white corners to tail.

Varied Thrush

Ixoreus naevius

The Varied Thrush is a common but often shy bird of taiga and of moist coastal and montane forests in the Northwest. In the Far North it also breeds in riparian alders.

Description
10″ (25.5 cm). Male in spring has orange eye stripe above black mask, bold orange wing bars, orange wing stripe, and black chest band. Female similar but duller; gray chest band may be lacking.

Voice
A protracted, nasal, whistled note, followed by similar note on higher or lower pitch. Call note a *chuk;* also querulous whining.

Range
Breeds in forested Alaska and from central Yukon to Oregon, California, Idaho, and Montana. Winters along coast from Kodiak Island and southern British Columbia to Baja California. Very rare but regular winter visitor in East.   *Daniel D. Gibson*

Wrentit

Chamaea fasciata

Without its loud, clear call the Wrentit would be difficult to detect; this bird sings frequently from a hidden perch throughout the year. Wrentits are found in dense, continuous chaparral and low tangles of vegetation. In general habits, they resemble small wrens.

Description
6″ (15 cm). The Wrentit is brown above with a grayish cast to the face and head; it is slightly paler brown below. The flanks are dark brown and the throat and breast have indistinct dusky streaking. The pale eye is conspicuous at close range. The tail is longer than the wings, narrow at the base, and rounded at the tip; it is often held at an angle to the body. Populations from the northern, humid parts of its range are darker than southern populations.

Voice
Ringing series of *yip-yip-yip*, similar to song of Brown Towhee and with a "bouncing ball" quality. Call a low, rattlelike, churring noise.

Similar Species
Wrens lack conspicuous, pale eye and streaked breast; have shorter, barred tails.

Range
Permanent resident along narrow coastal strip of Oregon from Columbia River south; inland in extreme southwest Oregon to north-central California, and south throughout the Coast Ranges and western Sierra Nevada below about 5000′ to northern Baja California. Absent from Central Valley of California.
Larry R. Ballard

Adult
1. Orange eye stripe.
2. Black mask.
3. Bold orange wing bars.
4. Brick-red underparts.

Males have bold black breastband.

Adult
1. Brownish plumage.
2. Pale eye.
3. Long tail.

Small size.
Secretive habits.
Chaparral habitat.
Ringing call.

Mimic-Thrushes

(Family Mimidae)
This New World family contains a group of medium-size, often
elongate birds; most species have longish tails that they frequently
hold cocked above the plane of the back. The birds in this family are
usually associated with dense, low vegetation; most family members
feed on the ground. These birds generally fly in a low and direct
fashion; their wings are short and rounded. Mimic-Thrushes have
strong, stout legs, and many members of the family choose to run to
escape, rather than to fly. The bills of most mimids are medium to
long and somewhat pointed; the thrashers have extremely long and
decurved bills. Most North American species have plumage that
consists primarily of shades of brown or gray; more colorful blues
and blacks occur on some more tropical species. There is a lack of
marked sexual or seasonal difference in plumage. Most mimids do
not normally occur in flocks. Thrashers and mockingbirds are well
known for their loud, clear, and complex songs; some species are
skillful mimics of other bird and even neighborhood noises. (World:
31 species. North America: 11 species.)   *Scott B. Terrill*

Gray Catbird

Dumetella carolinensis
This common bird inhabits undergrowth, brush, and gardens, and
usually stays near dense cover. It has a musical song and a varied
repertoire. When giving its catlike call, it often flicks its tail.

Description
9″ (23 cm). Slim, medium-size; dark gray above and below with black
cap, rust undertail coverts, and long tail.

Voice
Song soft, disjointed on 5–6 pitches; interspersed with pauses,
mews, and imitations. Commonest call a catlike scold. Also a grating
tcheek-tcheek, soft cluck, and sharp snapping notes.

Range
S. British Columbia to Nova Scotia, south to E. Oregon, E. central
Arizona, and N. Texas to central Georgia. Winters from Se. Texas
to Se. Virginia (small numbers to Massachusetts) and south through
Florida to Central America.   *Paul W. Sykes, Jr.*

Northern Mockingbird

Mimus polyglottos
This common, conspicuous, long-tailed songbird frequents open
country and is widespread across much of North America. It sings
incessantly throughout the year but most vigorously in spring and
summer. An expert mimic of other birds and sounds, it repeats most
phrases of its songs many times, singing from high, exposed perches
and in flight, often at night. It inhabits a wide variety of open
habitats, from cities to gardens, woodland edges, and deserts. It
flies with slow wingbeats. When perched, it often flicks its tail from
side to side or flashes its wings and fans its tail slightly.

Description
11″ (28 cm). Soft gray above (with faint brownish tone in some parts
of range); white to light gray below. Two white wing bars and large
white patch on upperwing at base of black primaries (visible in
flight); white areas diagnostic. Tail long, rounded, mostly black,
with several white outer feathers. Juvenile similar but with faint
spotting on breast.

Gray Catbird
Northern Mockingbird
Bahama Mockingbird
Sage Thrasher
Brown Thrasher
Long-billed Thrasher
Bendire's Thrasher
Curve-billed Thrasher
California Thrasher
Crissal Thrasher
Le Conte's Thrasher

Adult
1. *Black cap.*
2. *Gray plumage.*
3. *Rust undertail coverts.*

   Catlike, mewing call.

Adult
1. *Soft gray plumage.*
2. *White wing bars.*
3. *White patches in wings.*
4. *Long black tail with white outer tail feathers.*

Voice
Song a rich, varied, musical medley interspersed with imitations and harsh notes. Usually repeats each note 3–6 or more times before shifting to another imitation or phrase. Call note a loud *tchak;* also a *chair.*

Similar Species
See Northern and Loggerhead shrikes. Townsend's Solitaire darker gray, has different posture, white eye-ring, and buff wing bars. See Bahama Mockingbird*.

Range
Resident in recent years in scattered localities across southernmost Canada from Alberta to Newfoundland, particularly southern Ontario and Quebec; generally resident from northern California, northern Utah and southern North Dakota, to southern Maine; south through Florida, Bahamas, Greater Antilles, and into southern Mexico. Some birds in northern parts of range move southward in winter.   *Paul W. Sykes, Jr.*

Sage Thrasher

Oreoscoptes montanus
This smallest thrasher is common throughout most of its range in western North America. It inhabits open country year-round, occurring in summer in the sage and scrub of basin and range country; in winter it frequents a variety of more southerly deserts. This highly migratory bird flies swiftly with rapid wingbeats.

Description
8–9″ (20.5–23 cm). This species' short, straight, slender bill is unlike the bills of conventional thrashers. The upperparts are gray-brown, darker on the tail and wings; there are 2 white wing bars. The tail is conspicuously tipped with white. There is an indistinct eyebrow and mustache; the iris is yellow. The off-white underparts have narrow brown wedges on the breast that become streaks on the sides and flanks. The lower belly and undertail coverts often have a buff wash. Immatures are browner above and have more diffuse streaking below and darker eyes.

Voice
Song a long series of rich, warbling notes similar to songs of other mimids, especially Northern Mockingbird. Call a solid *chuck.*

Similar Species
Bendire's Thrasher has short bill; Curve-billed has long bill; both faintly spotted below, brown above, and lack wing bars. See other thrashers. Juvenile Mockingbird has distinctive wing pattern. Thrushes spotted below, brown above, and have shorter tails.

Range
Breeds largely between Sierra Nevada-Cascade axis and Rocky Mountains from southern British Columbia, Montana, and Wyoming south to east-central California, southern Nevada, northern Arizona and New Mexico, and northwestern Texas. Winters from southern Arizona to western Texas and south to northern Mexico, with scattered pockets in central and southern California, southern part of breeding range, and southern Texas. Early spring migration; fall migration protracted; size and location of wintering populations quite variable.   *Richard Webster*

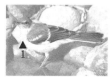

Juvenile
1. *Faint spotting on breast.*

Adult
1. *Short, straight bill.*
2. *Gray-brown uperparts.*
3. *Streaked underparts.*

Adult
1. *Two white wing bars.*
2. *White tips to tail feathers.*

Brown Thrasher

Toxostoma rufum
The fox-red Brown Thrasher haunts the wood lots, hedgerows, and gardens of eastern North America. Despite its skulking manner, the Brown Thrasher may deliver its song from a prominent, exposed perch.

Description
11½" (29 cm). The Brown Thrasher is entirely rufous on the crown, back, wings, and tail, with 2 dull white wing bars. The face is dull gray-brown. The underparts are whitish, strongly washed with buff on the breast and sides, and heavily streaked with dark brown. The eyes are usually yellow (rarely orange), and the bill is dark with a pale base to the lower mandible.

Voice
Song has quality between Northern Mockingbird's and Gray Catbird's: rich melodious phrases, motifs usually in pairs, sometimes tripled. Calls include a low *spuck*, a hard cracking sound, and a 3-note whistle, *pitcheree*.

Similar Species
Brown-backed thrushes have shorter tails, dark eyes, more or less spotted (not streaked) underparts. Long-billed and Brown thrashers occur together in southern Texas in winter; Long-billed has orange eyes, longer, more decurved, all-black bill; face generally grayer; sides of chest appear dull white with more blackish streaking (but this difference is subtle); upperparts appear slightly 2-toned rather than uniformly rufous. See Sage Thrasher.

Range
Breeds from southeastern Alberta east to New England and south to Colorado, northern and eastern Texas, Gulf Coast, and southern Florida. Common in winter in South from Texas eastward, ranging north in Mississippi Valley to Illinois and along coast to Massachusetts; sparse farther west and farther north. Rare visitor as far west as Pacific Coast in migration and winter.
Kenn Kaufman

Long-billed Thrasher

Toxostoma longirostre
This shy skulker inhabits dense woods and river thickets of south Texas, where the Brown Thrasher is also found in winter.

Description
11½" (29 cm). Similar to Brown Thrasher, but brown upperparts look slightly 2-toned, tail more rufous; back dull gray-brown. Face and sides of neck medium gray. Dull white below with heavy blackish streaks. Eyes orange; bill black, long, slightly decurved. Immatures similar; may have paler, yellowish eyes.

Voice
Long series of musical phrases and notes; also a *spuck* call and mellow, whistled *choowee* (rising) and *teeyook* (falling).

Similar Species
See Brown Thrasher.

Range
S. Texas and E. Mexico; permanent resident north at least to Del Rio and San Antonio; accidental in W. Texas.   *Kenn Kaufman*

Adult

1. *Buff-white underparts with brown streaks.*

Adult

1. *Bright rufous upperparts.*
2. *Long tail.*
3. *Buff-white underparts with brown streaks.*
4. *Yellow eyes.*

   Slender build.

Adult

1. *Dull brown back.*
2. *Long rufous tail.*
3. *Dull white underparts with black streaks.*
4. *Black bill, slightly decurved.*
5. *Orange eyes.*

   Texas only.

Bendire's Thrasher

Toxostoma bendirei
Bendire's Thrashers are found in deserts with scrub and cactus; they also breed in southern Great Basin desert scrub from monotypic sage to piñon-juniper-sage communities. This species is an early migrant, usually moving north in late January and withdrawing by late July or August. In winter, Bendire's is local and uncommon in the Phoenix-to-Tucson basin; there it is found from saltbush flats to agricultural and residential areas, but seldom in breeding habitats in the same region. In spring, these birds are fairly conspicuous, and can be seen flying near roadsides or singing from low perches.

Description
8½–11½″ (21.5–29 cm). Bendire's is dark grayish-brown above, and rather small and short-tailed for a thrasher; white corners on the outer tail feathers are visible in flight. The whitish underparts have pale grayish spotting on the breast (greatly reduced with wear). The bill is short; the upper mandible often appears straight but is sometimes slightly curved; the lower one is straight with a pale base, which is diagnostic but difficult to see.

Voice
A soft, thin warble with the "double effect" of 2 notes delivered simultaneously, or nearly so; different from typically loud, clear songs of mimids. Call note a low *chuck*.

Similar Species
Bendire's easily confused with Curve-billed Thrasher (especially immature), but Curve-billed generally larger-looking, with longer, more curved bill and longer tail; has pale plumage, primarily grayish or grayish-brown, and is shaped more like Crissal Thrasher (Bendire's is shaped more like Sage); adult has both mandibles curved with dark base to lower mandible. Curve-billed has bolder malar stripe and larger, more indistinct, rounder spots below in nonworn plumage, but young and worn birds of both species can be similar below. Curve-billed's loud *whit-wheet* call diagnostic.

Range
Breeds in southeastern California (primarily San Bernardino County), southern Nevada, western New Mexico, and Sonora. Winters from central-southern Arizona to Sinoloa. Rare in fall to southern coast of California.   *Scott B. Terrill*

Curve-billed Thrasher

Toxostoma curvirostre
In the desert regions of southern Arizona, southern New Mexico, and Texas, the Curve-billed Thrasher is the most abundant and conspicuous species in this group. In deserts with extensive thorny scrub (palo verde and mesquite) and dense large cactus (saguaro and cholla), and in brushy riparian and residential areas, these birds are easily seen perched or flying about. Their very loud, liquid *whit-wheet* call is especially noticeable. This species' flight is low, brief, and often rapid, like that of other thrashers; as the bird banks to land, the whitish corners of the outer tail feathers flash boldly.

Description
9½–11½″ (23.5–29 cm). This large thrasher has a long, evenly decurved bill, a long tail, and a bright orange to yellow eye. The upperparts are entirely pale grayish-brown. Most birds have conspicuous whitish corners on the outer tail feathers; birds east of central to southern Arizona show fairly prominent wing bars. However, both the wing bars and the white on the tail can be

Adult
1. Short bill with pale base, curved upper mandible, and straight lower mandible.
2. Grayish-brown upperparts.
3. Short tail with white at tips of outer feathers.

Adult
1. Fine spots on underparts.

Adult
1. Long, decurved bill.
2. Pale gray-brown upperparts.
3. Lightly spotted underparts.

Whit-wheet *call.*

absent, especially in birds in westerly localities. The tail is the same
color as the upperparts, but is variably darker. The underparts are
whitish, washed with gray or gray-buff, and have more or less
longitudinal dark gray to blackish spots; these spots vary greatly
according to the bird's range, age, and sex, and the amount of wear
on the throat, breast, sides, and flanks (usually most conspicuous on
the breast). Immature birds have shorter, straighter bills, shorter
tails, and poorly defined spotting on the underparts.

Voice
Call a very loud, liquid *whit-wheet.*

Similar Species
See Bendire's Thrasher.

Range
Breeds from central Arizona (and probably southernmost Nevada),
southeastern Colorado, northwestern Oklahoma, and western and
southern Texas south to southern Mexico. Winters from southern
Arizona and New Mexico southward. Casual west to southeastern
California in winter.   *Scott B. Terrill*

California Thrasher

Toxostoma redivivum
This active bird inhabits chaparral and is common in most of its
range. It spends much time on the ground in its brushy habitat.

Description
12″ (30.5 cm). Almost identical to Crissal: dark chocolate-brown
above, slightly paler below, with whitish throat, vague eyebrow,
mustache, and long, decurved black bill.

Voice
Song of deep, rich, slow phrases, like songs of other mimids;
patterns vary among individuals. Calls a *chuck* and *quip.*

Similar Species
See Crissal and Le Conte's thrashers. Brown Towhee similar in
pattern but shorter, with stubby bill.

Range
In California on west slope of Sierra Nevada, in Central Valley
(rare), and Coast Ranges from just south of Oregon border to
northern Baja.   *Richard Webster*

Crissal Thrasher

Toxostoma dorsale
The Crissal Thrasher inhabits the more heavily vegetated areas of
southern deserts. It is common at lower elevations in dense
mesquite and similar riparian vegetation, and where underground
water supports thickets, becoming uncommon in other habitats.

Description
11–12″ (28–30.5 cm). The Crissal is virtually identical to the
California Thrasher. The entire upperparts are an unmarked dark
chocolate-brown; the face is also chocolate-brown, with a faint pale
eyebrow and ear coverts faintly flecked with white. The chin and
throat are whitish with a more or less distinct mustache. The breast
and belly are buff-brown, becoming cinnamon on the lower belly and
more rufous on the undertail coverts. The strong, decurved black
bill is about the same length as the head. Immatures have shorter
bills and buff edges to the wing coverts.

Voice
Song a series of repeated, whistled phrases typical of thrashers;

Immature
1. Short, dark bill with no pale base.
2. Poorly defined spotting on underparts.

Immature easily mistaken for adult Bendire's Thrasher.

Adult
1. Long, decurved bill.
2. Dark mustache.
3. Plain buff-brown breast.
4. Dark brown upperparts.

Slender build. Usually seen on ground.

Adult
1. Long, decurved bill.
2. Vague moustache.
3. Plain breast.
4. Brown upperparts.
5. Reddish lower belly and undertail coverts.

more deliberate and less musical than song of mockingbird. Calls are 2- or 3-syllable whistles: *chi-deary* or *toit-toit.*

Similar Species
California Thrasher very similar; compared to nearest populations of Crissal is grayer above, especially in fresh plumage (fall through winter); however, gray cast wears off in spring and summer; has more distinct white throat and dark mustache; lower belly and undertail coverts grayer; tail slightly shorter. Calls also distinctive. See Le Conte's Thrasher. Other thrashers have pale eyes and streaked or spotted breasts. Abert's Towhee similar in pattern but shorter, with stubby bill.

Range
Resident in southeastern California, southern Nevada, southwestern Utah, most of Arizona, southern half of New Mexico, western Texas, and northern portions of Baja California, Sonora, and Chihuahua. Limited movement away from colder areas in winter does not take individuals out of normal range of species. Occurs from sea level to 6000'.   *Richard Webster*

Le Conte's Thrasher

Toxostoma lecontei
Le Conte's Thrasher inhabits the hottest, driest, most barren deserts of the Southwest. This very shy bird is rather local within its fairly extensive 4-state range; even where it is relatively common, the populations are spread over large territories.

Description
10–11" (25.5–28 cm). The upperparts are a plain, pale grayish- or sandy-brown, contrasting with a dark brown to blackish tail. The white throat shows a fine black mustache. The rest of the underparts are pale buff to gray, becoming rich buff on the lower belly and undertail coverts. The long black bill is sturdy and decurved. Freshly molted birds in fall as well as populations in the southern San Joaquin Valley of California, which have brighter undertail coverts, often appear a bit darker.

Voice
Song a series of rich, warbled phrases with less repetition than songs of other thrashers; songs may last several minutes and include much imitation. Low, whistled calls a *tu-wheep* and a rising *whit.*

Similar Species
California and Crissal thrashers larger, darker; upperparts and tail same color; occur in denser areas. Bendire's and Curve-billed spotted below, have pale eyes; Bendire's has short bill. Other thrashers streaked below, have wing bars.

Range
Resident in southern San Joaquin Valley of California and across deserts east of Coast Ranges and Sierra Nevada to southern Nevada and southwestern Utah, south to Baja California, northern Sonora, and western and south-central Arizona.   *Richard Webster*

Immature
1. *Bill shorter than adult's.*
2. *Buff edges to wing coverts.*
3. *Reddish undertail coverts.*

Adult
1. *Long, decurved bill.*
2. *Pale sandy-brown plumage.*
3. *Long, dark tail.*

Wagtails and Pipits

(Family Motacillidae)
For North American reference, this family may be conveniently
divided into 2 genera, *Motacilla*, the wagtails, and *Anthus*, the
pipits. Both groups include smallish birds of slim build with small,
slender bills; these birds have long legs—on which they walk and
run rather than hop—and long toes. The wagtails have long, slender
tails that they almost constantly wag or flip around. These
extremely elongate, slender birds are usually associated with water.
Most are brightly colored or boldly patterned. There is some sexual
and seasonal plumage difference in the genus, and a high degree of
geographical variation in several species. Pipits are primarily
brownish or olive-brown above and pale buff or whitish below; all
pipits recorded in North America are marked with more or less
extensive streaking and light superciliary stripes and wing bars.
Most all pump the tail continuously. The Old World species recorded
here represent a complex field identification problem; special
attention must be paid to subtle plumage features. (World: 54
species. North America: 10 species.)   *Scott B. Terrill*

Yellow Wagtail

Motacilla flava
A small, slender bird of open country, the Yellow Wagtail is smaller
than the White and Black-backed wagtails and not so prominently
long-tailed. It is also more tolerant of man than these species. It is a
common breeder on the coastal tundra of western Alaska and on
tundra in the northern foothills of the Brooks Range. This bird wags
its tail constantly as it walks. In spring plumage, the pipitlike
Yellow Wagtail is unmistakable.

Description
6½″ (16.5 cm). Adults are yellow below, becoming white at the
throat, with a broken, ill-defined breast band. The head is gray,
marked by a white eyebrow. The back is dark olive and the rump is
brighter olive; the tail is blackish with white outer feathers. The
juvenile has a whitish throat and an unstreaked buff breast and
belly. Poorly defined malar stripes meet at the pectoral band and
form a U. The eyebrow is buff and the head and back are a warm
olive-brown.

Voice
Call a distinctive, drawn-out, single-note, *tzeeep*.

Range
In North America, common on coast of western Alaska from Bristol
Bay north and in northern foothills of Brooks Range. Less numerous
farther east; reaches northernmost Yukon Territory. Migrant
through western Aleutian Islands. Also in Eurasia.
Daniel D. Gibson

Yellow Wagtail
Gray Wagtail
White Wagtail
Black-backed Wagtail
Brown Tree-Pipit
Olive Tree-Pipit
Pechora Pipit
Red-throated Pipit
Water Pipit
Sprague's Pipit

Adult
1. *White eyebrow.*
2. *Gray crown.*
3. *Gray mask.*
4. *Yellow underparts.*
5. *Dark olive back.*
6. *Black tail with white borders.*

Juvenile
1. *Buff eyebrow.*
2. *Whitish throat.*
3. *U-shaped breastband.*
4. *Buff breast and belly.*
5. *Warm olive-brown upperparts.*

White Wagtail

Motacilla alba
This shy, slender bird of open habitats near water reaches our area
only in coastal western Alaska, where it is a rare annual breeder.

Description
7″ (18 cm). Spring male has black throat, upper breast, crown, and
nape, and thin black line through eyes from bill to nape. Forehead,
cheeks, underparts, and wing bars white; flanks and back gray.
Long black tail has white outer feathers. Female has less black on
throat; juvenile has browner wings with thin bars, white throat.

Voice
Call a distinctive 2-note *chizzik*, inflected on second syllable.

Similar Species
Male Black-backed has black back and scapulars, large white wing
patch, whiter flanks; females probably inseparable.

Range
Alaska coasts and islands (St. Lawrence Island to Cape Lisburne);
casual inland in Alaska. Native to Eurasia.   *Daniel D. Gibson*

Black-backed Wagtail

Motacilla lugens
This rare spring migrant through the western Aleutians occurs
singly or in small groups along creeks and ponds near the coast.

Description
7″ (18 cm). Very similar to White Wagtail in Alaska; these are only
wagtails with black line through eye. Spring male has black back
and scapulars, large white wing patch, and broad white edging on
secondaries. Underparts and flanks clear white. Adult spring female
also has wing patch but has chin, throat, and back like both sexes of
White Wagtail. Juvenile identical to juvenile White Wagtail.

Voice
Call a 2-note *chizzik*, inflected on second syllable.

Similar Species
See White Wagtail; females and juveniles nearly identical.

Range
Rare in spring in W. Aleutians; casual on Bering Sea islands and
Pacific Coast east of Aleutians. Native to Asia.   *Daniel D. Gibson*

Olive Tree-Pipit

Anthus hodgsoni
This tail-pumping species often perches in trees or on other elevated
posts. It frequents tundra, fields, forest edges, and open woods.

Description
6½″ (16.5 cm). Dark olive-green above with faint black streaks on
back, distinct black streaks on crown, 2 buff wing bars, and white
outer tail feathers. Upper lores bright yellow-buff; eyebrow cream-
white with black border. Often small white patch behind eyebrow
and small black ear patch. Throat buff; breast and flanks buff with
heavy streaks. Belly and undertail coverts whitish. Legs pale.

Voice
Call note a reedy *tseep*, louder than Red-throated Pipit's.

Similar Species
See Water, Red-throated, and Sprague's pipits.

Range
Casual spring migrant in Western Aleutian and St. Lawrence
islands off Alaska. Native to Eurasia.   *Ben King*

Spring male
1. *Black-and-white head pattern.*
2. *Black throat and upper breast.*
3. *Gray back.*
4. *Long black tail with white outer feathers.*

Spring male
1. *Black back.*
2. *Large white wing patch.*

Adult
. *Olive-green upperparts with faint streaks on back.*
. *Creamy white eyebrow bordered with black.*
. *White patch below eyebrow.*

Red-throated Pipit

Anthus cervinus
While often found in more heavily vegetated areas than the Water
Pipit, the Red-throated Pipit is not particularly shy; unlike
Sprague's Pipit, this species does not use vegetation as a refuge.
The Red-throated Pipit is found on short tundra in the breeding
season; during winter and migration it inhabits damp grassy areas
near marshes and in river valleys. It sings from an elevated perch or
while in flight and pumps its tail occasionally.

Description
6½" (16.5 cm). The upperparts are a warm dark brown with bold
black streaks, 4 paler buff or whitish streaks on the back, 2 buff-
white wing bars, and white outer tail feathers. The throat, sides of
the head, and eyebrow are bright pinkish-rufous. The remaining
underparts are buff, with black streaks on the flanks and sometimes
on the breast. The legs are pale. Fall birds are similar, but the
pinkish-rufous is reduced in area and intensity, and is entirely
lacking in some birds; the breast and flanks are heavily streaked
with blackish. The juvenile is like the fall adult but has no pinkish-
rufous and has a buff throat and eyebrow.

Voice
Call note a thin, high-pitched *seee, seeep,* or *see-eep.* Song a
combination of reedy and musical notes, often prolonged; overall
effect rather insectlike.

Similar Species
Bright pinkish-rufous throat of breeding bird is diagnostic. Fall
Water Pipit may be confused with juvenile Red-throated, but has
dark brown ground color on more darkly streaked upperparts; legs
usually darker; call different. Sprague's Pipit has paler upperparts,
narrow necklace on breast (no heavy streaking), different call. Olive
Tree-Pipit has darker, less heavily streaked upperparts.

Range
Breeds in Bering Strait area of Alaska. Rare migrant on Aleutian
and Pribilof islands. Rare fall migrant to Pacific Coast. Native to
Eurasia and Africa.   *Ben King*

Water Pipit

Anthus spinoletta
In winter and migration, this bird inhabits shores and fields with
little or no vegetation; during the breeding season it is found on
tundra. It walks about in the open, often pumping its tail down and
up; it almost never perches in trees. It is normally found in pairs or
in small scattered flocks. Several races vary slightly in color.

Description
6½" (16.5 cm). Body and bill slender; tail long. In breeding plumage,
pale grayish above with faint dark streaks on crown and back, 2 buff
wing bars, and white outer tail feathers. Eyebrow rich pinkish-buff,
same color as breast or paler. Dark pinkish-buff below, with throat,
center of belly, and undertail coverts slightly paler. Flanks have
some blackish streaks; breast has moderately heavy necklace of
blackish streaks (not present in all birds). Wing linings buff; legs
brown to black. Fall plumage similar, but ground color of upperparts
dark brown; paler, duller, uniform buff below; breast and flanks
have heavy blackish streaks. Some fall birds have pale legs.

Breeding adult
1. *Bright pinkish-rufous throat.*
2. *Heavily streaked upperparts.*
3. *Pale legs.*

Fall adult
1. *Heavily streaked upperparts.*
2. *Breast and flanks streaked with blackish.*
3. *Pale legs.*

Fall adult
1. *Faintly streaked, dark brown back.*
2. *Heavily streaked breast and flanks.*
3. *Dark legs.*

Some fall birds have pale legs.

Voice
Call note a thin sharp *peet* or *pit* or *chip-it* or *pi-pi-pi-pit*. Song a
musical *chee* or *chawee*, repeated over and over.

Similar Species
Horned Lark has black patches on head and breast; different call.
Longspurs, sparrows, and finches have thick, conical bills and
different calls. See Sprague's and Red-throated pipits. Olive Tree-
Pipit olive-green above with white eyebrow, buff breast and lores,
whitish belly; more heavily streaked below and darker above than
breeding-plumage Water Pipit; Olive Tree-Pipit pumps tail more
often; call different.

Range
Breeds on Arctic tundra and in mountains in West and in Maine.
Common migrant throughout North America. Winters on Pacific
Coast from British Columbia south, and from the southern United
States south to Guatemala; rarely north along coast to New York.
Native to Eurasia.   *Ben King*

Sprague's Pipit

Anthus spragueii
An almost entirely terrestrial species, Sprague's Pipit is found only
in short-grass prairie. Secretive and a skulker, this bird is very
difficult to observe. Its presence usually goes undetected until it
launches itself abruptly into the air, uttering a distinctive, sharp,
explosive call note. These birds deliver their song from high in the
air. Unlike other pipits, Sprague's apparently does not pump its tail.

Description
6½″ (16.5 cm). The adult's upperparts are heavily streaked overall
with blackish and buff to buff-brown; there are 2 buff wing bars, and
the outer tail feathers are white. In fresh plumage there are faint,
fine buff scales on the back. The dark brown eye is conspicuous
against the pale buff lores and eye-ring and the rather plain buff
sides of the head. There is an indistinct buff eyebrow. The only
streaking on the underparts is a narrow necklace across the breast.
The breast is bright buff, grading to brownish-buff on the flanks and
pale buff or buff-white on the throat, belly, and undertail coverts.
The wing linings are white. The lower mandible and the legs are a
bright yellowish to pale pinkish color. The juvenal plumage is like
that of the adult except that the back is black with narrow buff
streaks and fine white scales.

Voice
Call note a forced, loud, reedy *tweep* or *tsweep;* often doubled. Song
a descending series of musical notes, often repeated many times in
flight.

Similar Species
Water Pipit has darker, less heavily streaked upperparts, dark legs,
streaked flanks, and different call. Juvenile Red-throated Pipit has
darker upperparts, more heavily streaked breast, streaked flanks,
and different call. Olive Tree-Pipit has darker, less heavily streaked
upperparts. Longspurs, finches, and sparrows have heavier, conical
bills and different calls.

Range
Breeds on northern Great Plains of Canada south to northern
United States. Migrant in Great Plains. Winters from southern tier
of Great Plains states south through Mexico. Strays to both East
and West coasts.   *Ben King*

Spring adult
1. *Pale grayish back.*
2. *Buff breast with few streaks.*
3. *Dark legs.*

Adult
1. *Heavily streaked back.*
2. *Pale sides of head and beady dark eye.*
3. *Pink legs.*

Adult
1. *Thin necklace of streaks on breast.*
2. *No streaks on flanks.*

Waxwings

(Family Bombycillidae)
Waxwings are sleek-plumaged, crested birds with black facial
markings, yellow-tipped tails, and red spots on the tips of the
secondaries that look like drops of sealing wax. The bill is broadly
based, short, and hooked at the tip. Vocal and gregarious, these
birds flycatch for insects and also eat a variety of berries. In fall and
winter, they are almost always found among fruit trees in towns and
cities. They typically feed in large erratic flocks; a flock can consume
all the fruit from trees in a single neighborhood within a few hours
before moving on to another area. (World: 3 species. North America:
2 species.)   *Kim R. Eckert and Scott B. Terrill*

Bohemian Waxwing

Bombycilla garrulus
In winter, throughout much of Canada and the northern United
States, the Bohemian replaces the Cedar Waxwing. A lone
Bohemian at this season is unlikely, since these birds typically travel
in large, unpredictable flocks that often number in the hundreds.
This species is partial to mountain ash, crabapple, and other fruit
trees that are normally found only in cities and towns; observers are
unlikely to encounter a flock of Bohemians in the depths of a
coniferous forest. A flock of these waxwings gives off an almost
incessant low-pitched buzzing. They can be abundant at a spot one
day and then disappear overnight once all the fruit has been
consumed. This species is remarkably like a Starling in its size,
flight profile, and flocking behavior.

Description
7½–8¾″ (19–22 cm). The Bohemian Waxwing appears uniformly
gray at a distance, except for the yellow-tipped tail and black mask
and throat markings. Seen in good light and from the side or below,
this large waxwing is best identified by the distinct dark rusty
undertail coverts. Bohemians also have white and (usually) yellow
wing spots. Like adults, juvenile Bohemians have pale rust-colored
undertail coverts and white marks on the wings, but are not as gray
and have diffuse streaking below.

Voice
A constant, trilled *zzrr zzrr zzrr*, similar to Cedar Waxwing's but
rougher, buzzier, and lower-pitched.

Similar Species
See juvenile Cedar Waxwing.

Range
Breeds from central Alaska, Yukon, southwestern Mackenzie, and
northern Manitoba south to northern parts of Washington, Idaho,
and Montana, central Saskatchewan, and central Manitoba. Winters
south to Washington, Colorado, Great Lakes, and Maine; east to
Ontario, southern Quebec, Nova Scotia, and northern tier of states;
irregularly to California, Arizona, northern New Mexico, and
northern Texas. Also found in northern Eurasia.   *Kim R. Eckert*

Bohemian Waxwing
Cedar Waxwing

Adult
1. *Crest.*
2. *Black mask.*
3. *Gray plumage.*
4. *White and yellow spots on wings.*
5. *Rust undertail coverts.*
6. *Yellow-tipped tail.*

   Large size.

Juvenile
1. *Streaked underparts.*
2. *Pale rust undertail coverts.*
3. *White wing spots.*
4. *Yellow-tipped tail.*

Cedar Waxwing

Bombycilla cedrorum
Found throughout most of the United States and Canada, the Cedar is the most familiar of the waxwings. Sleek and elegantly plumaged, the adult Cedar Waxwing never seems to have a feather out of place. This species is a berry-feeder, but when insects are present it often flycatches for them.

Description
6½–8" (16.5–20.5 cm). The adult Cedar Waxwing lacks the uniform gray appearance of the Bohemian and has a browner back and breast and a yellowish belly. The undertail coverts are white; the wings do not show white and yellow spots, although the Cedar does have a whitish edge on the secondaries that is visible when the bird is at rest. There is a yellow band on the tail. Juveniles tend to be grayer overall; they are diffusely streaked, especially on the underparts, and have little or no black around the eye and throat.

Voice
A hissing, high-pitched, lisping *ssse sssee seee*; notes sometimes slightly trilled. Similar to Brown Creeper's note.

Similar Species
Bohemian Waxwing grayer and a bit larger (although the size difference is not usually obvious without direct comparison); both adults and juveniles have rust-colored undertail coverts and white wing patches.

Range
Breeds from southeastern Alaska, central British Columbia, Alberta, Saskatchewan, central Manitoba, Ontario, southern Quebec, and Newfoundland south to northern parts of California, Nevada, Utah, Colorado, South Dakota, central Missouri, Illinois, Indiana, northern Georgia, western North Carolina, and Virginia. Winters from southern parts of British Columbia, Montana, Saskatchewan, Manitoba, Ontario, New York, and New England south to South America and West Indies.   *Kim R. Eckert*

Adult
1. *Crest.*
2. *Black mask.*
3. *Brownish upperparts.*
4. *Yellow band at tip of tail.*

   Pale undertail coverts.

Juvenile
1. *Streaked underparts.*
2. *Pale undertail coverts.*
3. *Yellow-tipped tail.*

   No white patches on wings.

Silky-Flycatchers

(Family Ptilogonatidae)
The Silky-Flycatcher family includes 4 species that are found from
the southwestern United States to Mexico and Central America.
Three of the 4 are very gregarious, slender, elongated, crested birds
with long tails; the exception is the Black-and-yellow Phainoptila.
All members of the family fly with erratic wingbeats, giving the
impression of a weak, jerky flight. Individuals call rather
continuously from overhead flocks or from perches near the tops of
trees and bushes. (World: 4 species. North America: 1 species.)
Scott B. Terrill

Phainopepla

Phainopepla nitens
Phainopeplas are found in a variety of southwestern habitats; they
move from region to region, and may breed in more than 1 area in
any given year. In deserts they are found primarily in washes,
riparian areas, and other habitats that support brushy growth of
mesquite, ironwood, and palo verde. In more northerly and coastal
areas, they are found in oak chaparral and riparian oak woodlands.
Phainopeplas feed heavily on mistletoe berries, and are often found
concentrated around mistletoe clumps; during the breeding season,
the birds become insectivores. When flying short distances, they
jerk about horizontally with weak, erratic wingbeats and almost
seem to hover just above vegetation. For longer flights, the bird
often climbs erratically upward and then takes off in a more direct
horizontal flight. At greater heights, Phainopeplas fly directly, but
not swiftly, with erratic wingbeats, displaying white wing patches.
In courtship, the male performs a steep climb, often singing, and
then glides with wings held in a stiff V alternating with deep
butterflylike wingbeats. Phainopeplas frequently call in flight; one
can hear their low, soft notes over an amazingly long distance.
Although the bird's crest may be flattened, even at a distance its
very slender, long-tailed look and characteristic flight identify it.

Description
7–7¾" (18–19.5 cm). Phainopeplas are slender birds with long,
slightly fanned tails, small bills, and long, thin, shaggy crests. They
often sit very upright with the crest sticking straight up. Males are
entirely glossy black except for 2 white wing patches (visible only in
flight) and deep red eyes. Females are shaped like the male but are
dark gray-brown with a pale brownish or gray wing patch.
Immatures are similar to females but browner and paler on the
underparts with more conspicuous pale edgings to the wings.

Voice
Call a low, liquid *whoip* or *wurp*. Also a harsh, nasal *korr* or *karak*.
Song a listless, wheezy series of disconnected warbled phrases.

Range

Northern California (interior), southern Nevada, southern Utah,
and southern New Mexico to trans-Pecos Texas, south to central
Mexico.   *Scott B. Terrill*

Phainopepla

Adult male
1. *Shaggy crest.*
2. *Glossy, black plumage.*
3. *White wing patches.*
4. *Long tail.*

Adult female
1. *Shaggy crest.*
2. *Grayish-brown plumage.*
3. *Long tail.*

Shows pale wing patches in flight.

Shrikes

(Family Laniidae)
Shrikes are grayish, predatory songbirds with black masks and
hooked beaks with a sharp, toothlike projection near the tip. The
wings and tails are black; the wings have bold white patches.
Shrikes prey on mice, large insects, and small birds, which they
impale on thorns and barbed wire. Like hawks, shrikes are solitary;
they hunt in open country, and are usually seen on conspicuous
perches. Their flight is direct, on rapid wingbeats. Shrikes often
drop low to the ground between perches, swooping upward again
suddenly to land again. (World: 74 species. North America: 3
species.)   *Kim R. Eckert and Scott B. Terrill*

Northern Shrike

Lanius excubitor
This shrike is a winter resident in many northern areas. It may hunt
for small birds from a conspicuous perch in open areas or frequent
feeding stations. Although the Northern Shrike is relatively easy to
see within its range and during the right season, it is usually wary
and difficult to approach; it will often fly off rapidly, in a straight
line, before its subtle field marks can be studied. Even on the
coldest winter days, the Northern Shrike may erupt into a
surprisingly musical song.

Description
9–10¾″ (23–27.5 cm). The Northern Shrike is pale gray above,
usually appearing palest on the crown and rump. Its black mask is
relatively narrow, often looking more like an eyeline than a mask,
and may be interrupted by gray feathers; the mask narrows and
stops where it meets the bill. Above the mask there is a noticeable
whitish line that extends over the bill. The bill is long, powerful-
looking, and obviously hooked. It is usually paler at the base,
especially on the lower mandible, but it darkens in late winter or
early spring and may then appear entirely black. The underparts are
finely barred, although the barring is often difficult to see.
Immature Northerns are more heavily barred and are brownish
overall, rather than gray, and have a duskier mask.

Voice
Usually silent; sometimes gives a long, varied, catbirdlike song of
harsh and musical phrases. Call notes a grating *jaaeg* and *shek shek*.

Similar Species
See Loggerhead Shrike. Plumage differences between shrikes often
subtle and difficult to see; best distinguished on basis of combination
of several features. Loggerhead may appear smaller; has different
breeding range.

Range
Breeds in Alaska, Yukon, southwestern Mackenzie, and northern
parts of Manitoba, Quebec, and Labrador. Winters from southern
Alaska and southern half of Canada south to northern California,
central Nevada, northern Arizona, northern New Mexico, Kansas,
northern Missouri, central Illinois, Indiana, Ohio, and Pennsylvania.
Also in Europe and North Africa.   *Kim R. Eckert*

Brown Shrike
Northern Shrike
Loggerhead Shrike

Immature
1. *Long, strongly hooked bill.*
2. *Brownish upperparts.*
3. *Brown barring on underparts.*

Adult
1. *Long, strongly hooked bill.*
2. *Narrow black mask.*
3. *White above bill.*
4. *Pale gray cap and upperparts.*

   Northern range.

Loggerhead Shrike

Lanius ludovicianus
Although the Loggerhead Shrike is more widespread than the
Northern, it is local and can be hard to find in much of the East; only
in the West can the Loggerhead be considered common. This species
often chooses lower and less conspicuous perches than the Northern
Shrike does. When it takes off, the Loggerhead often drops down,
flies low to the ground, and swoops up abruptly to its next perch.

Description
8–10″ (20.5–25.5 cm). Besides its slightly smaller size and more
southern range, the Loggerhead Shrike differs from the Northern in
several subtle plumage features. The Loggerhead often looks darker
gray above, especially on the crown and rump. Its mask is usually
wider, blacker, and of more uniform width, and at close range can be
seen to extend over the bill. There is no whitish line over the mask
or bill, as the Northern typically shows. The adult Loggerhead
Shrike is unbarred grayish-white below, although a Northern may
also appear unbarred at a distance. The best distinguishing mark,
which is visible with practice even at a distance, is the Loggerhead's
bill: it is shorter, less powerful-looking, and more conical, and it
lacks an obvious hooked appearance. Although the bill is usually
black, it may appear lighter at the base, like the Northern's, in fall
and winter. Juvenile Loggerhead Shrikes are grayish, not brownish,
and are lightly barred on the underparts like the adult Northern.

Voice
Usually silent. Song a chatlike series of notes or short phrases
repeated several times with long pauses in between; a common
phrase is a mechanical *zee-ert* or *surp-see*. Call notes similar to
Northern Shrike's.

Similar Species
Northern Shrike larger, appears paler gray above; has narrower
mask that stops at bill; has whitish line over mask and bill;
underparts finely barred; bill longer, more powerful-looking, less
conical and more hooked; immatures are brownish overall. Northern
Mockingbird longer, thinner, lacks black mask, has larger white wing
patches; has more leisurely flight with slower wingbeats.

Range
Breeds from central Alberta, central Saskatchewan, southern
Manitoba, Minnesota, central Wisconsin, central Michigan, and
southeastern Ontario south to Mexico and Gulf Coast; very rare
or absent from most of Appalachians, Pennsylvania, New York,
and New England. Winters in southern half of United States and
Mexico.   *Kim R. Eckert*

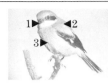

Juvenile
1. *Short, strongly hooked bill.*
2. *Grayish upperparts.*
3. *Faint barring on underparts.*

Adult
1. *Short, hooked bill.*
2. *Broad black mask extending over bill.*
3. *Gray cap and upperparts.*
4. *Unbarred underparts.*

Southern range.

Starlings

(Family Sturnidae)
This large Old World family includes mostly medium-size, robust
birds; many family members have short, squared tails and stocky,
strong legs and bills. Sturnids are highly gregarious omnivores.
Most members of the family have glossy plumage with a metallic
sheen; in most species, the sexes are quite similar. These skillful
mimics fly directly on rapidly beating wings. Two representatives,
the Crested Myna and the European Starling, have been
successfully introduced to North America. (World: 111 species.
North America: 2 species.)   *Scott B. Terrill*

European Starling

Sturnus vulgaris
Introduced from Europe less than a century ago, this aggressive,
gregarious, and adaptable species now occupies a tremendous
variety of habitats—from farms to cities, woodlands, and dumps—
throughout much of North America. The presence of the European
Starling has been a great detriment to other cavity-nesting species
here. Starlings are often seen walking energetically over grassy
areas where groups forage with military efficiency; these birds will
even pick over the edges of tidal flats. Large numbers often form
enormous roosts on building ledges, under bridges, or in trees,
especially from late summer until early spring. Starlings are shaped
like meadowlarks. They emit a wide variety of whistles, squeaks,
and squeals, as well as imitations of other birds. Their flight is direct
and swift: flaps alternate with brief glides, without the undulation
that can be seen in the flight of a blackbird. Dense flocks of
European Starlings are notable for their precise maneuvers, like
those of small shorebirds.

Description
7½–8½″ (19–21.5 cm). The European Starling is a stubby, chunky,
blackish bird with a long, pointed bill, triangular wings, and a short,
square tail. The bill is yellow in breeding season and dark at other
times. In good light and at close range, breeding birds show purple
and green iridescence; otherwise they look entirely blackish except
for the bill and the dull reddish legs. Outside of the breeding season,
Starlings have dark bills and are heavily speckled with whitish
marks, except on the wings and tail. Immatures are uniformly dusky
or mouse-brown, lighter on the throat and upper breast, and they
somewhat resemble the female Brown-headed Cowbird. In breeding
display, the Starling assumes an upright posture; it rotates the
wings or throws back the head and squeals.

Voice
A wide variety of whistles, clicks, clucks, squeaks, rattles, and
gurgles. Roosting birds keep up a continuous chorus of grotesque
utterances, even at night. A wolf whistle, *sweeeuu*, is common.
Underrated as a mimic: often convincingly imitates Eastern Wood
Pewee and Wood Thrush; less frequently and more surprisingly
imitates larger birds: Canada Goose, male Mallard, Green-backed
Heron, and Osprey.

European Starling
Crested Myna

Winter adult

1. *Long, pointed, dark bill.*
2. *Blackish plumage speckled with whitish.*
3. *Pointed, triangular wings.*
4. *Short, squared tail.*

Breeding adult

1. *Yellow bill.*
2. *Blackish, iridescent plumage.*

Dull reddish legs.

Similar Species
Blackbirds have longer tails, thicker bills, a more undulating flight.
Starlings engaged in aerial flycatching conceivably confused with
Purple Martins; latter have longer wings, shorter bill and slightly
forked tail. Female Brown-headed Cowbird resembles immature
Starling but has much blunter, shorter bill, longer tail. Meadowlark
has slower flight with longer glides between weaker wingbeats.

Range
Introduced to North America. Breeds from southeastern Alaska and
southern half of all Canadian provinces (almost all of Alberta) south
to Mexico, Gulf of Mexico, and southern Florida. Reached
Southwest in 1940s; still uncommon in such recently occupied parts
of range. Some migration in northern part of range. Range
expansion continuing. Also in Europe, North Africa, and Asia.
Henry T. Armistead

Crested Myna

Acridotheres cristatellus
A popular cage bird in Asia, this member of the Old World starling
family was introduced to North America at about the turn of the
century and is found in our range only in the region of Vancouver,
British Columbia, where it is moderately common. In 1927, the
Myna population in the Vancouver area was reported to be 20,000.
In 1960 a thorough census counted 2,500 birds. Since then the
population has further declined, possibly because of competition
with European Starlings. During most of the year, Crested Mynas
are found in pairs or small groups, sometimes with European
Starlings; but in winter, they sometimes form roosts of several
hundred birds. Mynas nest in bird boxes, drain pipes, building
ledges, and natural cavities.

Description
9–10½″ (23–26.5 cm). Adults are black with somewhat grayish
underparts. The bases of the primaries and outer secondaries are
white and sometimes show as a narrow horizontal white slash on
perched or sitting birds; when the bird is in flight, this area appears
as a large round white patch. The tail feathers are narrowly tipped
with white. Erect nasal plumes form a low crest or tuft at the base
of the bill. The bill itself is pale yellow to ivory-colored, with a rosy
base. The legs and feet are yellow. Sexes are similar, but the female
has a shorter crest. The juvenile is dark brown, lacks a crest, and
does not have white-tipped tail feathers.

Voice
Garrulous and an accomplished mimic. Many calls resemble those of
European Starlings but are more melodious. A single note, a rasping
jaay, similar to call of Steller's Jay, is characteristic. Also a loud,
melodious *sweet, sweet, sweet* and a rolling *prup-prup-prup*.

Similar Species
European Starling, Brown-headed Cowbird, and Brewer's Blackbird
have no crest and lack white markings; Brewer's Blackbird has
longer tail.

Range
In North America, found only in area of Vancouver, British
Columbia. Native to Southeast Asia.   *David Stirling*

Juvenile
1. *Dark bill.*
2. *Dusky-brown*
   plumage.

Adult in flight
1. *Blackish plumage.*
2. *White wing patches.*
3. *White tips to tail*
   feathers.
4. *Pale yellow bill.*

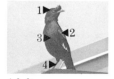

Adult
1. *Low crest.*
2. *Black upperparts.*
3. *Grayish underparts.*
4. *Yellow legs.*

Vireos

(Family Vireonidae)
Vireos are small to medium-size, usually dull-plumaged birds with
relatively large heads, stout bills, and a hooked upper mandible.
Vireos are generally plain greenish (less commonly grayish or
brownish) on the upperparts with whitish or yellowish-gray
underparts. Many species have eye stripes or eye-rings; some have
wing bars. Vireos superficially resemble dull wood warblers, but the
shape of the bill and the sluggish but deliberate foraging movements
will usually distinguish vireos. Vireos are not appreciably
gregarious, although they often appear in mixed-species flocks
during the nonbreeding season. Their songs are generally made up
of distinct, concise, repeated phrases. (World: 43 species. North
America: 12 species.)   *Scott B. Terrill*

White-eyed Vireo

Vireo griseus
The White-eyed Vireo is a common small bird of southeastern North
America. It inhabits moist deciduous thickets, woodland edges,
brambles, undergrowth, and hedgerows. Seldom ranging far from
the ground, this active, inquisitive bird is a persistent singer,
repeating its song over and over. Its diet consists mainly of insects,
but in winter it also eats a variety of small fruits.

Description
5–5½" (12.5–14 cm). The adult has a white iris; that of the immature
is dark. The upperparts are uniformly grayish-green; the underparts
are whitish or ashy. The lores, or spectacle markings on the face,
the forehead, the sides, and sometimes the breast are yellow. The 2
prominent wing bars are white.

Voice
Song a loud, emphatic *chick-a-per-weeoo-chick*, or *chip-whee-oo*.
Each individual has several songs. Various calls include harsh
mewing note, short *tick*, and loud whistle.

Similar Species
All other vireos have dark eyes, lack yellow on forehead. Solitary
Vireo has white spectacle and sharp contrast between dark head and
white throat. Bell's Vireo has an inconspicuous white spectacle or
broken eye-ring; has duller wing bars and less yellow on sides.
Yellow-throated Vireo has bright yellow chin and throat. See Thick-
billed Vireo*.

Range
Breeds from southeastern Nebraska and southern Iowa to southern
Michigan and eastern Massachusetts, south through eastern
Texas and Florida into eastern Mexico. Winters from southern
Texas across Gulf Coast, Florida, north to central coastal North
Carolina, south through the Bahamas, the Greater Antilles, and
Central America to Panama.   *Paul W. Sykes, Jr.*

White-eyed Vireo
Thick-billed Vireo
Bell's Vireo
Black-capped Vireo
Gray Vireo
Solitary Vireo
Yellow-throated Vireo
Hutton's Vireo
Warbling Vireo
Philadelphia Vireo
Red-eyed Vireo
Black-whiskered Vireo

Adult
1. *Yellow spectacles.*
2. *Whitish eyes.*
3. *Grayish-green upperparts.*
4. *Yellowish sides.*
5. *Two white wing bars.*

Immature
1. *Yellow spectacles.*
2. *Dark eyes.*
3. *Yellowish sides.*

Bell's Vireo

Vireo bellii
This species shows tremendous geographical variation, with birds in
the eastern part of the range generally green above and yellow
below, and birds from farther west appearing gray and white.
Throughout most of its range, Bell's Vireo is a riparian species and
is often found in willows bordering streams. In the arid Southwest,
this bird is also found along watercourses and marshes with
mesquite and in mesquite mixed with cottonwood, salt cedar,
elderberry, and desert hackberry. The rapid, loud, chattered song of
Bell's Vireo is unique and conspicuous. Like other members of its
genus, this species often sings all day long, and it is frequently one
of the few birds singing during the extreme heat of midday. In
California, the "Least" Bell's Vireo population has decreased
alarmingly, and the bird has disappeared from most of its former
habitat. Some observers also feel that eastern populations are also
on the decline. These decreases are probably, in part, the result of
the destruction of the bird's riparian habitat as well as of parasitism
by cowbirds.

Description
4½–5″ (11.5–12.5 cm). This small, stout vireo is highly variable. The
eastern populations are usually strongly washed with olive-green
above and yellowish below; southwestern populations can show this
color pattern, but for much of the year they are entirely gray above
and whitish below. This species can show whitish lores, a whitish
eye-ring, and a whitish eyebrow; any combination of these 3 features
is possible. Many birds have 1 fairly conspicuous wing bar; some
birds, however, have 2, and others have none. Midwestern
populations are short-tailed, while birds from the Southwest have
comparatively long tails.

Voice
Rapid, loud, nonmusical, chattering *chu-che-chu-che-chu-che-chu;*
sometimes ending with an upward inflection, other times a
descending last *chu* (only last note inflected), but always building in
volume toward end. Duration and complexity varies to *cheedle
cheedle-cheu*-type songs, but emphasis the same.

Similar Species
Warbling Vireo has longer proportions, longer bill, and longer,
generally more conspicuous eyebrow; calls very different. White-
eyed Vireo has eye-ring, yellow lores, and often yellow forehead.
Gray Vireo larger and more pure gray, with very different calls and
habitat.

Range
Breeds from southern California (local and rare), southern Nevada,
Arizona, southern New Mexico, north into Midwest (east of Rocky
Mountains) to North Dakota; east to Illinois and south to
southwestern Tennessee, Arkansas, northwestern Louisiana, Texas,
and Mexico. Winters from Mexico south to Nicaragua.
Scott B. Terrill

Southwestern form
1. *Gray upperparts.*
2. *Whitish eye-ring.*
3. *White wing bars.*

Small size.

Eastern form
1. *Olive-green upperparts.*
2. *Yellowish underparts.*
3. *Whitish lores, eyebrow, and eye-ring.*
4. *Whitish wing bar.*

Small size.
Birds vary in face pattern and number of wing bars.

Black-capped Vireo

Vireo atricapillus
In Texas and Oklahoma, this small, active, chunky vireo is local and uncommon; it favors low oak scrub of dry hillsides and ravines.

Description
4½" (11.5 cm). Adult male has glossy black crown, nape, and face; bold white spectacles around red eye; white throat. Back yellow-olive; wings and tail blackish with yellow-green edgings and 2 pale yellow wing bars. Dull white below with gray to yellow wash on sides and flanks. Female similar, usually with paler head markings.

Voice
Variable song of rapid phrases with grating and squeaking notes and clinking tone. Common call a *chidit;* also a scolding *tchee.*

Similar Species
See Solitary Vireo; other vireos lack white spectacles on dark face.

Range
Central Oklahoma locally through central and W. Texas to N. central Mexico. Winters mainly in W. Mexico.   *Kenn Kaufman*

Gray Vireo

Vireo vicinior
This rare to locally common vireo inhabits piñon-juniper and low, dense scrub in much the same range as the "Plumbeous" Solitary Vireo. It often flips and twitches its tail.

Description
5¾" (14.5 cm). Small, slender, with long gray tail. Gray above; wing and tail darker with variable paler edgings (may form whitish wing bar); dull white below with light gray wash on breast, sides, and flanks. Thin white eye-ring and whitish lores not always visible.

Voice
Song of rapid phrases with long pauses; similar to "Plumbeous" Solitary Vireo's.

Similar Species
See Solitary, Bell's, and Hutton's vireos.

Range
S. California, S. Utah, Sw. Colorado to central Mexico; winters from Sw. Arizona and Big Bend to Mexico.   *Scott B. Terrill*

Solitary Vireo

Vireo solitarius
The handsome, sweet-singing Solitary Vireo is a widespread species equally at home in open mixed northern hardwood forests and pine-oak woodlands of foothills and mountains in the western United States.

Description
5–6" (12.5–15 cm). The crown, nape, and sides of the head are slate gray, contrasting with an olive-green back, wings, rump, and upper tail coverts. There are 2 broad, whitish wing bars; a thick white eye-ring and connecting white loral area produce a prominent spectacled effect. The underparts are white, washed on the sides and flanks with yellow and olive-green. Birds of the Rocky Mountain and Great Basin race (*V. s. plumbeus*) are a duller, neutral gray above with little color contrast between the head and back, and with the sides and flanks less strongly washed with greenish-yellow. The Pacific Coast race, *V. s. cassini*, has dull yellow sides and a gray head contrasting somewhat with the greenish back.

Adult male

1. *Black crown, nape, and face.*
2. *White spectacles.*
3. *White throat.*
4. *Yellow-olive back.*
5. *Pale yellow wing bars.*

Small size.
Chunky build.

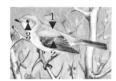

Adult

1. *Nondescript gray plumage.*
2. *Narrow whitish wing bar.*
3. *Thin white eye-ring.*

Flicks tail.

Rocky Mountain race

1. *White spectacles.*
2. *Gray head and upperparts.*
3. *Broad whitish wing bars.*

Voice
Song a deliberate series of short, sweet phrases with long pauses between each phrase; higher and slower than Red-eyed's. Phrases may run together into a rich warble. Scold note harsh, wrenlike.

Similar Species
White-eyed Vireo has yellow spectacles, lacks gray cap. Black-capped Vireo has black cap. Gray Vireo resembles *V. s. plumbeus*, but slimmer, smaller, with smaller bill, longer tail; has much fainter spectacles, 1 indistinct wing bar; twitches tail. In areas of overlap, songs of the 2 species nearly identical but Gray's phrases more rapidly delivered with longer pauses between phrases.

Range
Breeds from central British Columbia east through central Canada to northern Ontario and Newfoundland, south to North Dakota (locally), central Minnesota, southern Ontario, and in mountains to North Carolina; south to Guatemala and El Salvador. Winters from southern California (rare), Arizona, and South Carolina to Central America and Cuba.   *Wayne R. Petersen*

Yellow-throated Vireo

Vireo flavifrons
This rather uncommon eastern vireo frequents mature, moist, semiopen forest. It often sings from high in the deciduous canopy.

Description
6″ (15 cm). Only vireo with bright yellow throat and breast, yellow spectacles, and bold white wing bars. Whitish below, olive-green above with slate-gray lower back and rump. Immature resembles adult.

Voice
Slow, deliberate song of slurred notes (usually of 2 syllables) and fairly long pauses; 1 common phrase a descending *three-eight*.

Similar Species
See Pine Warbler and Yellow-breasted Chat.

Range
S. Manitoba and Minnesota to S. Quebec, Maine (rare); to E. Texas, Louisiana, Gulf of Mexico, and N. Florida. Winters mainly in Central and South America; a few in Florida.   *Henry T. Armistead*

Hutton's Vireo

Vireo huttoni
Hutton's Vireo is a bird of oak and mixed woodlands, especially evergreen oaks. It responds readily to "spishing" and owl calls.

Description
5″ (12.5 cm). Stout, stocky; grayish to olive above, paler below, often with yellow-green or buff wash along sides. Lores and thin broken eye-ring whitish; 2 bold whitish wing bars. Tail short, legs stocky. Bill stout with pale base, hooked upper mandible.

Voice
Song: nasal, 2-syllable, widely spaced phrases: *zuwee, zuwoo, zeeoo*. Call notes buzzy, whiny; typical vireo scold note.

Similar Species
Ruby-crowned Kinglet smaller with tiny black bill, smaller head and tail, tapered body; darkest area is patch behind second wing bar.

Range
Sw. British Columbia to Baja California, central Arizona, Sw. New Mexico, W. Texas, and N. Mexico; to Guatemala.   *Scott B. Terrill*

Eastern race
1. *White spectacles.*
2. *Slate-gray head.*
3. *Olive-green upperparts.*
4. *Broad whitish wing bars.*
5. *White throat.*
6. *Yellowish sides.*

Adult
1. *Bright yellow throat and breast.*
2. *Yellow spectacles.*
3. *White wing bars.*
4. *Olive-green upperparts.*

Adult
1. *Thick bill with pale lower mandible.*
2. *Broken eye-ring.*
3. *Gray-green upperparts.*
4. *Whitish wing bars.*

Has bullheaded appearance.

Warbling Vireo

Vireo gilvus
This widespread, rather nondescript vireo sings persistently from dense roadside shade trees, farmyards, aspen groves, and riparian willow and alder thickets. The Warbling Vireo is often best detected and identified by its husky, rambling song. In migration, it sometimes occurs with the Philadelphia Vireo.

Description
5–6″ (12.5–15 cm). The upperparts are light gray tinged with olive-green; the crown and nape are only slightly paler. There is a whitish line over the eye, and the lores are white. The underparts including the throat are whitish, often washed with yellow or greenish-yellow on the sides and flanks, particularly in young birds in later summer and early fall. Birds in juvenal plumage may exhibit a single, faint buff wing bar.

Voice
Song a husky, rambling warble reminiscent of Purple Finch's. Often ends abruptly on rising note. Scold note wheezy and querulous *tshay, tshay,* sometimes given between songs.

Similar Species
Philadelphia Vireo has pale yellow underparts and dusky lores; song different. Red-eyed Vireo has gray crown, olive-green back, and black-bordered straight white eyebrow. Tennessee Warbler greener above, with tiny, pointed bill.

Range
Breeds from northern British Columbia and southern Mackenzie southeast to southern Ontario and southern New Brunswick; south to northern Mexico, Alabama, and Virginia. Winters in Mexico and Central America.   *Wayne R. Petersen*

Philadelphia Vireo

Vireo philadelphicus
This vireo inhabits deciduous second-growth woods, alder thickets, and aspen parkland; in migration, it occurs in more varied habitats.

Description
5″ (12.5 cm). Plumper and shorter-tailed than Warbling Vireo; pale yellow below, palest on throat and belly; fall immature usually most richly colored. Gray-olive above with grayish crown, dusky lores.

Voice
Song very similar to Red-eyed Vireo's but slightly higher, sweeter, and slower in delivery. Scold note similar to Warbling Vireo's.

Similar Species
See Warbling and Red-eyed vireos, Tennessee Warbler, and Black-throated Blue Warbler.

Range
S. British Columbia and S. Alberta to Newfoundland and N. New England. Winters in Central and South America.
Wayne R. Petersen

Juvenile
1. Faint buff wing bar.

Adult
1. Whitish eyebrow.
2. Light gray crown and upperparts.
3. Whitish underparts.
4. Whitish lores.
5. No wing bars.

Husky, rambling song.

Adult
1. Grayish-olive upperparts.
2. Pale yellow throat and upper breast.
3. Dusky lores.
4. No wing bars.

Red-eyed Vireo

Vireo olivaceus
The repetitive, continuous song of the abundant Red-eyed Vireo is a
familiar sound in mixed and deciduous forests and suburban shade
trees throughout much of North America. Often heard through the
heat of the day, the song has a ventriloqual quality; this, combined
with the sluggish behavior of the Red-eye, can make this bird
difficult to locate. A thorough knowledge of this species' song can be
useful, since a number of other birds have similar vocalizations.

Description
5½–6½″ (14–16.5 cm). The upperparts, wings, and tail are olive-
green, contrasting with a black-bordered gray crown, whitish
eyebrow stripe, and black eyeline. The underparts are white; the
sides and flanks are washed with yellowish-olive. The eyes are red in
adults, brown in immatures. The Mexican and Central American
race, *V. o. flavoviridis* ("Yellow-green"Vireo), has occurred casually
as a breeder and wanderer in our range. These birds have more
yellow on the upperparts, bright yellow sides and undertail coverts,
and less distinct head stripes.

Voice
Song a continuous series of short, robinlike phrases, given with
slightly rising inflection and separated by short pauses. Scold note a
harsh *wheree.*

Similar Species
See Warbling and Black-whiskered vireos. Philadelphia Vireo
smaller, duller above and more yellow below, with no strong
eyebrow stripe.

Range
Breeds from southwestern British Columbia and southern
Mackenzie southeast to central Ontario and Maritime Provinces,
south to northern Oregon, eastern Colorado, western Oklahoma to
central Texas, Gulf Coast, and central Florida. Very rare but
regular migrant in California and Arizona. "Yellow-green" very rare
in summer in southern Texas, casual to southern Arizona; casual fall
vagrant to coastal California. Also breeds in Central and South
America.Winters in South America.   *Wayne R. Petersen*

Black-whiskered Vireo

Vireo altiloquus
This rather tame West Indian species occurs commonly along the
Florida coast in mangrove and West Indian hardwood hammocks. It
is very similar to the Red-eyed, and often sings throughout the day.

Description
6¼″ (16 cm). Very similar to Red-eyed Vireo: adult has gray crown,
black-bordered white eyebrow, and black whiskers. Back olive-
green; ashy or whitish below; eye red. Immature browner above
with buff chin and throat, faint yellow wing bar, and brown eyes.

Voice
Song like Red-eyed's, but has paired phrases, less variable pitch.

Similar Species
Red-eyed lacks whiskers; generally overlaps only in migration.

Range
Florida coasts to Keys and West Indies; some records from elsewhere
on Gulf Coast. Winters in N. South America.   *Paul W. Sykes, Jr.*

Adult
1. *Gray crown with thin black border.*
2. *Whitish eyebrow.*
3. *Black line through eye.*
4. *Red eyes.*
5. *Olive-green upperparts.*
6. *Whitish underparts.*

"Yellow-green" Vireo
1. *Bright yellow sides and undertail coverts.*
2. *Indistinct head stripes.*

Adult
1. *Gray crown.*
2. *Whitish eyebrow.*
3. *Black whisker.*
4. *Olive-green back.*
5. *Pale underparts.*

Wood Warblers

(Subfamily Parulinae)
Until quite recently, the wood warblers were considered a separate
family, the Parulidae; however, recent observations have caused
experts to combine the wood warblers and several other groups into
one large family, the Emberizidae. The wood warblers have been
reclassified as a subfamily, the Parulinae. The other groups that
were formerly considered separate families that are now part of the
Emberizidae are the bananaquits (subfamily Coerebinae); the
tanagers (Thraupinae); the cardinals and their allies (Cardinalinae);
the New World sparrows and their allies (Emberizinae); and the
New World blackbirds and their allies (Icterinae). Because the
family that includes all of these groups is so large and diverse, these
subfamilies have here been treated separately.
Wood Warblers are, for the most part, active little insectivores with
small, thin bills. In most tropical and subtropical members of this
group, the sexes are similar and often brilliantly plumaged. But in
temperate regions, most species are sexually dimorphic—the males
have bright, flashy breeding plumage; females and fall males are
more dully plumaged and can be more difficult to identify. Broad
groups among these species can be formed on the basis of the
presence or absence of wing bars, tail spots, eye-rings, and eyelines,
and by general characteristics of the call note. Distinguishing among
less obvious species becomes a matter of detecting subtle differences
in plumage, behavior, and voice. Although the songs of some
members of this subfamily are loud and generally diagnostic, many
species have an array of different song types. Some wood warblers
are solitary, while others are highly gregarious; some are ground-
dwelling species, and others spend most of their time in trees. Most
birds that breed in the temperate regions of North America are
highly migratory. (World: 125 species. North America: 57 species.)
Scott B. Terrill

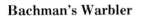

Bachman's Warbler

Vermivora bachmanii
This is the rarest songbird in North America: in the past 25 years,
only lone birds have been seen at widely scattered spots in the
Southeast. Because comparatively little is known about Bachman's,
the reasons for its decline are not clear. It migrates early in spring
and fall and nests in canebrakes and thickets in and along the
margins of mature deciduous swamp forests.

Immature

Description
4¼–4½″ (11–11.5 cm). Both sexes have a blackish-brown, slightly
down-curved bill, with the lower mandible paler than the upper. The
legs and feet are pale. The distinctive male has a bright yellow
forehead, eye-ring, and chin; a small area at the bend of the wing
and the belly is also bright yellow. The forward part of the crown
and the throat are black; the rear of the crown, the ear patch, and
the nape are gray. The rest of the upperparts are olive-green, the
undertail coverts are whitish, and there are inconspicuous
subterminal white spots on the outer 3 or 4 tail feathers. The female

Bachman's Warbler
Blue-winged Warbler
"Brewster's" Warbler
"Lawrence's" Warbler
Golden-winged Warbler
Tennessee Warbler
Orange-crowned Warbler
Nashville Warbler
Virginia's Warbler
Colima Warbler
Lucy's Warbler
Northern Parula
Tropical Parula
Yellow Warbler
Chestnut-sided Warbler
Magnolia Warbler
Cape May Warbler
Black-throated Blue Warbler
Yellow-rumped Warbler
Black-throated Gray Warbler
Townsend's Warbler
Hermit Warbler
Black-throated Green Warbler
Golden-cheeked Warbler
Blackburnian Warbler
Yellow-throated Warbler
Grace's Warbler
Pine Warbler
Kirtland's Warbler
Prairie Warbler
Palm Warbler
Bay-breasted Warbler
Blackpoll Warbler
Cerulean Warbler
Black-and-white Warbler
American Redstart
Prothonotary Warbler
Worm-eating Warbler
Swainson's Warbler
Ovenbird
Northern Waterthrush

Louisiana Waterthrush
Kentucky Warbler
Connecticut Warbler
Mourning Warbler
MacGillivray's Warbler
Gray-crowned Yellowthroat
Common Yellowthroat
Hooded Warbler
Wilson's Warbler
Canada Warbler
Red-faced Warbler
Painted Redstart
Slate-throated Redstart
Fan-tailed Warbler
Golden-crowned Warbler
Rufous-capped Warbler
Yellow-breasted Chat
Olive Warbler

Male
1. *Black crown.*
2. *Yellow face.*
3. *Black throat.*
4. *Yellow breast and belly.*

is duller, with less yellow in the plumage, lacks any black markings and has a gray crown, ear patch, and nape. There are diffuse dusky streaks across the breast; the eye-ring is yellow or white. Immatures of both sexes are duller than the corresponding adults.

Voice
Song a distinct, rapid 8-note trill on same pitch, *bzz-bzz-bzz-bzz-bzz-bzz-bzz-bzz;* suggestive of Worm-eating Warbler or Chipping Sparrow but higher, with quality closer to song of Northern Parula.

Similar Species
Male Hooded Warbler has complete black hood; female has no gray on head or throat; both have white tail spots. Male Wilson's entirely yellow below with black cap; female lacks gray areas on head and throat. Nashville Warbler has white eye-ring and gray forehead.

Range
Formerly bred from northeastern Arkansas and southeastern Missouri to central Alabama and coastal South Carolina and Georgia. May still breed in South Carolina. Migrates through Florida and Bahamas to Cuba.   *Paul W. Sykes, Jr.*

Blue-winged Warbler

Vermivora pinus
The Blue-winged Warbler is an inhabitant of overgrown fields with scattered trees, second-growth woods, and brushy hillsides. It is usually seen in undergrowth or on the lower branches of trees, although males may sing from treetops.

Description
4–4½″ (10–11.5 cm). Spring adults have a bright yellow crown and underparts (except for white undertail coverts) and greenish-yellow backs. A black eyeline runs from the base of the bill to a short distance behind the eye. The wings and tail are bluish-gray with 2 conspicuous white wing bars, and white spots (usually concealed) in the tail. In fall, the yellow crown is concealed by greenish feather tips. Immatures are duller, with no contrast between the crown and back, but usually with a yellow eyebrow. In areas where the Blue-winged hybridizes with the Golden-winged Warbler, individuals may show some variation.

Voice
Primary song a buzzy *bee-buzz*, with second note longer; many variations. Secondary song a *trill-buzz*. May sing primary song of Golden-winged. Calls are undistinguished chips.

Similar Species
Other bright yellow warblers lack white wing bars. See Pine Warbler.

Range
Breeds from eastern Nebraska, southern Ontario, and southern Maine south to northeastern Oklahoma and northern Georgia in interior and to northern Virginia and Delaware on coastal plain. Winters mainly in Central America. Breeding range expanding locally to some areas at expense of Golden-winged Warbler. *Kenneth C. Parkes*

Adult female
1. *Gray crown, ear patch, and nape.*
2. *Yellow face and throat.*
3. *Diffused dusky streaks across breast.*
4. *Yellow underparts.*

Adult
1. *Bright yellow crown.*
2. *Black eyeline.*
3. *Yellow underparts.*
4. *Blue-gray wings with 2 white wing bars.*

Immature
1. *Greenish crown and nape do not contrast with rest of upperparts.*
2. *Yellow eyebrow.*

"Brewster's" Warbler and "Lawrence's" Warbler

The breeding ranges of the Blue-winged and Golden-winged warblers overlap broadly, and these species frequently hybridize over much of this common range. The first generation hybrid, once described as a new species, is called "Brewster's" Warbler; the much rarer hybrid with genetically recessive characteristics was described as "Lawrence's" Warbler.

Description

"Brewster's" Warbler represents the combination of dominant genetic characteristics; it looks somewhat like a Golden-winged Warbler without the facial pattern—instead, both sexes have the black eyeline of the Blue-winged Warbler. The underparts are intermediate: white heavily washed with yellow. The wing bars are also intermediate: there are usually 2, as in the Blue-winged Warbler, but they are distinctly yellowish, as in the Golden-winged. Backcrossing of first generation "Brewster's" Warblers with Golden-winged Warblers produces another variant that has, like the Golden-winged, pure white underparts and broad yellow wing bars; the wing bars merge in males. The much rarer combination of recessive genetic characteristics produces "Lawrence's" Warbler, which is just the opposite of "Brewster's" Warbler; "Lawrence's" has the facial pattern of the Golden-winged Warbler and the body and wing-bar color of the Blue-winged Warbler. The facial mask and throat patch are almost always inherited as a unit; *very* rarely these may dissociate, so that a hybrid will have a mask but no throat patch or some black on the throat but no mask. Hybrids of the Blue-winged and Golden-winged warblers rarely if ever mate with other hybrids, even in areas where hybrids are relatively frequent. They mate with either Blue-winged or Golden-winged warblers, producing a number of hybrid variants as well as individuals indistinguishable from the pure parental species. Backcrossing may also produce individuals that most closely resemble one of the parental species, but show some signs of intermediacy. Examples include Blue-winged Warblers with 2 yellowish (not white) wing bars, or Golden-winged Warblers heavily washed with yellow on the underparts and greenish on the back. Note that immature Golden-winged Warblers in the fall are often lightly washed with yellow and greenish.

Voice

Hybrids may sing the primary song of either parental type, sometimes both.

Similar Species

Very rare male Bachman's Warbler yellow with black throat patch like "Lawrence's" Warbler, but lacks facial mask and wing bars; has black crown. Immature Chestnut-sided Warbler may lack chestnut on flanks; greenish on back with somewhat yellower crown and white underparts and yellowish wing bars; may look somewhat like "Brewster's" but has brighter green back, usually with at least faint streaking, and lacks black eyeline.

Range

Hybrids may be found anywhere within area of overlap of breeding ranges of Blue-winged and Golden-winged warblers, and within winter range of either species.   *Kenneth C. Parkes*

**Backcross
"Brewster's"
Warbler**

1. *Yellow crown.*
2. *Black eyeline.*
3. *White underparts.*
4. *Yellow wing bars.*

**"Brewster's"
Warbler**

1. *Yellow crown.*
2. *Black eyeline.*
3. *Yellow wash on
   white underparts.*
4. *Yellow wing bars.*

*Wing bars are white
in some birds.*

**Male "Lawrence's"
Warbler**

1. *Yellow crown.*
2. *Black mask.*
3. *Black throat.*
4. *Yellow underparts.*

Golden-winged Warbler

Vermivora chrysoptera
The Golden-winged Warbler is a strikingly patterned species of open deciduous woods, second-growth woods, and overgrown pastures. It generally occupies higher and drier areas than the Blue-winged · Warbler, although the 2 species overlap broadly in habitat.

Description
4½–5″ (11.5–12.5 cm). The adult male Golden-winged Warbler has a bright yellow crown, a neutral gray back, and white underparts. The conspicuous facial pattern includes a white eyebrow, a black mask extending from the base of the bill to the cheeks, a white mustache, and a broad black patch from the chin to the upper breast. The bright yellow tips to the wing coverts are very broad, appearing as a single patch rather than as 2 wing bars. The white spots on the tail are usually concealed. Adult females are similar to males, but have a duller yellow crown; the black of the face pattern is replaced by gray. The white underparts are often washed with gray, resulting in very little contrast between the slightly darker gray of the throat and upper breast and the paler gray of the posterior underparts. The yellow wing bars are usually slightly separated. Immatures in fall often have the gray of the back washed with yellow-green and the white underparts washed with pale yellow. This is not a sign of hybridization with the Blue-winged.

Voice
Primary song buzzy in quality; typically a *zee* followed by 2–5 repetitions of a short *bee* at a lower pitch. Secondary song a *trill-buzz* like that of Blue-winged Warbler. Rarely, Golden-winged Warblers may sing Blue-winged's primary song. Calls are undistinguished chips.

Range
Breeds from southeastern Manitoba, central Ontario, northern Michigan, and southern New England south to Iowa, northern Illinois, northern Indiana, Ohio, and Pennsylvania; south in Appalachians to northern Georgia. Breeding range, especially in Northeast and Appalachians, has been diminishing, partly as a result of displacement by Blue-winged Warblers. Winters from Yucatán Peninsula and Guatemala south to northern Colombia and northern Venezuela.   *Kenneth C. Parkes*

Tennessee Warbler

Vermivora peregrina
The relatively common Tennessee Warbler breeds in northern coniferous and deciduous woodland, and is found in a wide variety of wooded habitats during migration. Its numbers may vary greatly from year to year in response, at least in part, to significant increases in the occurrence of the spruce budworm. The Tennessee Warbler regularly feeds far up in the foliage. In spring and summer, it is often heard—but not seen—singing high above the observer.

Description
4½–5″ (11.5–12.5 cm). The breeding adult male has a blue-gray crown and nape contrasting with an unmarked forest-green back and rump; the wings and tail are also unmarked forest-green. There is a white eyebrow and a dusky line through the eye; the white underparts are unmarked. The female has a greener crown; the eyebrow may be washed with yellow, and the throat or upper breast lightly washed with yellow. Nonbreeding adults have dingier crowns and a wash of yellow to the throat or breast. Immature Tennessee

Female

1. *Gray mask.*
2. *Gray throat.*
3. *Yellowish crown.*
4. *Gray back.*
5. *Yellow wing bars.*
6. *White underparts.*

Male

1. *Black mask.*
2. *Black throat.*
3. *Yellow crown.*
4. *Gray back.*
5. *Yellow wing bars.*
6. *White underparts.*

Breeding male

1. *Blue-gray crown and nape.*
2. *White eyebrow.*
3. *Dusky line through eye.*
4. *Forest-green upperparts.*

White underparts.

Warblers have unmarked lime-green upperparts; there is a yellow eyebrow and usually a faint wing bar. The unmarked underparts are variably washed with yellow: in some individuals, the yellow is restricted to the throat and upper breast; in others this color extends to the lower breast and, more rarely, to the undertail coverts.

Voice
Song a fairly loud, staccato *sidit-sidit-sidit-sidit-swit-swit-sit-sit-sit-sit-sit-sit*, increasing in speed toward end. Call note a high, thin *seet;* also gives a rich *chip* reminiscent of call note given by Yellow Warbler or American Redstart, but slightly higher in pitch.

Similar Species
Brightly colored Orange-crowned Warbler deeper olive-green above, has thin broken eye-ring, yellow undertail coverts, less white belly, and often dusky streaking on breast; voice also different. Philadelphia and Warbling vireos stouter, with thicker bills; behavior more sluggish. Warbling Vireo much less green above; most immature Philadelphias have yellow undertail coverts. In Alaska, Arctic Warbler may appear similar but is slightly larger, with stouter bill.

Range
Breeds from southeastern Alaska (rare), southern Yukon, northern Ontario, and southern Labrador south to southern British Columbia, northern Michigan, and southern Maine. Winters primarily from Mexico south as far as northern South America. Rare migrant in western United States. Rare but regular in winter in coastal California, very rare in southern Texas; casual elsewhere in Southeast.   *Paul Lehman*

Orange-crowned Warbler

Vermivora celata
This is a common warbler in western North America but is less numerous in much of the East. It occurs in a variety of woodland and brushy habitats. There are several different races with significant variations in plumage.

Description
4½–5½" (11.5–14 cm). This warbler has unmarked olive-green upperparts and plain wings that occasionally have a thin wing bar. There is a greenish-yellow eyebrow, a thin, broken yellow eye-ring, and a variable amount of diffuse, dusky olive streaking on the breast. The race *lutescens* of the West Coast is the brightest yellow below and the greenest above. *Sordida*, which is restricted to southwestern California and particularly the Channel Islands, is darker and somewhat duller. *Orestera* breeds in the Great Basin and Rocky Mountains; it is duller yellow below than *lutescens* and has a gray head. The nominate race, *celata*, breeds across Canada from Alaska to Quebec and occurs throughout the East. It is the dullest

Nonbreeding adult
1. *Unmarked green upperparts.*
2. *Underparts washed with yellow.*
3. *Yellow eyebrow.*

Immature
1. *Unmarked green upperparts.*
2. *Underparts washed with yellow.*
3. *Yellow eyebrow.*
4. *White undertail coverts.*

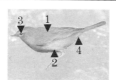

West Coast race
1. *Olive-green upperparts.*
2. *Olive underparts with yellow tinge.*
3. *Greenish-yellow eyebrow.*
4. *Yellow undertail coverts.*

plumaged of the different races, particularly the immature, which
may appear quite grayish overall with yellow undertail coverts.
Many individuals of all races show a narrow, pale yellowish-white
area along the leading edge of the shoulder at the bend of the wing.
The orange crown patch is almost never seen.

Voice
Song a series of staccato notes, with slight rising or lowering in
pitch towards end. Calls a high, thin *seet* and a hard, somewhat
metallic *chip*.

Similar Species
See Tennessee Warbler. Bright Orange-crowned may also be
confused with female Yellow or Wilson's warblers: Yellow has
beady-eyed look, lacks dusky breast streaking, has yellow edgings
to primaries and secondaries, yellow tail spots, and shorter tail.
Wilson's also has beady eyes and lacks dusky streaking on breast;
usually has suggestion of darker forecrown. Both species have
different call notes. In Alaska, Arctic Warbler darker with some
brown above, dull whitish below, with no streaking; has whitish
eyebrow and wing bar.

Range
Breeds from central Alaska eastward to northern Manitoba and
southern Labrador and south to northern Baja California, western
Texas, southern Manitoba, and east-central Quebec. Winters from
Oregon (uncommon), northern California, central Arizona, Texas,
and southeastern Virginia south to Central America; casually north
along Atlantic Coast to Massachusetts.   *Paul Lehman*

Nashville Warbler

Vermivora ruficapilla
This plain little *Vermivora*, with neither wing bars nor tail spots,
occurs most frequently in open second-growth woodlands, brushy
bogs, or regenerating areas that have been burned or cut. Aspen
and birch are often good indicators of the Nashville Warbler's
habitat, and the species' persistent song will readily lead the
observer to the bird. Despite its ground-nesting habit, the Nashville
Warbler regularly forages in the tree tops.

Description
4½–5″ (11.5–12.5 cm). The male in breeding plumage has the top,
back, and sides of the head and neck bluish-gray with a concealed
chestnut crown patch and a conspicuous white eye-ring and whitish
loral streak. The back, wings, and tail are an unmarked yellowish-
green. The underparts, including the throat and undertail coverts,
are bright yellow except for a whitish belly. Females, males in
winter plumage, and fall immatures have paler gray or brownish-
gray heads, paler yellow underparts, and buff-white eye-rings. In

Great Basin race
1. *Duller yellow below than West Coast race.*
2. *Diffuse streaking on breast.*
3. *Yellowish undertail coverts.*

Northern and eastern race
1. *Duller than other races.*

Breeding male
1. *Gray head.*
2. *White eye-ring.*
3. *Yellow throat and breast.*
4. *Yellow-green upperparts.*

Has chestnut-crown patch.

late summer, birds in juvenal plumage may exhibit 2 yellowish wing bars.

Voice
Song in 2 parts, first higher and slower than second: *see-it see-it see-it, ti-ti-ti-ti-ti-ti.* Frequently intersperses alternate variations of same notes with original song. Call note a sharp, metallic *pink* or *clink.*

Similar Species
See Virginia's Warbler. Connecticut Warbler has eye-ring but is larger, with brownish throat. See Mourning, MacGillivray's, and Wilson's warblers.

Range
Breeds from southern British Columbia, southern Saskatchewan, southern Manitoba, northern Ontario, and Nova Scotia south to central California, northern Utah, southern Minnesota, southern Michigan, northern West Virginia, and western Maryland. Winters from California (in small numbers), southern Texas, and southern Florida (rarely) south to Guatemala.   *Wayne R. Petersen*

Virginia's Warbler

Vermivora virginiae
This species represents the Nashville Warbler complex in the interior mountains of the Southwest. Virginia's is very similar to the Nashville in its calls and behavior, but twitches its tail more conspicuously. In the Rockies and other arid mountains of the interior, Virginia's prefers scrubby brush interspersed with piñon-juniper and yellow pine. At high elevations, this bird is found in fir and spruce as well as riparian willow and alder thickets.

Description
4–4½″ (10–11.5 cm). In breeding plumage, Virginia's is similar to the Nashville but much paler, with almost entirely gray upperparts and much less yellow on the underparts. The yellow is confined to the breast (where it is often greatly reduced in females) and to the rump and undertail coverts. The belly and throat are whitish. The reddish crown patch is usually concealed. The sides are washed with grayish. The lores are whitish, and there is a conspicuous white eye-ring. Immatures vary but often have browner or more olive-brown upperparts and reduced or duller yellowish on the rump. The undertail coverts are often the only yellow area on the underparts, although there may be a reduced yellowish spot on the breast.

Voice
Call note a very sharp, high-pitched, bell-like *pink;* also, less commonly, a harder *chip* (reminiscent of Yellow Warbler). Songs variable, but generally a series of somewhat musical 1- or 2-syllable notes; on same pitch or ascending toward end.

Similar Species
Adult Nashville has greener upperparts and more extensive yellow on underparts; fall birds also extensively yellow below with white vent. Western Nashville Warblers have reduced yellow on underparts, especially in immatures; back color in young birds can be very similar to young Virginia's, even showing contrasting yellowish rump. Immature Nashvilles show more yellow on breast and throat than immature Virginia's; lack neutral gray upperparts. Lucy's Warbler lacks conspicuous white eye-ring, has no yellow in plumage. Virginia's passes through Big Bend as uncommon spring migrant and may overlap with superficially similar Colima Warbler; but Colima larger, less active, with stouter bill; has grayer throat

Immature
1. *Brownish-gray head.*
2. *Pale yellow underparts.*
3. *Buff-white eye-ring.*

Adult female
1. *Gray head and upperparts.*
2. *White eye-ring.*
3. *Yellow rump.*
4. *Yellow undertail coverts.*

   Yellow tinge on breast.

Adult male
1. *Gray head and upperparts.*
2. *White eye-ring.*
3. *Yellow patch on breast.*
4. *Yellow rump.*
5. *Yellow undertail coverts.*

and belly, with only faint greenish-yellow wash on breast (not bright
yellow spot as in Virginia's); Colima's rump and undertail coverts
slightly deeper yellow.

Range
Breeds from southeastern California (rare in east-central part of
state), northern Nevada, southeastern Idaho, and northern
Colorado south through Arizona, New Mexico, and Trans-Pecos
Texas. Winters in western Mexico. Regular but rare in early fall to
coastal southern California.   *Scott B. Terrill*

Colima Warbler

Vermivora crissalis
This Mexican warbler reaches our range only in the Chisos
Mountains, where it lives at about 6000 feet in low oak, piñon-
juniper, maple, and Arizona cypress.

Description
5½" (13.5 cm). Fairly dark gray above, paler below; no sharp
division between above and below. White eye-ring creates large-
eyed look. Rump and undertail coverts yellow; may have yellow-
green wash on breast. Rufous crown patch usually indistinct.

Voice
Song a musical trill on 1 pitch with 1 or 2 lower notes at end. Call a
hard *tsick*, like call of Virginia's; sometimes a more liquid *fsht*.

Similar Species
See Virginia's Warbler.

Range
Chisos Mountains W. Texas, and in highlands of Ne. Mexico.
Winters in Sw. Mexico.   *Kenn Kaufman*

Lucy's Warbler

Vermivora luciae
This active bird is a very early migrant and abundant in summer in
parts of the Southwest. It frequents riparian areas, washes, ponds,
and well-vegetated deserts, becoming restricted to riparian areas at
higher elevations. It flicks its tail often, its wings less frequently,
and flies with weak, jerky wingbeats. There is much regional
variation, perhaps reflecting elevational distinctions.

Description
4½" (11.5 cm). Small, drab, with tiny, thin bill. Uniformly gray
above except for rufous crown patch (usually concealed; reduced in
females) and rufous rump. White to grayish-white below. Eye-ring
thin, whitish, often indistinct; may have grayish eyeline or pale
eyebrow (most conspicuous in immatures). Fall adults washed with
buff, primarily below. Immatures more strongly washed with light
brownish or buff above and buff below, with varying amounts of
reddish on rump. Juveniles grayer. Adults in first breeding season
may be washed with faint buff.

Immature
1. *Olive-brown upperparts.*
2. *Yellowish rump patch.*
3. *Yellow undertail coverts.*

Adult
1. *Dark upperparts.*
2. *Gray underparts with greenish-yellow on breast.*
3. *White eye-ring.*
4. *Yellow rump.*
5. *Yellow undertail coverts.*

Adult
1. *Thin bill.*
2. *Gray upperparts.*
3. *White eye-ring.*
4. *Whitish underparts.*
5. *Rufous rump.*

   Small size.

Voice
Song a rapid series of staccato, metallic, trilled notes, slowing
toward end and often changing pitch; trill ends with clear, *sweet-
sweet* notes, like song of Yellow Warbler but often on a higher pitch.
At higher elevations may give song like Virginia's. Call a high-
pitched, bell-like *tink* or *pink;* when excited, a hard, kisslike *chip.*

Similar Species
Bell's Vireo in arid Southwest very gray but larger, stockier; has
much heavier, decurved bill with slightly hooked upper mandible;
calls very different. Immature Virginia's and Nashville warblers
have brighter eye-ring, yellow rump and undertail coverts. Grayish
Orange-crowned Warbler (migrant and winter visitor) has dry call
note like Chipping Sparrow's, heavier bill, bolder eyebrow, and
usually some greenish or yellowish on undertail coverts.

Range
Southeastern California (local away from Colorado River plain),
southern Nevada, southern Utah, and southwestern Colorado south
into extreme western Texas and northwestern Mexico. Winters in
arid interior of central Mexico.   *Scott B. Terrill*

Northern Parula

Parula americana
This very small bird is one of our most adaptable warblers, breeding
from northern spruce forest to southern swamps.

Description
4½" (11.5 cm). Blue-gray above with broken white eye-ring, 2 bold
white wing bars, and suffused greenish-yellow patch on upper back;
throat and chest yellow, lower underparts white. Adult males bright
with sharply defined markings and band of black and rufous-orange
on upper chest; adult females duller, lack chest band. Immatures
may be quite dull but have same general color scheme.

Voice
Song a wiry buzz that winds unsteadily upward and ends abruptly
on a lower note: *zzzzzzeeeeurp.* May begin with a series of buzzy
notes on 1 pitch. Call note resembles *chip* of Yellow Warbler.

Similar Species
Nashville and immature Mourning may have roughly similar face
patterns, but are larger and lack wing bars. The 2 parulas must be
carefully distinguished. Adult male Northern has broken white eye-
ring, distinct chest band; Tropical lacks these, has black on face.
Female and immature Northerns have broken eye-ring, which
Tropicals lack (but may be faint). Extent of yellow below a good
mark: malar tract of feathers (extending back from base of lower
mandible) blue-gray in Northern, continuous with side of head, but
in Tropical this area is yellow, same color as throat; this detail hard
to discern but makes yellow throat area appear wider on Tropical.
Smaller yellow throat area of Northern seems "pinched in" at base
because gray extends downward at sides of neck and upper chest.
Yellow below on Tropical extends to belly; ends at mid-breast on
Northern. Lower wing bar of Tropical sometimes less extensive, has
white tips on fewer of great coverts.

Range
Breeds from southeastern Manitoba to Nova Scotia and south locally
to central Texas and south-central Florida. Winters mainly in
southern Florida, Mexico, Central America, and West Indies; also
rarely on Gulf Coast and casually in West. Regular wanderer in
West; isolated nesting records in California, New Mexico, and
northwestern Mexico.   *Kenn Kaufman*

Immature
1. *Buff tinge on upperparts.*
2. *Buff tinge on underparts.*

Reddish tinge on rump.

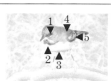

Adult male
1. *Broken white eye-ring.*
2. *Black and rufous chest bands.*
3. *Yellow throat and chest.*
4. *Blue-gray upperparts with green on back.*
5. *White wing bars.*

Female
1. *Broken white eye-ring.*
2. *Blue-gray upperparts.*
3. *White wing bars.*
4. *Yellow throat and chest.*

Small size.

Tropical Parula

Parula pitiayumi
This tropical edition of the Northern Parula, found in very small
numbers in southern Texas, is best detected by the male's song.

Description
4½" (11.5 cm). Adult male very similar to Northern Parula but lacks
eye-ring, has black patch from base of bill to ear coverts; upper
chest may have dull orange wash. Females and immatures duller
gray above, yellow below, and may lack most of black patch on face.

Voice
Buzzy song very similar to that of Northern Parula.

Similar Species
See Northern Parula.

Range
Widespread but local in tropics to Argentina. In very small numbers
from S. Texas north to near Kingsville; in most years a few winter
in woods along Rio Grande.   *Kenn Kaufman*

Yellow Warbler

Dendroica petechia
The most widespread North American wood warbler, the Yellow
Warbler breeds from Alaska to Newfoundland and from southern
California to the Florida Keys, Mexico, and Central America south
to Peru. At least 7 different races are recognized, and some
ornithologists believe 2 or more species may be involved. It may be
more useful to consider the Yellow Warbler complex as a
superspecies with numerous, partially distinct forms. All the
subspecies are strictly allopatric. Aptly described as "a bit of
feathered sunshine" by Frank Chapman, the Yellow Warbler is
easily recognized and is a familiar sight about the ornamental
shrubbery and hedgerows of our suburbs. Yellow Warblers also
commonly inhabit willow and alder thickets bordering streams and
swamps as well as thickets in cut-over woodlands. The "Golden"
Yellow Warbler of the Florida Keys is restricted to coastal
mangroves. Yellow Warbler nests are heavily parasitized by Brown-
headed Cowbirds; this warbler thwarts the cowbird by covering the
unwanted intruder's eggs with additional nest linings. Yellow
Warblers migrate extremely early, and some adults may be found
moving south by late July.

Description
4½–5¼" (11.5–13.5 cm). This is the only yellow warbler with
obvious yellow patches on the inner web of most tail feathers, a
yellow eye-ring, and yellowish wing bars and edges to the flight
feathers. Males are bright yellow below with thin chestnut breast
stripes, yellow-green upperparts, darker wings and tail with yellow
edges, and sometimes a reddish tinge to the crown. Females are
somewhat duller; the chestnut breast stripes are usually faint and
are absent in some birds. Immature males resemble females.
Immature females are drab olive-green birds lacking breast stripes;
the yellow tail spots are restricted to the outer 2 or 3 tail feathers.
The Alaska race tends to be small and dull olive-green; the Sonoran
form is pale. The "Golden" Warbler of the Florida Keys is most
distinct: males are warm, bright yellow with rusty crowns and more
heavily streaked breasts. All Yellow Warblers show a rather
distinct beady black eye and are short-tailed.

Voice
Lively, cheerful song: usually 3–4 well-spaced *tseet-tseet-tseet* notes

Adult male

1. *Black mask with no eye-ring.*
2. *Blue-gray upperparts.*
3. *White wing bars.*
4. *Yellow throat and breast.*

Texas only.

Adult male

1. *Bright yellow face.*
2. *Bright yellow underparts with bold chestnut streaks.*
3. *Yellow wing bars.*

In flight, shows yellow tail patches.

Adult female

1. *Yellow underparts with faint chestnut streaks.*
2. *Yellow-green upperparts.*

followed by more rapid *sitta-sitta-see*. Full song: *tseet-tseet-tseet sitta-sitta-see*. Call note a distinctive soft, clear *chip*. Flight note a high, thin *zeet*.

Similar Species
Female and immature Wilson's Warbler olive-green above and lemon-yellow below; have dark tails that lack yellow spots, yellow face sharply framed with olive-green along crown and nape. All Wilson's lack yellow wing bars and wing edges, have more flat-looking crown. See Orange-crowned Warbler.

Range
Breeds from Arctic Circle in Alaska across Canada to central Labrador, Newfoundland; south to southern California, northern Oklahoma, northern Georgia; disjunct population in Florida Keys through West Indies. Also resident from Mexico to Colombia and Peru. Winters mostly from southern Mexico to Peru and Brazil; small numbers regularly in southern California, more rarely in southern Arizona.   *Peter D. Vickery*

Chestnut-sided Warbler

Dendroica pensylvanica
Probably more than any other wood warbler in eastern North America, the Chestnut-sided Warbler has benefited from the changing land uses brought about by the development and subsequent decline of agriculture. In the early 19th century, Chestnut-sided Warblers were so rare that in his lifetime John James Audubon apparently encountered just a single individual. As farming diminished in the Northeast, abandoned pastures and fields became overgrown with shrubs and vines. Similarly, the brushy regrowth of clear-cut forests provided excellent habitat for Chestnut-sided Warblers. The species flourished, and today these birds are a familiar sight along country roadsides and overgrown fields that have not yet reverted to forest. Chestnut-sided Warblers are not shy birds; the colorful males can often be seen drooping their wings and cocking their tails as they pour forth their loud, clear, emphatic song.

Description
4½–5¼" (11.5–13.5 cm). Adult male Chestnut-sideds have a bright lemon-yellow crown, white underparts with thin chestnut stripes along the sides and flanks, and 2 yellow wing bars. The back is streaked with yellow-green and black, the face is patterned with black and white, and the tail spots are white. The females are similar but duller, with less black on the face and less pronounced chestnut flank stripes. Immature birds are bright yellow-green above and off-white below, with pale gray faces, a bold white eye-ring, and 2 yellow wing bars. Adults Chestnut-sideds in fall plumage lose the black facial markings; they are bright yellow-green above with chestnut flank stripes.

Voice
Loud, clear song, last 2 syllables accented: often interpreted as *so pleased, so pleased, so pleased to meet cha;* also transcribed as: *I wish, I wish to see Miss Beecher;* accent on last two syllables. Second song longer and more variable. Call note a rich *chip*, similar to Yellow Warbler's.

Similar Species
Ruby-crowned Kinglet resembles immature Chestnut-sided but has white wing bars; is smaller, duller, and more energetic. Immature

Immature, Alaska race
1. *Uniform dull olive-green plumage.*

Shows yellow patches in tail.

Adult male
1. *Yellow crown.*
2. *Black-and-white facial pattern.*
3. *Chestnut sides and flanks.*
4. *White underparts.*
5. *Yellow wing bars.*

Adult female
1. *Yellowish crown.*
2. *Reduced facial pattern.*
3. *Reduced chestnut on sides and flanks.*
4. *White underparts.*
5. *Yellow wing bars.*

Bay-breasted Warbler has white wing bars, different face pattern; has dull yellowish-buff underparts; also larger.

Range
Breeds from south-central Saskatchewan, Manitoba, and southern Ontario to Nova Scotia, south through Minnesota, eastern Nebraska to northern Indiana and northern New Jersey, and south along Appalachian mountains to northern Georgia. Winters in Nicaragua, Panama.   *Peter D. Vickery*

Magnolia Warbler

Dendroica magnolia
In open stands of young spruce and fir, particularly along woodland roads or in old, neglected pastures, the active and colorful Magnolia Warbler is a common nesting species. Although these warblers frequently fan their tails, revealing a white median band, Magnolias can be difficult to observe: they tend to forage near the center of trees, rather than at the outer edges. From below, the tail appears white with a black terminal band. This is 1 of only 3 warblers that display a bright yellow rump.

Description
4¼–5¼″ (11–13.5 cm). In breeding plumage the adult male has a gray crown, black back, and yellow rump. The sides of the head are black, and there are 2 very wide white wing bars that nearly form a wing patch. A broad, rectangular white band crosses most of the middle of the tail, except for the 2 central tail feathers. The throat and underparts are bright yellow; the breast, sides, and flanks are heavily streaked with black, and the undertail coverts are white. Females in breeding plumage are similar but duller, with reduced white wing bars. Immatures and fall adults resemble females in breeding plumage but have a grayish head, a thin, pale eye-ring, olive-green back (sometimes spotted), faintly streaked sides and flanks, and a distinctive, narrow, nearly complete gray breastband.

Voice
Song a short, variable, rising *wee-o wee-o wee-chy*, resembling Yellow Warbler in tone. Note a unique *tlep*.

Similar Species
Yellow-rumped Warbler has white breast. Cape May Warbler male has chestnut cheeks, lacks white median tail band. Immature Prairie Warbler wags tail, lacks tail band, and has dusky jaw stripe.

Range
Breeds from southern Mackenzie east to northern Saskatchewan, northern Ontario, central Quebec, and Newfoundland; south to central British Columbia, southern Manitoba, northern Minnesota, central Michigan, southern Ontario; locally to central West Virginia and Virginia, central Pennsylvania, northwestern New Jersey, and western Massachusetts. Winters from Mexico to Panama; also in West Indies.   *Wayne R. Petersen*

Immature

1. *Bold white eye-ring.*
2. *Yellow-green upperparts.*
3. *Yellow wing bars.*
4. *Off-white underparts.*

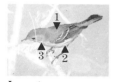

Immature

1. *Olive-green upperparts.*
2. *Yellow, faintly streaked underparts.*
3. *Narrow gray breastband.*

In flight, shows white tail patches.

Adult male

1. *Gray crown.*
2. *Black sides of head.*
3. *Yellow underparts with black streaks.*
4. *Black back.*
5. *White wing bars.*

In flight, shows white tail patches.

Cape May Warbler

Dendroica tigrina
These birds are uncommon warblers in the mature spruce woods of
eastern Canada, but, like the Bay-breasted Warbler, they
occasionally undergo local population explosions in areas heavily
infested with spruce budworms. Much of their summer foraging and
singing is confined to the upper branches of spruce and fir trees;
during migration, however, they may occur in a variety of
situations, often seeming to prefer pines, where they methodically
explore dense clusters of needles or hover momentarily at the tips of
branches.

Description
4¾–5½" (12–14 cm). Adult males in breeding plumage are yellowish-
green above, spotted with black, with white wing patches and tail
spots and bright yellow rumps. They have a chestnut cheek patch,
bordered above by a yellow eyebrow stripe, and yellow underparts
that are heavily streaked with black. Females in spring are less
heavily streaked below; they lack chestnut cheek patches, have the
underparts whitish or lightly washed with yellow, and show a yellow
neck patch. Adults and immatures in fall resemble spring females
but are duller, having olive-gray upperparts obscurely spotted with
brown, greenish-yellow rumps, and dusky streaks below, variably
washed with yellowish. A diffuse yellow neck patch is always
present but may be obscure. The tail in all plumages is short.

Voice
Song a very high, sibilant *seet seet seet seet*, all on same pitch. Call
note a distinctive, high, sharp *seet*.

Similar Species
Immature Yellow-rumped Warbler also has yellow rump but is
larger, lacks yellow neck patch, and has different note. Palm
Warbler in fall wags tail; usually found close to ground.

Range
Breeds from southwestern Mackenzie and northeastern British
Columbia east to central Manitoba, southern Quebec, and Nova
Scotia; south to northeastern North Dakota, central Minnesota,
northern Michigan, northern New York, and northern New
England. Very rare to casual in West. Winters in the West Indies.
Wayne R. Petersen

Black-throated Blue Warbler

Dendroica caerulescens
The husky song of the Black-throated Blue Warbler is a familiar
summer sound on the beech- and maple-covered slopes of the
northern hardwood forests of eastern Canada and the northeastern
United States. In the southern Appalachians, the species is often
associated with dense mountain laurel thickets; farther north,
hardwood sprout growth with an understory of shrubs—especially
American yew—is preferred. This is the only warbler that
sometimes flashes a white wing stripe in flight.

Description
4¾–5½" (12–14 cm). Males in all plumages are recognizable by their
dark grayish-blue upperparts (tinged with greenish in immatures);
the black sides of the head, throat, upper breast, and sides and the
white underparts are also distinctive. They have a conspicuous
white wing patch and white patches in the outer tail feathers.
Females are unstreaked olive-green above, often with traces of blue
on the crown and upper tail coverts, a brownish cheek patch, and

Breeding male
1. Chestnut cheek patch.
2. Yellow neck patch.
3. Yellow-green back with black spots.
4. Yellow underparts streaked with black.
5. White wing patches.

Immature
1. Yellow neck patch.
2. Streaked underparts.
3. Olive-gray upperparts with indistinct spots.
4. White wing bars.

Female
1. Partial eye-ring.
2. Dark cheeks.
3. Olive-green upperparts.
4. White wing spot.
5. Olive-yellow underparts.

usually a white wing spot—which may sometimes be concealed—at
the base of the primaries. There is a whitish stripe over the eye, and
the lower eyelid is white. The underparts are a dull olive-yellow.
Immatures basically resemble adults.

Voice
Song a lazy *zwee-a zwee-a zwee-a zweee*, last note ascending. One
variation resembles Cerulean Warbler's song. Call note a juncolike
smack.

Similar Species
Tennessee Warbler in fall greener above; lacks dark cheek patch and
white wing spot. Female Cerulean Warbler has 2 white wing bars.
Philadelphia Vireo lacks wing spot, has paler cheeks and stouter bill.

Range
Breeds from southeastern Manitoba and central and western
Ontario east to southern Quebec and Nova Scotia, south to central
Minnesota, western Pennsylvania, Connecticut, Rhode Island, and
in Appalachians to northeastern Georgia. Rare wanderer to West.
Winters primarily in West Indies.   *Wayne R. Petersen*

Yellow-rumped Warbler

Dendroica coronata
Included here are 2 forms that were considered full species until
recently; studies have shown that they interbreed freely where their
summer ranges meet in southwestern Canada. However, their
comparative distribution and status is still worth recording, and it is
acceptable (and commendable) for birders to continue using the
name "Myrtle" Warbler for the white-throated eastern form and
"Audubon's" Warbler for the yellow-throated western form. The
"Myrtle" is the winter warbler of the East. Inland it may overwinter
only sparsely, but on the Atlantic Coast—where thickets of
bayberry and wax myrtle provide edible berries as well as shelter—
its winter concentrations can be awesome. Hordes flush ahead of the
advancing birder, filling the air with hard *check* calls and flashing a
yellow rump patch above 2 white tail spots. In summer the "Myrtle"
Warbler is found throughout the coniferous woods of the North.
Replacing the "Myrtle" as a breeding bird in the conifers of the
mountainous West, "Audubon's" is very much like that form.

Description
5–6″ (12.5–15 cm). The adult male "Myrtle" in summer is blue-gray
above, with black back streaks, a small yellow crown patch, and a
yellow rump. The wings are gray with 2 white wing bars. A thin
white eyebrow and broken eye-ring set off a black ear patch. The
white throat area curves up behind the ear patch. Black streaks
cover the chest and extend down the sides and flanks, interrupted
by a yellow patch on the side; the lower underparts are white. The
tail feathers are gray, with white spots on the inner webs of the
outer 3 or 4 pairs. The female in summer has the same basic pattern
duplicated in shades of grayish-brown. The breast streaks are less
extensive, and fewer tail feathers (just the outer 2 or 3 pairs) have
white spots. The adult male in winter resembles the summer female.
Winter females and immatures are duller and variable, some
immatures having very faint breast streaking and little or no yellow
on the sides or crown. The adult male "Audubon's" in breeding
plumage is similar to the corresponding plumage of the "Myrtle,"
but the pale throat area is yellow instead of white; it covers a
smaller area and does not curve up behind the ear coverts. The ear
coverts do not show up as conspicuously as they do on the "Myrtle,"
especially since there is little or no pale eyebrow outlining them

Adult male
1. *Grayish-blue crown and upperparts.*
2. *Black face, throat, and flanks.*
3. *White wing patch.*

Breeding male "Myrtle" Warbler
1. *Blue-gray, streaked upperparts.*
2. *Black ear patch.*
3. *White throat.*
4. *Black streaks on breast and flanks.*
5. *Yellow on sides of breast.*
6. *Yellow rump.*

Breeding male "Audubon's" Warbler
1. *Yellow throat.*
2. *Broad white wing patch.*
3. *Solid black breast.*
4. *Yellow on sides of breast.*

Has yellow rump. Soft chep call.

above. The greater coverts generally have broad white edgings,
creating a large white wing patch instead of 2 discrete wing bars.
The black on the chest and sides tends to be more solid and less
streaked, and there is more white in the tail (usually white spots on
inner webs of the outer 5 pairs of tail feathers). Female and
immature "Audubon's" and winter males duplicate the summer
male's pattern in duller and paler tones of brownish-gray. They have
less white in the tail than adult males (but more than the typical
"Myrtle") and never show a white wing patch; on some immatures
the yellow of the throat is represented only by dull pale buff. (Adult
males breeding in southern Arizona have more extensive black on
the chest, broader black back streaks, and darker faces.)

Voice
"Myrtle's" song a musical trill, the elements vaguely doubled: *tuwee-
tuwee-tuwee* or *tyew-tyew-tyew*, often changing to higher or lower
pitch near the end. In spring migration a weaker, disorganized
warbling song. Call note a loud, hard *check*. "Audubon's" song very
like "Myrtle's" but some variations seem to have richer tone quality.
Call note a *chep*, softer and less metallic than that of "Myrtle."

Similar Species
Magnolia, Palm, and Cape May can show a yellow rump area.
Magnolia yellow below. Palm has strong cap and eyebrow; wags tail.
Some immature Cape Mays similar to dullest "Myrtles" but have
shorter tails, finer bills, and usually pale neck spots. Not all Yellow-
rumpeds can be assigned to either "Myrtle" or "Audubon's," because
they interbreed regularly; but area of contact is small, so
intergrades make up very small percentage of population.

Range
"Myrtle" breeds from Alaska east to Newfoundland and south to
northern British Columbia, southern Manitoba, Michigan, New
York. Winters in southeastern United States, north sparsely to
Great Lakes, Maritime Provinces; also on Pacific Coast from
Washington to Baja and uncommonly in Southwest; also south to
Panama and West Indies. "Audubon's" breeds from central British
Columbia east to southern Saskatchewan and south through
mountains of western United States to central Mexico; also in
southern Mexico and Guatemala. Winters from southern British
Columbia south through lowlands of Pacific coastal states and
throughout Southwest east to Texas (and south into Central
America). Accidental east to Atlantic Coast.   *Kenn Kaufman*

Black-throated Gray Warbler

Dendroica nigrescens
Pleistocene shifts in the distribution of forests in North America
shaped the evolution and current distribution of a group of strongly
patterned *Dendroica* warblers, the Black-throated Gray,
Townsend's, Hermit, Black-throated Green, and Golden-cheeked
warblers. The 5 are largely separated geographically, and, where
overlap occurs, there is some ecological separation. They share
many common characteristics: black, yellow, and white face
patterns; largely white underparts, usually with streaks along the
side; 2 white wing bars; white outer tail feathers; "wheezy" songs;
sharp, metallic call notes; and a preference for conifers. All are
active, arboreal insect-hunters, and all are entirely migratory.
Each species can easily be distinguished by its head pattern,
especially by the presence or absence of a dark cheek patch and by
the color of the crown and face. Within each species, the adult male
and female can be distinguished by the presence (in the male) of an
entirely black throat; females also have fewer streaks on the sides,

Immature "Myrtle" Warbler

1. *Brownish streaked back.*
2. *Whitish throat.*
3. *Yellow on sides of breast.*
4. *Streaking on chest.*

Has yellow rump. Hard check call.

Fall adult "Audubon's" Warbler

1. *Yellow throat.*
2. *Plain face.*
3. *Streaked or mottled breast.*

Has yellow rump. Soft chep call.

Adult male

1. *Black crown.*
2. *White eyebrow.*
3. *Black cheek.*
4. *White stripe below cheek.*
5. *Black throat.*
6. *Gray upperparts with faint black streaks.*
7. *Streaked flanks.*

flanks, and back than the males, and have less white in the tail.
Adults in fall differ only slightly from adults in spring. Immatures
resemble dull females and show only slight differences between the
sexes. The Black-throated Gray Warbler is the most distinct of the
group. It has no yellow in its plumage other than a tiny spot on the
lores. Its range overlaps those of the Hermit and Townsend's
warblers, but it prefers dry forests in warm climates. It often
breeds in areas where the trees are widely spaced with much
intervening brush. Oak woodland is the preferred habitat, although
the piñon-juniper woodland runs a close second; some pine and fir
communities are also used, generally in the north and particularly if
oaks are present. This species is common through most of its range.

Description
4½–5″ (11.5–12.5 cm). On the adult male the crown, most of the
lores, the cheeks, and the throat are black. The cheek is bordered by
2 white lines, 1 below and the other behind the eye. The underparts
below the throat are white, with black streaks along the sides and
flanks. The back is gray, faintly streaked with black. The wings
have 2 white bars. The outer 2 tail feathers are white; this white
shows in flight and makes the underside of the folded tail almost
entirely white. Adult females are very similar but show gray in the
crown and white in the throat. Immatures have the black in the
plumage largely replaced by gray, and the throat is mostly or all
white; some may be very pale, but show the pattern of the adults.

Voice
Song a *weezy weezy weezy weezy-weet*. Call a dull *chut*, intermediate
between call notes of Yellow-rumped and Townsend's warblers.

Similar Species
Other 4 warblers in group have similar patterns but show yellow on
face. Black-and-white Warbler has white stripe down center of
crown, white streaks on back; behaves like a creeper. Various
chickadees have all-white cheeks, no wing bars.

Range
Breeds from southwestern British Columbia, Washington, Idaho,
Wyoming, and Colorado south, mostly in mountains, to
northernmost Mexico. In winter, rare to locally uncommon in
southern California and southern Arizona; most winter in Mexico.
Migrates widely through lowlands of West, occurring east into
western Texas.   *Richard Webster*

Townsend's Warbler

Dendroica townsendi
Coniferous forest is the habitat of the Townsend's Warbler for most
of the year. It breeds in the Pacific Northwest, where it may spend
most of the summer singing, feeding, and nesting at infuriatingly
high levels of the trees. In winter it occupies conifers of a curiously
disjunct range: in coastal Oregon and California, and from central
Mexico south to Nicaragua. As a migrant it is widespread, occurring
in the lowlands and in a variety of habitats. Active insect-eaters,
Townsend's Warblers may be found by themselves, in small groups,
or mixed in with other warblers foraging from high to low in trees;
in migration, they are frequently found in chaparral and desert
scrub.

Description
4½–5″ (11.5–13 cm). The crown, cheek, throat, and upper breast of
the adult male are black. The black cheek is bordered from above by
a yellow eyebrow and from below by a broad yellow stripe on the
side of the throat. The back is dull olive-green spotted with black.

 *Wood Warblers*

Adult female
1. *Grayish crown.*
2. *White throat.*

Immature
1. *Gray crown.*
2. *Gray cheek.*
3. *White throat.*

Immature
1. *Olive-green crown.*
2. *Olive-green cheek.*
3. *Yellow throat.*

The lower breast is yellow, and the belly is white; the sides and
flanks are streaked with black. The 2 wing bars are white, as are
most of the 2 outer tail feathers. The adult female is similar, but has
an olive-green crown, a dusky cheek, a largely yellow throat, and
less black in the back and white in the tail. Immatures tend to have
olive-green cheeks and yellow throats.

Voice
Song a series of 5–7 high, buzzy *zee* or *swee* notes; quite variable and
generally similar to songs of Townsend's relatives. Call a sharp *tsik*.

Similar Species
Hermit Warbler has entirely golden cheek, no yellow on breast, few
or no streaks on side, and primarily gray back. Black-throated Gray
Warbler has paler cheek, lacks yellow on breast. Hybrids of
Townsend's and Hermit warblers are rare, but are encountered
annually. These most closely resemble Black-throated Green
Warblers, and vagrants of that species occur along the Pacific Coast
with roughly the same frequency as hybrids. If a confusing bird is
encountered, a detailed description should be made on the spot.

Range
Breeds from central and southern Alaska and southern Yukon south
through British Columbia to Washington, central Oregon, northern
Idaho, western Montana, and northwestern Wyoming. Locally
common in winter in coastal California and Oregon, occurring
sparsely elsewhere in those states and in Arizona; the majority
winter in Mexico and Central America. Migrates broadly through
lowlands and highlands and mountainous western states, occurring
regularly as far south and east as western Texas. Casual in East.
Richard Webster

Hermit Warbler

Dendroica occidentalis
The Hermit Warbler is fairly common within its narrow range along
the Pacific Coast. Nesting Hermit Warblers tend to occupy well-
forested areas that are higher and drier than those of Townsend's.
The zone of overlap is narrow, and little interbreeding occurs. In
spring the Hermit moves north through the lowlands and mountains
of Baja California and Arizona and continues north into its breeding
range; it is only at this time that the Hermit Warbler is commonly
found outside coniferous forests. The return migration largely
follows the same route, but through montane forests. As a breeder
and migrant, the Hermit Warbler occurs commonly in only 4 states.

Description
4½–5″ (11.5–12.5 cm). The face and forehead of the spring male are
a light, bright yellow; the nape is dusky; the back is gray with black
streaks; and the wing bars are white, as are most of the 2 outer tail
feathers. The throat is black; the rest of the underparts are white
(rarely faintly streaked on the sides). Females have a grayer back

Adult male
1. *Black crown.*
2. *Yellow eyebrow.*
3. *Black cheek.*
4. *Black throat and upper breast.*
5. *Yellow breast.*
6. *Streaked flanks.*

Adult female
1. *Olive-green crown.*
2. *Dusky cheek.*
3. *Largely yellow throat.*

Female
1. *Yellow forehead and face.*
2. *Largely yellow throat.*
3. *Gray, streaked upperparts.*
4. *White wing bars.*

and more yellow and white and less black in the throat. Immatures have a faint suggestion of a cheek patch, are much paler, and have little or no black in the throat, which is off-white to dull yellow. Fall adults and immatures may show a tinge of olive-green on the back.

Voice
Songs are very similar to Townsend's and others, and are equally variable. Typically high and slightly wheezy, ending briskly: *zwee zwee zwee zwee zeek-zeek.* Call a sharp *tsik*, very like Townsend's.

Similar Species
See Townsend's Warbler.

Range
Breeds in Cascades and coastal ranges of southwestern Washington and western Oregon, continuing uncommonly in Coast Ranges of northern and central California and commonly through the southern Cascades into the Sierra Nevada. Rare in winter in conifers on California coast; winters in southern Mexico and Central America.
Richard Webster

Black-throated Green Warbler

Dendroica virens
The Black-throated Green Warbler is a common bird in coniferous and mixed forests, especially where birch and aspen are prevalent in the North and where cypress is dominant in southern swamps. As with a number of canopy-dwelling warblers, this species is often first detected by its distinctive, lazy song that comes from high in a tree.

Description
4½–5½" (11.5–14 cm). Males in breeding plumage have upperparts that are yellowish-green, sometimes lightly spotted with black, 2 broad white wing bars, and white outer tail feathers. The forehead, face, and sides of the neck are yellow, contrasting with a black throat and upper breast; there is a faint olive line through the eye and bordering the ear coverts. The lower breast and belly are white with black side streaks. The adult female in breeding plumage is similar except that the black on the underparts is reduced and the chin and throat are mostly yellow. There is a slight yellow tinge to the vent. Adults and immatures in fall are similar to spring birds in having yellow faces; however, they usually have the black throat veiled with whitish feather tips or else have a yellowish white throat with only a few dusky streaks at the sides.

Voice
Song a husky *zee zee zee zoo zee;* also *zoo zee zoo zoo zee.* Call note a high, thin *seet* and a dull *tsip*, similar to Black-and-white Warbler's.

Similar Species
See Golden-cheeked and Townsend's warblers.

Range
Breeds from northern Alberta east to central Ontario and Newfoundland, south to central Alberta, southern Manitoba, central Minnesota, Pennsylvania, and northern New Jersey; south in mountains to northern Alabama and Georgia. Winters from southern Texas and southern Florida south to South America and West Indies. *Wayne R. Petersen*

Breeding male
1. *Bright yellow face and forehead.*
2. *Black throat.*
3. *Gray streaked upperparts.*
4. *White underparts.*

Adult male and female
1. *Yellow face.*
2. *Black throat and upper breast.*
3. *Yellow-green upperparts*
4. *White wing bars.*

Female has less black below.

Immature
. *Yellowish face.*
. *Little black on throat.*
. *Yellow-green upperparts.*
. *White wing bars.*

Golden-cheeked Warbler

Dendroica chrysoparia
Early every spring the Golden-cheeked Warbler returns to its sole nesting ground, the hill country of central Texas. Even there it is local, favoring hillsides and canyons with a good mix of junipers and oaks. Males sing from the treetops in late March and April, but the species becomes harder to find after singing begins to decline in May; by early August, most of these birds have departed.

Description
5" (12.5 cm). Adult male black on crown, nape, back, throat, and breast; wings black with 2 white bars and extensive white edgings. Tail blackish with large white spots on inner webs of outer feathers (visible from below or in flight). Face (including eyebrow, ear patch, and sides of neck) bright golden-yellow; bold black eyeline becomes broader behind eye and curves down at back of ear patch. Lower underparts white with black streaks on flanks. Adult female similar but duller; mostly green crown and back have some black streaking; bib reduced to dark smudges. Immature dull green above, often with very little black on back; mostly white below with some dark smudges at sides of throat and chest and faint streaks on flanks; face yellow, usually with hint of eyeline.

Voice
Song buzzy, usually of 4 or 5 syllables; frequent patterns include ascending *zee, dee, sidee-zee* and a dropping then rising *zee, zoo, sidee, zeep*. Call note a *chup*, similar to Black-throated Green's.

Similar Species
Female and immature similar to Black-throated Green Warbler (migrant through central Texas); Golden-cheeked usually has at least some black on back (virtually always lacking on Black-throated Green, except adult male); lower belly pure white (faintly washed with yellow in Black-throated Green); some indication of dark eyeline. Hybrids of Townsend's and Hermit might duplicate these characteristics, so Golden-cheekeds, except adult males, probably not safely identified outside normal range.

Range
Breeds in Edwards Plateau area of central Texas north very locally to near Dallas. Winters from southern Mexico to Nicaragua. Accidental in California and Florida.   *Kenn Kaufman*

Blackburnian Warbler

Dendroica fusca
The brilliant orange throat of the male Blackburnian Warbler in breeding plumage makes this bird unmistakable; however, its preference for the upper canopy of coniferous trees renders it difficult to observe in the northern forests that are its summer home. Even though its variable song is a common sound in the north woods, it is often overlooked or mistaken for that of some other species. During migration, the Blackburnian Warbler may show up in a variety of woodland habitats.

Description
4½–5½" (11.5–14 cm). Males in breeding plumage have black upperparts striped with white, a black face patch bordered with orange, an orange crown patch, a large white wing patch, and extensive white in the outer tail feathers. The underparts below the orange throat and breast are whitish with black stripes on the sides. Females in spring and adults and immatures in the fall are similar in pattern to the breeding male, except that the orange throat is

Adult female

1. *Yellow face with dark eyeline.*
2. *Green crown and back with dark streaks.*
3. *White belly.*
4. *Black streaks on flanks.*

Central Texas only.

Adult male

1. *Black crown, nape, and upperparts.*
2. *Golden-yellow face with black eyeline.*
3. *Black throat and upper breast.*

Fall plumage

1. *Yellow throat.*
2. *Yellowish eyebrow.*
3. *Brownish-olive facial pattern.*
4. *Streaked back.*
5. *White wing bars.*
6. *Streaks on sides.*

replaced by yellow, the black face patch and side streaks are brownish-olive, and the crown patch is obscured.

Voice
Song very thin and wiry, consisting of 2 or 3 parts. Variations are *sip sip sip titi tzeeee*, last note very high and ascending; also *zillup zillup zillup zizizizi*, like Nashville Warbler's. Call a rich *chip*.

Similar Species
Yellow-throated Warbler has unstreaked gray back and white above eye. Female Townsend's Warbler lacks pale back stripes and median crown stripes; has different call.

Range
Breeds from central Saskatchewan east to central Quebec and Nova Scotia, south to central Manitoba, northeastern Ohio, northern Rhode Island, and in Appalachians to South Carolina and northern Georgia.   *Wayne R. Petersen*

Yellow-throated Warbler

Dendroica dominica
The Yellow-throated Warbler, common in southeastern North America, inhabits big timber along river banks, swamps, and bottomlands, as well as open stands of pines, live oaks, and mixed forests. In the South, it seems to prefer areas with abundant Spanish moss. This bird tends to stay in the treetops, foraging with rather deliberate, creeping movements.

Description
4¾–5½" (12–14 cm). The Yellow-throated Warbler has a black-and-white head pattern with a white eyebrow stripe (partly yellow in the southeastern race *dominica*), an unmarked gray back, 2 white wing bars, a bright yellow chin and throat, and white underparts with black streaks on the sides. The rare "Sutton's" Warbler, a hybrid of the Northern Parula and the Yellow-throated Warbler, has a greenish patch on the back and no side streaking.

Voice
Song a loud musical series of clear syllables given faster as they descend with abrupt higher note at end: *tee-ew, tew-ew, tew-ew, tew-ew, tew-wi* or *sweetie, sweetie, sweetie;* sounds like Northern Parula's song repeated twice. Call note a rich *chip*.

Similar Species
Grace's Warbler has different face pattern, yellow eyebrow stripe, and different range.

Range
Breeds from central Missouri, southern Ohio, eastern Maryland, and southern New Jersey south to southeastern Texas, Gulf Coast, and central Florida. Wanders north to Great Lakes and Maritime Provinces. Winters from southeastern Texas, Gulf Coast, and Florida north along coast to northeastern South Carolina; south through Bahamas, Greater Antilles, and eastern and southern Mexico to Costa Rica.   *Paul W. Sykes, Jr.*

Breeding male
1. *Orange crown patch.*
2. *Orange eyebrow.*
3. *Orange throat.*
4. *Black back with white streaks.*
5. *White patch on wing.*
6. *Streaked flanks.*

Adult
1. *Black-and-white head pattern.*
2. *Bright yellow throat.*
3. *Gray unstreaked back.*
4. *White wing bars.*
5. *Streaked flanks.*

Male "Sutton's" Warbler
1. *Reduced streaking on side of breast.*
2. *Greenish-yellow patch on back.*

Grace's Warbler

Dendroica graciae
These common birds of southwestern pine forests are easy to spot in spring, but remain very high in the trees later in the season.

Description
5" (12.5 cm). Gray above with black forehead, sides, and crown; back, sides, and flanks streaked with black. Eyebrow yellow before eye, shading to white; lores dark. Chin, throat, and breast bright yellow. Wings have 2 bold white bars; outer tail feathers have white outer webs and subterminal spots.

Voice
Song rapid, staccato, musical trill: *chee-chee-che-che*; many variations. Call a thin, loud, sharp *tsip* or saucier *chip*.

Similiar Species
See Townsend's, Yellow-throated, and Blackburnian warblers.

Range
S. Nevada, S. Utah, and Sw. Colorado in highlands to Nicaragua. Winters from Nw. Mexico south.   *Scott B. Terrill*

Pine Warbler

Dendroica pinus
The Pine Warbler is a common passerine found in mature pine forests, pine barrens, and open mixed woodlands of eastern North America; in migration, however, this species may occur in a large variety of habitats. The Pine Warbler feeds in a creeping manner on insects from the ground to the tree tops, and in winter takes seeds and small fruits. It will sometimes alight on the trunks of pine trees in the manner of nuthatches or creepers. It is usually found in pines, as its name implies, and tends to stay in the tops of the trees. The Pine Warbler's song is pleasant and not loud; this bird occasionally sings in winter. It is one of the few North American wood warblers whose winter range includes much of its breeding area.

Description
5–5¾" (12.5–14.5 cm). The upperparts are unstreaked olive-green; there is a faint yellowish eyebrow stripe, 2 prominent white wing bars (fainter in immatures), and white spots on the corners of the tail. The legs are black. The amount of yellow on the underparts is highly variable. The male has a yellow chin, throat, and breast; the breast has indistinct grayish-olive to blackish streaking, and the belly and undertail coverts are white. The female is similar to the male but duller on the underparts. The immature has brownish-olive upperparts (brown in immature females) and whitish or ashy underparts with or without a trace of yellowish wash, particularly on the sides and breast.

Voice
Song is musical trill varying slightly in pitch, like Chipping Sparrow's song but softer, lower, and less rapid: *zit, zit, ziz-ziz-ziz-ziz-ziz-ziz-ziz-ziz-ziz-ziz*. Call note a soft, lisping *chip* or a high, thin *seet*.

Similar Species
Yellow-throated Vireo has heavier bill, no streaking on underparts, and yellow spectacles. Immature Blackburnian, Bay-breasted, and Blackpoll warblers have streaked backs; Blackpoll has pale feet and usually pale legs. Immature Cape May Warbler has pale neck spot, subdued yellowish rump, and streaked breast, sides, and flanks. Blue-winged Warbler has black eyeline and unstreaked yellow flanks.

Adult
1. *Yellow throat and breast.*
2. *Eyebrow yellow in front of the eye, white behind it.*
3. *Gray upperparts with black streaks.*
4. *Streaked flanks.*

Adult female
1. *Duller underparts than male.*

Adult male
1. *Unstreaked olive-green upperparts.*
2. *Two prominent white wing bars.*
3. *Faint yellowish eyebrow.*
4. *Yellow underparts with faint streaks.*

Range
Breeds from southeastern Manitoba to southern Quebec and central
Maine, south to eastern Texas and southern Florida (absent from
Keys, but occurs at Dry Tortugas in migration); rare or absent in
the upper Mississippi and Ohio river valleys. Winters from
Arkansas, southern Illinois, Tennessee, and Virginia, sparingly
north along coast to Massachusetts, and south to southern Florida,
Gulf Coast, and eastern Texas south into Mexico.
Paul W. Sykes, Jr.

Kirtland's Warbler

Dendroica kirtlandii
One of the rarest songbirds in North America, Kirtland's Warbler is
almost never seen except on its nesting ground in Michigan. When
sighted in migration, it is usually solitary and unwary, moving
deliberately at low elevation in shrubbery and semi-open areas. This
yellow-breasted, dark-backed, tail-bobbing species is relatively large
for a warbler. During migration (chiefly in May and September) it
occurs mainly in a direct path between Michigan and the Bahamas.

Description
6" (15 cm). The first feature of the full-plumage male that catches the
eye is its bright yellow underparts with black spots forming streaks
at the sides of the breast. The front of the face is black without any
yellow markings, giving prominence to thin white crescents
outlining the top and bottom of the eye. The upperparts are blue-
gray streaked with black, becoming brownish in fall. All of these
marks are subdued in some males, which may have fine scattered
spots on the front of the breast, and all females, which have pale
yellow breasts, no black on the face, and few or no black spots on
the sides. All have 2 dull whitish wing bars, but these are not
conspicuous.

Voice
Loud, emphatic, distinct notes without trill or buzz, low-pitched for
a warbler, with quality like Northern Waterthrush's and suggesting
parts of House Wren's song but shorter. Some individual variation
in song, with 1–3 quick introductory or closing notes. Also some
males sing a chatter song of a brief, rapid series: *ch-ch-ch-ch*. Call a
faint *chip*, seldom heard. Male sings in spring migration.

Similar Species
Prairie and Palm warblers also bob tails, but both have yellowish or
pale faces in all plumages. Fall Magnolia Warbler has yellow on
rump and prominent white marks in tail.

Range
Breeds only in extensive tracts of small jack pines in a few counties
of northern Lower Michigan, but nonbreeding strays occasionally
found in similar habitat in Wisconsin, southern Ontario, and
southern Quebec. Winters in Bahama Islands.
Harold F. Mayfield

Immature
1. *Brownish-olive upperparts.*
2. *Dull underparts.*

Breeding male
1. *White crescents above and below eye.*
2. *Black face.*
3. *Dark blue-gray upperparts.*
4. *Yellow underparts.*
5. *Streaked flanks.*

   Bobs tail.

Female
1. *Pale yellow underparts.*
2. *No black on face.*

   Breeds in Michigan only.

Prairie Warbler

Dendroica discolor
The misnamed Prairie Warbler, an eastern bird, is one of the
prettiest and most distinctive warblers. It is bright yellow below
and yellowish olive-green above, with black streaks along the sides
and 2 black marks on the face. The streaks and face marks are
barely discernible in immatures. Prairies prefer dry, scrubby areas,
old fields, barrens, and low, semiopen second growth, especially
with scrub oak, cedars, and pines. In Florida they also inhabit
mangroves. In such scrubby, sapling-filled areas the ascending,
sizzling song of these birds is heard. Prairie Warblers pump their
tails but not as much as Palm Warblers do. Because the trees in this
species' favorite habitat grow too tall for the birds within a few
years, Prairie Warblers appear and disappear as such areas develop
or change. Their spotty distribution corresponds to the occurrence
of suitable habitat. The Prairie Warbler nests and lives close to the
ground, but males often sing at the very top of moderate-size trees.

Description
4½–5″ (11.5–12.5 cm). The male is bright yellow below with black
streaks on the sides and 2 black facial marks, 1 through the eye and
1 along the jaw. The upperparts are yellowish olive-green. The
chestnut spots on the back are hard to see, and, in fact, are often
concealed. There are 2 distinct but inconspicuous yellow wing bars.
Like other *Dendroica* warblers, the Prairie has white in the tail; this
feature is most readily glimpsed when the bird flies. Females are
similar but duller, with a much less bold facial pattern and streaks.
In immatures, which are duller still, these features are barely
detectable, and the cheek is often gray. This species' habit of
bobbing the tail is a good field mark.

Voice
A distinctive, ascending, thin, buzzy song, variable in speed and
length; sizzles up chromatic scale and usually runs together at end.
Consists of 5–16 or more notes, usually 8–14, *zee, zee, zee, zee, zee,
zee, zee, zee, zee*. Call note a *chip*, sweet and weak yet emphatic,
with a little snap.

Similar Species
Palm Warbler also bobs tail but is usually less yellowish (especially
below), has more extensive streaking, brownish cap; more apt to be
seen in open areas (except on breeding grounds). Pine Warbler
duller, less uniformly yellow below, has more prominent white wing
bars; is bigger, chunkier, and has larger bill; often stays higher up in
trees. See Magnolia Warbler.

Range
Breeds from northern parts of Missouri, Illinois, and Michigan,
southern Ontario, northern New York, and southern Maine south to
eastern Texas, northern Louisiana, and southern parts of
Mississippi, Alabama, and Florida. Winters from northern Florida
(occasionally farther north) south to West Indies and Central
America. Rare in southwestern states, especially California in fall.
Henry T. Armistead

Immature
1. *Gray tinge on face.*
2. *Reduced streaks on face and sides.*
3. *Yellow underparts.*

Bobs tail.

Adult male
1. *Black streaks on face.*
2. *Black streaks on sides.*
3. *Yellow underparts.*
4. *Yellow-green upperparts.*

Bobs tail.

Female
1. *Reduced streaks on face and sides.*
2. *Yellow underparts.*
3. *Yellow-green upperparts.*

Bobs tail.

Palm Warbler

Dendroica palmarum
In summer the Palm Warbler dwells in northern muskeg, but during migration it is most often seen in low bushes or on the ground in weedy fields. One of the earliest warblers to arrive in spring and among the latest to depart in fall, its continual tail-wagging helps to identify it at any season.

Description
4½–5¾" (11.5–14.5 cm). Adults in breeding plumage have a chestnut crown and yellow eyebrow stripe with the cheeks, sides of the neck, and back grayish-brown, tinged with olive and with light dusky streaks. The wings have 2 indistinct buff wing bars, the tail has white spots in the corners, and the rump is greenish-yellow. In the race *D. p. palmarum*, the throat, upper breast, and undertail coverts are bright yellow, and the lower breast and belly are dull yellow, mixed with grayish-white. The race *D. p. hypochrysea* has the entire underparts bright yellow. Both races are streaked on the sides of the throat, across the breast, and on the sides with dark chestnut. In winter plumage, adults and immatures have a brownish crown, a whitish or yellowish eyebrow stripe, and either buff-white underparts (*palmarum*) or yellowish underparts (*hypochrysea*). The undertail coverts remain yellow in both races.

Voice
Song a buzzy trill given on 1 pitch; like Chipping Sparrow's song but less emphatic. Note a *check*, higher than Yellow-rumped Warbler's.

Similar Species
Prairie Warbler wags tail but lacks crown patch and has dusky jaw stripe and ventral stripes only on sides. Yellow-rumped Warbler has bright yellow rump.

Range
Breeds from southern Mackenzie and northern Alberta east to central Quebec and southern Newfoundland south to northeastern British Columbia, central Alberta, northern Minnesota, southern Quebec, Maine, and Nova Scotia. Winters from southeastern Texas east to North Carolina (occasionally southern New England); rare but very regular in coastal California; south to Central America and Caribbean.   *Wayne R. Petersen*

Bay-breasted Warbler

Dendroica castanea
This warbler is one of a complement of birds of northern coniferous forests whose wiry song is often confused with those of its congeners. The Bay-breasted requires spruce and fir—often in secondary growth or with lots of edge—for breeding, and it tends to forage at about the middle of the tree. A rather rapid but late spring migrant, the Bay-breasted is among the earliest warblers to go south in the fall; it often moves in August, a full month ahead of the main flight of the Blackpoll, which it closely resembles at that season. Like the Cape May, the Bay-breasted has local population explosions coinciding with infestations of spruce budworm.

Description
5–6" (12.5–15 cm). Males in breeding plumage have a chestnut crown, black face, large buff neck patch, and upperparts that are greenish-gray streaked with black. The wings have 2 white wing bars and there are small white tail spots. The throat, upper breast, sides, and flanks are deep chestnut; the rest of the underparts are

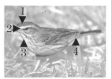

Breeding adult
1. *Chestnut crown.*
2. *Yellow eyebrow.*
3. *Yellow throat and breast with streaks.*
4. *Yellow undertail coverts.*

Wags tail.
Forages on or near ground.

Fall immature
1. *Brown crown.*
2. *Whitish eye stripe.*
3. *Yellow undertail coverts.*

Immature
1. *Greenish-gray streaked upperparts.*
2. *Buff underparts with no streaks.*
3. *Trace of bay on flanks.*
4. *Buff undertail coverts.*
5. *Dark legs.*

buff-white. Females are similar except that the extent of chestnut
varies, usually reduced to a wash on the sides, and the buff neck
patch is often inconspicuous. Adults and immatures in fall resemble
fall-plumage Blackpoll Warblers except that they have unstreaked
underparts, buff undertail coverts, and usually show a trace of bay
on the flanks. Most have dark legs; all have dark feet.

Voice
Song a weak, short, high-pitched *seetzy seetzy seetzy see;* resembles
Black-and-white Warbler's song in pattern and American Redstart's
in quality. Call note a mellow *chip* and a high, thin *seet.*

Similar Species
Chestnut-sided Warbler in spring has yellow crown; fall birds lack
colorful crown patch. See Blackpoll Warbler.

Range
Breeds from northeastern British Columbia east to central
Manitoba, northeastern Minnesota, central Ontario, northeastern
New York, and northern New England. Casual in West. Winters in
Panama and South America.   *Wayne R. Petersen*

Blackpoll Warbler

Dendroica striata
The Blackpoll is widespread and abundant in summer in the spruce-
fir forests of boreal Canada and Alaska. It is one of the latest
Dendroica warblers to arrive in spring, and its sluggish actions and
preference for tall tree tops make it difficult to observe at that
season. In the autumn it often forages at lower levels. In
September, the Blackpoll is an abundant northern Atlantic Coast
migrant, filling its favored oaks and birches with its loud *chip* notes.

Description
5–5¾" (12.5–14.5 cm). Males in breeding plumage have a black cap
and white cheeks, 2 white wing bars, white tail spots, and olive-gray
upperparts that are streaked with black. The underparts are white,
striped with black on the sides of the neck and body. Females in
breeding plumage have a similar pattern except that they have a
pale eyebrow stripe, a greenish cap and upperparts with dusky
streaks, and underparts washed with yellowish and finely striped on
the sides. Adults and immatures in fall resemble females in spring
but are greener above, have faint side streaks and greenish-yellow
underparts, and white undertail coverts. The legs and feet are
usually pinkish or straw-colored.

Voice
Song extremely high *sit sit sit sit sit sit sit*, on 1 pitch and loudest in
middle. Call note a loud *smack*, easily imitated by kissing back of
one's hand. Also a high, thin *seet* and chipmunklike *chip* notes.

Similar Species
Black-and-white Warbler has striped crown. Black-throated Gray
Warbler has black cheek patch. Immature Pine Warbler has dark
legs and unstreaked gray or brownish back, larger bill, and darker
ear coverts. Immature Bay-breasted plumper, more yellow-green
above, unstreaked buff or buff-white below and on undertail coverts,
often with trace of bay on flanks; has dark legs and feet.

Range
Breeds from northern Alaska to northern Labrador and
Newfoundland south to southern Alaska and central British
Columbia and east to western Massachusetts and southern Nova
Scotia. Wanders regularly to California in fall. Winters in South
America.   *Wayne R. Petersen*

Breeding male
1. *Chestnut throat.*
2. *Buff neck patch.*
3. *Chestnut flanks.*
4. *White wing bars.*

Breeding male
1. *Black cap.*
2. *White cheek.*
3. *Streaked olive-gray upperparts.*
4. *White wing bars.*
5. *Streaked flanks.*

Immature
1. *Greenish streaked upperparts.*
2. *Yellowish-green underparts with faint streaks on sides.*
3. *Pale legs.*

Cerulean Warbler

Dendroica cerulea
This rather local, uncommon, small warbler of the East is usually
found high up in the canopy of mature, open deciduous forests in
bottomland swamps and wooded hillsides along streams. Ceruleans
are most common in the Ohio River valley. They build their nests
high in hardwoods and well out from the trunk, and can be difficult
to see well because of this preference for the tops of big trees.
Ceruleans are locally common, and breeding birds are often
concentrated in a favorable habitat. The male is light bluish above
and white below with wing bars, a narrow black ring across the
breast, and streaked sides. Its vigorous song suggests the Northern
Parula. Females and immatures are subtly marked and a source of
probable confusion; they are blue-gray (especially on the head) and
olive-green above, yellowish-white below, with wing bars and a pale
eyebrow stripe.

Description
4–5″ (10–12.5 cm). Males are light bluish or grayish-blue above,
brightest on the crown. The underparts are white with streaks on
the sides, a dark band (sometimes incomplete) across the chest, and
white wing bars. Females are much more nondescript: the dull blue-
gray or bluish-green on the head and upper back merges into olive-
green on the rest of the back. They are dull whitish below, tinged
with yellowish, and have white wing bars and a pale whitish
eyebrow stripe. Immatures are similar to females, but slightly more
greenish above and more yellowish below. The immature male may
be a bit bluer above, with a suggestion of a breastband. The
immature female may have more extensive yellow below and duller
upperparts. The plumage of adults in both sexes is also variable.

Voice
An energetic, rapid song, somewhat suggestive of Northern
Parula's, usually with 3–5 introductory short, chanted notes ending
with a higher, drawn-out note. Variously transcribed as *zray, zray,
zray, zray, zreeeee* and *just a little sneeze.* Like Black-throated Blue
Warbler's song but faster and less slurred.

Similar Species
Black-throated Blue Warbler has black throat. Bluish-backed Parula
has true yellow on some of underparts. Spring Tennessee Warbler
slightly similar to female Cerulean but lacks wing bars. Spring
female Blackpoll Warbler heavily streaked, much more black-and-
white. Fall Blackpoll Warbler similar to female Cerulean but
greener above, has streaks on back and less prominent eyebrow.
Female Black-throated Blue Warbler lacks wing bars.

Range
Breeds from southeastern Minnesota, central Wisconsin, southern
parts of Michigan, Ontario, New York, and western New England
south to northeastern Texas, northern parts of Louisiana,
Mississippi, Alabama, and northern North Carolina. High
Appalachian areas split breeding range somewhat. Northeastern
range expanding slightly. Always rare on Atlantic coastal plain.
Winters in northern South America. Casual in southwestern states.
Henry T. Armistead

Immature
1. *Blue-green upperparts.*
2. *White wing bars.*
3. *Yellowish underparts.*

Adult male
1. *Light bluish upperparts.*
2. *White underparts with dark breastband.*
3. *White wing bars.*

Song like Northern Parula's.

Adult female
1. *Blue-gray upperparts.*
2. *Whitish underparts.*
3. *White wing bars.*

Black-and-white Warbler

Mniotilta varia

The Black-and-white Warbler's notably long, thin bill with its arched culmen seems especially well suited to this bird's particular method of foraging for insects and larvae on the trunk and lower branches of trees. This bark-gleaning feeding behavior has freed this species from the need for a green canopy overhead. Not surprisingly, Black-and-whites are among the first warblers to migrate north and generally appear well before the foliage has emerged. This species prefers deciduous and mixed forests, especially damp woodlands, but in the north may be found in coniferous areas.

Description
4½–5½" (11.5–14 cm). The shiny adult male is boldly streaked with black and white above and below, with a white stripe through the center of the crown, a white eyebrow, 2 white wing bars, and white tail spots. The black throat and streaked sides and flanks extend as black spots onto the undertail coverts. The throat usually becomes whitish in winter. Females are dull black with a brown wash, especially on the flanks. The throat is white. Thin black streaks on the flanks continue as black spots onto the uppertail coverts. Immatures resemble females, but often have more heavily streaked sides.

Voice
Unhurried, high, thin song of 6–8 *wee-see* couplets, with stress on first syllable. Also a more complex variation. Call note a sharp *pit*, often in series, and a high, thin *seet*.

Similar Species
Male Blackpoll Warbler has solid black crown and pure white undertail coverts, lacks white eye stripe.

Range
Breeds from southern Northwest Territories (Mackenzie River), Alberta, and central Saskatchewan to Newfoundland; south to eastern Montana, central Texas, North Carolina; infrequently south to Louisiana, Alabama, and Georgia. Winters in southern Texas, coastal South Carolina, and Florida; rare transient in West; also to Bahamas, West Indies through Mexico, Central America to Venezuela, Ecuador, and Colombia.   *Peter D. Vickery*

American Redstart

Setophaga ruticilla

One of our most abundant wood warblers, the American Redstart prefers open, second-growth deciduous and mixed woodlands. As Frank Chapman aptly recounts, the bird displays its "brilliant plumage in a manner to set at defiance all laws of aggressive coloration. With what dainty grace he spreads his tail, half opens his wings, and pirouettes from limb to limb like a village belle with coquettishly held skirts tripping the mazes of a country dance."

Description
4¼–5¼" (11–13.5 cm). Adult male shining black with orange blaze across wing and broad orange band across basal half of all but 2 central tail feathers. Sides and flanks bright salmon-orange; lower belly white. Female has gray head, olive-gray back, dull white underparts; sides and flanks orange-yellow. Tail and wing pattern like male's but yellowish. First spring male like female but has a few black feathers on the body and brighter orange flank, wing, and tail markings.

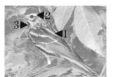

Adult male
1. *Black-and-white streaked plumage.*
2. *White eyebrow.*
3. *Black throat.*

Creeps on tree trunks like a nuthatch.

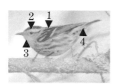

Female
1. *Black-and-white streaked plumage.*
2. *White eyebrow.*
3. *White throat.*
4. *Black spots on undertail coverts.*

Creeps on tree trunks.

Adult female
1. *Olive-gray upperparts.*
2. *Dull white underparts.*
3. *Orange-yellow on sides.*

Shows yellow on wings and tail.

Voice
Variable. Song usually shrill, strident, not especially tuneful, and slow enough to hear each note. Most frequent song has 5 or 6 rapid notes with last 2 syllables strongly accented: *zee-zee-zee-zawaah* (down-slurred), *zee-zee-zee-zee-zweee* (up-slurred). Second song similar to Black-and-white Warbler's. Call note a sharp *chick*.

Range
Breeds from southeastern Alaska, east to southern Northwest Territories (Mackenzie), through central Canada to Labrador and Newfoundland; south to Utah, southeastern Oklahoma, and east Texas to South Carolina; infrequently to central Alabama and Georgia; rarely in New Mexico. Winters in southern Texas and southern Florida south to Brazil.   *Peter D. Vickery*

Prothonotary Warbler

Tail

Protonotaria citrea
Primarily a summer bird of wooded swamps, cypress, gum, and tupelo bottomlands in the Southeast, this spectacular warbler is always exciting to see. Its ringing, loud song is distinctive. Prothonotaries spend most of their time fairly close to the ground in their preferred habitat. In flight, the adult male Prothonotary looks like a glowing, golden coal of molten yellow. Common in many parts of the South, this bird is aptly nicknamed the "Golden Swamp Warbler."

Description
5½" (14 cm). The entire head, breast, and sides are a brilliant yellow suffused with orange; these colors are the bird's most noticeable feature. The unbarred wings and the rump are blue-gray, and the back is olive. The undertail coverts are white. The black eye and the long bill are both prominent. There are white areas in the tail, which is otherwise blackish-gray. The legs are dark bluish. Females and immatures are not nearly as bright orange-yellow as adult males but nevertheless have the same plumage pattern.

Voice
A loud, emphatic, clear *zweet, zweet* on 1 pitch (usually repeated 5–9 times or more). Call note a clear, metallic *tink*, similar to that of waterthrushes. Male occasionally gives a sweet, canarylike flight song while hovering: *che-wee-che-wee-chee-chee.*

Similar Species
Blue-winged Warbler has somewhat similar color pattern but blue-gray wings have conspicuous white wing bars; has black eyeline but lacks orange cast. Yellow Warbler has yellowish wings, greenish-yellow back, and much yellow instead of white in tail.

Range
Southeastern Minnesota, southern Ontario, and southwestern New York to southeastern Pennsylvania and southern New Jersey; through eastern Plains States to eastern Texas, Gulf of Mexico, and central Florida. Absent from greater Appalachian area. In migration, occurs very rarely in California, Arizona, New Mexico, Canada, and New England. Winters very rarely in Florida and elsewhere in extreme South; vast majority migrate to Central America and northern South America.   *Henry T. Armistead*

Adult male

. *Black head, back, and breast.*

. *Orange patches on wings.*

. *Orange patches on tail.*

Often fans tail.

Adult male

. *Orange-yellow head and breast.*

. *Blue-gray wings.*

. *Olive back.*

. *Dark tail with large, white patches.*

Loud, ringing song.

Adult female

. *Duller orange or yellow head and breast.*

Worm-eating Warbler

Helmitheros vermivorus
This rather unfamiliar warbler is fond of shady deciduous hillsides
and wooded ravines. It often walks with its tail slightly cocked and
creeps over trunks and limbs. It can be common at the center of its
range.

Description
5½" (14 cm). Very plain with 4 blackish stripes on buff head; 2
stripes on crown, 1 through each eye. Back, wings, and tail dull
olive; buff below. Bill thick, light brown; legs yellowish-pink.

Voice
Song a thin, high, dry, insectlike trill. Call note a rich *chip*.

Similar Species
Swainson's Warbler lacks bold head stripes, has rufous cap.

Range
E. Iowa to S. New England south to N. Gulf States, N. Georgia,
Piedmont and mountain areas of Carolinas, and Virginia. Winters in
West Indies, Mexico, and Central America.   *Henry T. Armistead*

Swainson's Warbler

Limnothlypis swainsonii
This uncommon, local bird of canebrakes, swamps, and thickets of
the Southeast spends most of its time on or near the ground.

Description
5½" (14 cm). Olive-brown above, plain yellowish-white below, with
reddish-brown cap and light eyebrow. Bill large, thick at base and
tapering to sharp point. Immature similar to adult.

Voice
Song clear, loud, ringing; starts with 3 or 4 even or falling notes
followed by 4 or 5 syllables; *tee-o, tee-o, whit-sut-say, bee-o, tee, toot-
sut-say, bee-u, whee, whit-sut-say, bee-o*. Call note a *chip*.

Similar Species
Worm-eating Warbler has black-and-buff striped head.

Range
E. Texas, to S. Illinois and S. Delaware, N. Florida, and Gulf Coast.
Winters in Caribbean and Se. Mexico.   *Paul W. Sykes, Jr.*

Ovenbird

Seiurus aurocapillus
The Ovenbird breeds abundantly throughout eastern North America
in open dry deciduous woods devoid of thick brush and tangles. It
will also accept wet swampy conditions and, in the north, nests in
jack pine or spruce forests. Ovenbirds and waterthrushes, primarily
ground-feeders, are notable because they walk rather than hop.

Description
5½–6½" (14–16.5 cm). Large, heavy-bodied warblers, Ovenbirds
have an unmarked, dull brownish olive-green back, wings, and tail.
The round crown has an orange stripe bordered with broad dark
brown stripes. There is a prominent white eye-ring and a clear
white throat bordered by a thin dark line. The long, slender bill is
somewhat curved and notched at the tip. The breast and flanks are
heavily marked with elongated dark brown spots that often form
brown stripes. The flanks are washed with greenish-olive; the lower
belly and undertail coverts are white. Females are slightly duller,
especially on the crown.

Adult
1. Black and buff head
   stripes.
2. Olive-green
   upperparts.
3. Plain buff
   underparts.

   Dry, insectlike song.

Adult
. Reddish-brown cap.
. Pale eyebrow.
. Large, pointed bill.
. Olive-brown
   upperparts.
. Plain yellowish-
   white underparts.

   Loud, ringing song.

Adult, side view
Olive-green
upperparts.
Orange crown
bordered with
brown.
White eye-ring.

Walks on forest
floor.

Voice
Most frequent song a vigorous, clear *teacher-teacher-teacher-teacher*, growing louder; accented on first or second syllable. Also a *teach-teach-teach-teach*. Evening flight song a rapid jumble of bubbling, warbling notes, usually ending with *teacher-teacher* notes. Call note at nest a sharp *cheep;* also *chock*.

Similar Species
Louisiana and Northern waterthrushes have prominent white or buff eye stripes, brown upperparts; wag their tails. Thrushes larger and lack orange-and-brown striped crown; hop rather than walk.

Range
Breeds from northeastern British Columbia, southern Mackenzie, central Alberta, and across southern Canada to Newfoundland; south to eastern Colorado, eastern Oklahoma, northern Arkansas, and Mid-Atlantic States to northern Georgia. Winters in coastal South Carolina, Florida, Gulf States, coastal Texas, West Indies, Mexico, and Central America south to Venezuela and Colombia. *Peter D. Vickery*

Northern Waterthrush

Seiurus noveboracensis
Waterthrushes are aberrant, ground-dwelling warblers that teeter and bob as they walk. The Northern Waterthrush is common, but shy and retiring; it chooses cool, dark wooded swamps, brushy bogs, and lake shores for breeding and is particularly fond of areas with standing water.

Description
5–6″ (12.5–15 cm). The entire upperparts are an unmarked olive-brown. The prominent eyebrow stripe is narrow and of uniform thickness; it is usually yellowish or buff, but varies in some races. The throat is yellowish or off-white, typically with tiny spots. The entire underparts range in color from yellowish to nearly white (rare), and have sharp, heavy, dark brown spots and streaks; these spots sometimes form a necklace across the upper breast.

Voice
Song loud and clear with accelerating staccato ending, *sweet sweet sweet swee-wee-wee chew chew chew;* from a distance only ending is clearly audible. Call note a sharp *chip* or *chuck*.

Similar Species
See Louisiana Waterthrush.

Range
Breeds from northern Alaska and northern Yukon south to southern Alaska and eastern Oregon (sparingly), east to northern Pennsylvania, northern New Jersey, Rhode Island, and Newfoundland. Winters from Mexico to South America; also in Bahamas and Cuba.   *Wayne R. Petersen*

Adult, front view
1. *Olive-green upperparts.*
2. *Boldly streaked underparts.*

   Vigorous teacher-teacher *song.*

Adult
1. *Narrow yellowish eyebrow.*
2. *Spots usually present on throat.*
3. *Brown upperparts.*
4. *Yellowish streaked underparts.*

   Teeters and bobs when walking.

Adult
1. *Narrow yellowish eyebrow.*
2. *Throat usually spotted.*

Louisiana Waterthrush

Seiurus motacilla
The elusive Louisiana Waterthrush is the southern breeding
counterpart of the Northern Waterthrush over much of the eastern
United States. This bird prefers running brooks, streams, and cool
ravines for breeding; this preference can be useful in distinguishing
the 2 waterthrushes in summer. An early arrival in spring, the
Louisiana Waterthrush is rare in many areas after mid-August.

Description
5¾–6⅜″ (14.5–16 cm). This species is very similar to the Northern
Waterthrush, but has a wider eyebrow stripe, especially behind the
eye, which often seems to extend slightly farther back on the head.
This stripe is mostly bright white (rarely flecked with buff) and
washed with grayish-buff in front of the eye. The throat is usually
pure white, occasionally lightly spotted. The ventral streaks in the
Louisiana tend to be browner and more diffuse, seldom producing a
necklace effect. The underparts are whitish; a buff wash on the
flanks often creates a patch. The Louisiana's bill is generally longer,
thicker, and more obvious than the Northern's; however, this,
feature can only be detected at close range.

Voice
Song a loud *see-you see-you see-you chew chew to-wee;* 3 slurred
introductory notes distinctive. Call note a sharp *chick,* slightly
higher and more emphatic than Northern Waterthrush's.

Similar Species
Northern Waterthrush has narrower yellow or buff eyebrow stripe;
throat yellowish or off-white; underparts have sharp, heavy spots
that sometimes form necklace.

Range
Breeds from eastern Nebraska, central Iowa, and east-central
Minnesota to central New York and New England; south to eastern
Texas, central Louisiana, central Georgia, and Carolinas. Winters in
West Indies, Mexico, and northern South America.
Wayne R. Petersen

Kentucky Warbler

Oporornis formosus
This small, common yellow songbird inhabits moist, shaded
deciduous and mixed woodlands with well-developed ground cover in
bottomlands, ravines, and swamp borders. It spends most of its time
on the ground but sings from lower limbs of trees. This bird is a
persistent singer and feeds mainly on insects.

Description
5–5¾″ (12.5–14.5 cm). The Kentucky Warbler has solid olive-green
upperparts, unmarked bright yellow underparts, yellow spectacles,
and a black sideburn below the eye. The sexes are more or less
similar, although the male has more extensive black on the forehead
and forecrown, and a larger sideburn. The immature is similar to the
adult but slightly more brownish above; the sideburn is often
reduced or absent.

Voice
Song a series of 2-syllable notes repeated 5–10 times: *tur-dle, tur-
dle,* or *chur-ree, chur-ree,* or *chur-ry, chur-ry,* or *tor-ry, tor-ry.*

Adult
1. *Broad white eyebrow.*
2. *Throat usually plain and white.*

Adult
1. *Broad white eyebrow.*
2. *Brown upperparts.*
3. *White underparts with brown streaks.*

Teeters and bobs when walking.

Adult male
1. *Black crown.*
2. *Yellow spectacles.*
3. *Black sideburns.*
4. *Olive-green upperparts.*
5. *Bright yellow underparts.*

Usually on ground. Loud, ringing song.

Song suggests Carolina Wren's but not as loud or musical. Call note
a low-pitched *chuck;* alarm call a metallic *check, chuck,* or *chip.*

Similar Species
Adult male Common Yellowthroat has black mask; both male and
female have white bellies, lack spectacles.

Range
Breeds from southeastern Nebraska, southwestern Wisconsin,
southern Michigan, central Ohio, southern Pennsylvania, and
southeastern New York south to eastern Texas, southern Alabama,
central Georgia, and eastern North Carolina. Casual in West,
primarily in southwestern states. Winters from Mexico south to
northern South America.   *Paul W. Sykes, Jr.*

Connecticut Warbler

Oporornis agilis
The birds of the genus *Oporornis* are rather robust wood warblers
characterized by long pinkish legs, a rather heavy bill, a rather
short tail, long undertail coverts, and a lack of wing bars. The
Connecticut, Mourning, and MacGillivray's warblers have a more or
less distinctly hooded appearance, an olive back, and yellow lower
underparts. The Connecticut is the rarest and largest of the 3,
breeding locally in spruce and tamarack bogs and open poplar or
jack pine woodland. It is also the most terrestrial and walks on the
ground with a peculiar mincing gait, bobbing head, and elevated tail,
in a fashion reminiscent of an Ovenbird. The Connecticut Warbler's
very long wings and short tail accentuate its body size, so that when
this shy and furtive species disappears into the undergrowth in
rapid, direct flight, it gives the impression of a *Seiurus* warbler or
small thrush.

Description
5¼–6″ (13.5–15 cm). All plumages show a conspicuous complete
white or buff-white eye-ring, relatively dull yellow lower
underparts, and very long undertail coverts that reach more than
halfway to the end of the tail. The adult breeding-plumage male has
a slate-gray hood, slightly paler on the throat. In nonbreeding
plumage, the top of the head and nape are strongly washed with
brown. The hood of the adult female in breeding plumage is grayish-
brown or brownish-olive, and the throat is buff-gray or brownish-
buff. The nonbreeding plumage is similar but browner. The
immature has a brown or olive-brown hood that blends into the
brownish-olive back but contrasts with the dull yellow lower
underparts even in the center of the breast. The throat is brownish-
buff or buff-white.

Tail

Voice
Song a loud, clear, jerky, repetitive chant of 2- or 3-note phrases,
usually accented on last syllable of each phrase. Somewhat
resembles song of Ovenbird or Common Yellowthroat. Call note a
loud, sharp, metallic *cheep* or *peek.*

Similar Species
MacGillivray's Warbler has incomplete eye-ring. Most Mourning
Warblers either lack an eye-ring or have an interrupted one, but

Adult female
1. Gray on crown.
2. Smaller black sideburns than male's.

Breeding male
1. Uniform gray hood.
2. Complete white eye-ring.
3. Dull yellow lower underparts.
4. Long pinkish legs.

Female
1. Grayish-brown hood.
2. Buff-gray throat.
3. Complete buff-white eye-ring.
4. Undertail coverts extend more than halfway to end of tail.

occasionally females or immatures appear to have a complete one. Mourning Warbler with complete eye-ring can be distinguished, with care, from Connecticut by smaller size and shorter undertail coverts, lack of peculiar walking gait, less prominent and less uniform eye-ring, and brighter yellow underparts; immature Mourning has less extensive and less brownish hood, and yellow or yellow-tinged throat. Much smaller, more arboreal Nashville Warbler superficially like male Connecticut but always has bright yellow throat and shorter legs. Dull female Yellow Warbler or Common Yellowthroat with complete eye-ring could possibly be mistaken for Connecticut but both are smaller and have yellow or yellowish throat.

Range
Breeds in Canada east of Rocky Mountains from northeastern British Columbia and north-central Quebec to northern Minnesota and central Ontario. Winters in South America. Fall migration route from breeding range to northeastern United States and presumably over western Atlantic directly to South America. In spring, moves north across Caribbean and west of Appalachians to Canada.
David F. DeSante

Mourning Warbler

Oporornis philadelphia
This eastern *Oporornis* inhabits the shrubby undergrowth of woodland and forest edges as well as shrubby burned-over land, young second growth, and the edges of swamps and bogs. While rather uncommon outside its breeding range, the Mourning Warbler is considerably less rare than the Connecticut.

Description
5–5¾″ (13–14.5 cm). The adult male in breeding plumage has a dark slate-gray hood, gray lores, considerable black on the lower throat and upper breast, and lacks an eye-ring. In nonbreeding plumage, the black upper breast is more or less veiled with gray. The adult female in breeding plumage is similar but much duller, with no black on the upper breast and with a paler gray or buff-gray throat. In nonbreeding plumage, the hood is rather strongly tinged with brownish. A few breeding-plumage females, and many in nonbreeding plumage, have an eye-ring; this is usually faint and incomplete (broken at least in front), but sometimes quite complete. All immatures have an eye-ring that is nearly always broken in front and usually also behind, and have much less prominent hoods than do adult birds. The underparts are mostly yellow; there is generally some yellow on the throat, but the sides (at least) of the upper breast are tinged with olive or grayish to produce the vague appearance of a hood. There is usually a faint, pale, often yellowish area above the lores that connects with the upper eye-ring to produce a vaguely "spectacled" or even eyebrowed appearance.

3   *Tail*

Voice
Song a fairly loud, variable, rather liquid chant of 2-note phrases in 2 parts; second part a bit slower and usually lower-pitched, but sometimes higher; *chirry chirry chirry chorry chorry*. Call a loud, low-pitched, rather rough *check* or *tcheck*, rougher than Connecticut's but usually sharper and less rough than MacGillivray's.

Similar Species
See Connecticut and MacGillivray's warblers. Female Common Yellowthroat similar to those immature Mournings with considerable yellow on throat and very little suggestion of hood, but Yellowthroat smaller with whitish or dull yellowish abdomen.

Immature
1. *Olive-brown hood.*
2. *Buff throat.*
3. *Complete buff-white eye-ring.*

Breeding male
1. *Gray hood.*
2. *Gray lores.*
3. *No white eye-ring.*
4. *Blackish on upper breast.*
5. *Long pinkish legs.*

Breeding female
1. *Dull gray hood.*
2. *Faint incomplete eye-ring (often lacking).*
3. *Undertail coverts extend less than halfway to end of tail.*

Orange-crowned Warbler smaller, with stronger eyebrow and vague streaking below; shorter legs; different call.

Range
Breeds east of Rocky Mountains across Canada and northern United States from northeastern British Columbia to Newfoundland, south to North Dakota and central New England and south through Appalachians to Virginia. Winters in Central America and northwestern South America (west of Andes) from Nicaragua to Ecuador. Migrates in spring and fall across Gulf of Mexico, avoiding southern Atlantic States.   *David F. DeSante*

MacGillivray's Warbler

Oporornis tolmiei
This western counterpart of the Mourning Warbler is a common breeder in the dense understory of open montane forests and brushy mountain hillsides and in shrubby mountain riparian locations. This bird migrates the shortest distance of the 3 "hooded" *Oporornis* and is characterized by shorter wings and a relatively longer tail; these features are especially evident in flight. MacGillivray's flies in a somewhat hesitant fashion and typically shows a bit of tail "pumping," much like a Common Yellowthroat.

Description
5–5¾″ (12.5–14.5 cm). All plumages show a conspicuous eye-ring, broken both in front and back. The adult male in breeding plumage has a bluish slate-gray hood, black lores, and some black on the upper breast. In nonbreeding plumage, the black upper breast is veiled with gray. The adult female in breeding plumage is similar but much duller, with no black on the upper breast and with a paler whitish-gray throat. In nonbreeding plumage, the hood is strongly tinged with olive or brownish. Immatures have a grayish-olive or olive-brownish hood that often shows little contrast with the back but that always shows strong contrast with the yellow lower underparts. The throat is grayish-white or buff-white and generally lacks any tinge of yellow.

Tail

Voice
Song similar to Mourning Warbler's but generally a bit higher-pitched, clearer, and less liquid; second part often has single-note phrases: *chu-weet chu-weet chu-weet chewp chewp*. Call note a loud husky *tcheck*, somewhat rougher and huskier than Mourning's. Resembles call of Common Yellowthroat but higher-pitched, clearer, and less husky.

Similar Species
See Connecticut Warbler. Mourning Warbler very similar but often lacks an eye-ring and has relatively shorter tail that is rarely pumped in flight. Adult male Mourning generally has paler lores and more black on upper breast. Adult female Mourning with broken eye-ring may be impossible to distinguish from MacGillivray's, but usually has eye-ring fainter, narrower, and more nearly complete (especially in back). Under careful scrutiny, immature Mourning

Immature
1. *Hood less evident than in MacGillivray's Warbler.*
2. *Incomplete eye-ring.*
3. *Yellowish tinge on throat.*

Breeding male
1. *Bluish, slate-gray hood.*
2. *Black lores.*
3. *Bold, incomplete eye-ring.*
4. *Blackish on upper breast.*

Female
1. *Duller hood than male's.*
2. *Bold, incomplete eye-ring.*
3. *Whitish-gray throat.*
4. *Undertail coverts extend less than halfway to end of tail.*

seen to differ from MacGillivray's in these features and usually has
some yellow on throat, a less hooded appearance (especially across
center of breast), and stronger spectacles or eyebrows. Female
Common Yellowthroat lacks hooded appearance, has yellowish
throat and whitish or dull yellowish abdomen. Smaller Nashville
Warbler has complete eye-ring, bright yellow throat, and shorter
legs. Certain grayish races of Orange-crowned Warbler superficially
similar (with vague hooded appearance, grayish throat, and broken
white eye-ring) but smaller, with shorter legs; have at least a faint
eyebrow and are vaguely streaked below.

Range
Breeds throughout mountains of western North America from
southern Alaska and southwestern Yukon to southern California and
central New Mexico. Winters from northern Mexico to Panama.
David F. DeSante

Common Yellowthroat

Geothlypis trichas
The wide-ranging Common Yellowthroat breeds from Alaska to
Newfoundland and south throughout North America to California,
Mexico, and Florida. Considering this extensive breeding range, it
is not surprising that there are numerous recognized races across
the continent. The black-masked male, scolding vigorously as it hops
like an energetic wren, is a familiar sight. Common Yellowthroats
are equally at home wherever bushes, vines, tangles, or cattails
provide sufficient cover; this species can be found nesting along
streams, ponds, marshes, roadsides, wood margins, brushy
pastures, rejuvenated clear-cut forests, and even brushy openings
well within the forest. In addition to their well-known song,
territorial males also perform flight songs, flying upward a few feet
while uttering a jumbled series of notes.

Description
4½–5½″ (11.5–14 cm). The adult male has plain brown-olive
upperparts. A broad black mask, present throughout the year,
extends from the bill and forehead over the eyes across the cheeks
to the side of the neck. The mask is bordered posteriorly with a pale
blue-gray band. The bright, warm yellow chin, throat, and breast
contrast with the buff-brown flanks and the dingy white belly. The
undertail coverts are yellow. The adult female lacks the mask. The
olive upperparts are tinged gray or brown; the forehead and face are
usually more obviously brown and are set off by a dingy white eye-
ring and a pale, ill-defined eye stripe. The throat is yellow,
sometimes pale buff, and is sharply defined by the darker cheeks.
The breast is usually yellow and contrasts with the browner flanks
and dull white belly. The undertail coverts are greenish-yellow.
Immature males are duller and browner than adult males and have
only partially developed masks that do not have the pale gray
posterior margin. Immature females are duller and paler than adult
females; the throat is only tinged with yellow. The adult western
race, *G. t. occidentalis*, is brighter with more yellow on the breast
and less buff-white on the belly, which on some individuals is yellow.
Males have a more obvious white-gray border to the mask.

Voice
Song usually transcribed as *witchity-witchity-witchity* but there can
be considerable variation. Evening flight song a series of jumbled

Immature
1. *Incomplete eye-ring.*
2. *Grayish throat with no tinge of yellow.*
3. *Distinct hooded effect across center of breast.*

Adult male
1. *Black mask with white or gray border.*
2. *Bright yellow throat and breast.*
3. *Brown-olive upperparts.*
4. *Buff-brown flanks.*

Witchity song.

Adult female
1. *Yellow throat.*
2. *Dull whitish eye-ring, with no mask.*

notes usually concluding with several *witchity-witchity* notes. Call note a sharp, husky *tcheck*.

Similar Species
Adult males distinct. Kentucky Warbler similar to immature male Yellowthroat but always has distinct yellow spectacles and completely yellow underparts. Female Nashville Warbler resembles female Yellowthroat but has blue-gray crown, distinct, clear white eye-ring, and yellow flanks.

Range
Breeds from southeastern Alaska and northern Alberta to central Ontario, central Quebec, southern Labrador, and Newfoundland south throughout lower 48 states to southern Mexico. Winters along Pacific Coast from northern California across southern Arizona, central Texas, and southern Arkansas to Gulf States; along Atlantic Coast from New Jersey (sparingly), Virginia, and Delaware to Florida. Also Bahamas, West Indies, Mexico, Central America, infrequently to Colombia and Venezuela.   *Peter D. Vickery*

Hooded Warbler

Wilsonia citrina
The beautiful Hooded Warbler is primarily found in the Southeast. It often flycatches and flicks its tail open, revealing white tail spots. This bird spends most of its life in the dense, low understory of damp woods; its loud, ringing song is the best clue to its presence.

Description
5–5¾″ (12.5–14.5 cm). The male has bright yellow underparts, olive-green upperparts, and a spectacular black hood enclosing a yellow face and forehead. Females are similar but lack the hood, although they often have a trace of it, especially on the forehead behind the cheek and, less often, on the throat. Immatures resemble females but are duller. In all plumages Hooded Warblers lack wing bars and streaks but have white tail spots and prominent large black eyes.

Voice
Very easily confused with song of Magnolia Warbler, which has similar pattern. Hooded's song variable but usually can be transcribed as *weeta, weeta, wee-tee-o*, the *tee* much higher than rest of song, and also louder and more emphatic than comparable part of Magnolia's. Hooded's song loud, clear, rapid, and ringing, with snap on last phrase. Call note a loud, metallic *chip*.

Similar Species
Male distinctive. Female Wilson's Warbler very similar to female Hooded but lacks olive around sides of neck and white tail spots; does not spread tail; is smaller, has different call, and breeds in far North. Female Bachman's Warbler variable but lacks Hooded's bright solid yellow underparts, has less (if any) white in the tail, complete eye-ring, and grayish head and breast. Fall Nashville and Canada warblers also have distinct eye-rings, are grayer above, but without white tail spots.

Range
Breeds from southeastern Iowa, northern Illinois, and extreme southern Michigan and Ontario, southern New York, and New England; south to eastern Texas, Gulf of Mexico, and northern Florida. Winters from Mexico to Panama. Rare in migration, particularly in spring, to Northeast; casual in West.
Henry T. Armistead

Immature male

1. *Partially developed mask.*

Adult male

1. *Yellow face.*
2. *Black hood.*
3. *Olive-green upperparts.*
4. *Bright yellow underparts.*

Shows white spots in tail.
Loud ringing song.

Adult female

1. *Yellow face and underparts.*
2. *Trace of hood on crown.*
3. *Olive-green upperparts.*

Shows white spots in tail.

Wilson's Warbler

Wilsonia pusilla
Wilson's Warbler is a common and widespread species that most often occurs in willow and alder thickets and tangles near water, where it seldom ventures more than 10 feet off the ground. It is a very active, flycatching warbler, often engaging in aerial cartwheels that are punctuated by a sharp snap of the bill. This species frequently twitches its longish, unspotted tail in a circular motion and flicks its wings like a kinglet.

Description
4¼–5″ (11–12.5 cm). Adult males have a black cap and a contrasting yellow forehead and eyebrow stripe. The upperparts and wings are a featureless olive-green; the entire underparts are lemon-yellow. Females and immatures are similar but they usually lack the black cap or else have it reduced and obscured by greenish feather edgings. Their dark eyes are prominent in an otherwise unmarked face.

Voice
Song a rapid, staccato chatter dropping in pitch at end: *chi chi chi chi chet chet.* Call note a flat *chuck* or *chuff.*

Similar Species
Yellow Warbler has yellow wing bars and tail spots, shorter tail. Female and immature Hooded Warblers larger, with flashing white tail spots and different head pattern.

Range
Breeds from northern Alaska, northern Yukon, northern Ontario, southeastern Labrador, and Newfoundland; south to southern California, central Nevada, northern Utah, northern New Mexico, central Ontario, northern New England, and Nova Scotia. Winters from southern California and southern Texas to Panama.
Wayne R. Petersen

Canada Warbler

Wilsonia canadensis
The Canada Warbler is at home in the luxuriant, moist undergrowth of mature northern and eastern woodlands. Like Wilson's Warbler, it has no wing bars or tail spots and is an active, fly-catching species that confines most of its activity to within a few feet of the ground.

Description
5–5¾″ (12.5–14.5 cm). Distinctive. Adult males have plain bluish-gray upperparts and wings with black on the sides of the head and neck and black spots on the forehead. Yellow spectacles, or yellow lores with a white inner eye-ring, and a necklace of black breast spots contrast with the otherwise bright yellow underparts and white undertail coverts. Adult females are similar but have a fainter necklace and the black facial markings are replaced with gray. Fall immatures are like females except the necklace is further reduced and the back is often washed with olive-brown.

Voice
Song an explosive burst of rapid, irregularly arranged, staccato

Adult male
1. *Black cap.*
2. *Yellow eyebrow.*
3. *Yellow underparts.*
4. *Olive-green upperparts, with no wing bars or tail spots.*

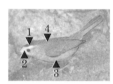

Adult female
1. *Black cap rarely present.*
2. *Yellow eyebrow.*
3. *Yellow underparts.*
4. *Olive-green upperparts, with no wing bars or tail spots.*

Adult female
1. *Yellowish spectacles.*
2. *Gray markings on face.*
3. *Trace of necklace on yellow breast.*
4. *Bluish-gray upperparts.*

notes, often with a characteristic *ditchety* phrase, and introduced or
terminated by a single *chip*. Call note a loud *chick*, quite similar to
call note of Lincoln's Sparrow.

Similar Species
Kentucky Warbler has similar face pattern but lacks black necklace
and gray upperparts.

Range
Breeds from central Alberta east to central Quebec and south to
southern Manitoba, central Minnesota, southern Michigan, and
through Appalachians to northern Georgia. Winters in South
America.   *Wayne R. Petersen*

Red-faced Warbler

Cardellina rubrifrons
This unmistakable warbler of streamside canyons and open
mountain forests is most easily seen from early to mid-spring.

Description
5¼″ (13.5 cm). Face, throat, and upper breast scarlet; black cap on
rear of crown, upper nape, and rear sides of head; whitish spot
between cap, throat, and gray back. Other upperparts gray except
for round white rump patch and 2 faint wing bars. White to grayish
below. Immature resembles adult but faded.

Voice
Song a loud, clear, sweet, and rapid *a-sweet-a-sweet-teta-teta,
tsweet, sweet-a tsue;* variable.

Range
In mountains from Arizona and Sw. New Mexico into Nw. Mexico.
Winters from W. central Mexico to Guatemala.   *Scott B. Terrill*

Painted Redstart

Myioborus pictus
The Painted Redstart is one of the flashiest birds in North America.
Both sexes are glossy jet-black on the upperparts with a scarlet
breast and pure white wing and tail patches. They forage with wings
and tail held stiffly and half spread; often, they fan the wings and
tail. They frequently flycatch in a weak, fluttery manner, and their
flight is usually jerky. These highland birds are common breeders in
evergreen oak woods, primarily those mixed with other trees. They
are especially common in moist mountain canyons and somewhat
concentrated along flowing streams. They are usually not
gregarious.

Description
5–5¾″ (12.5–14.5 cm). The entire upperparts, the throat, and the
upper sides are glossy black except for broad conspicuous white
wing coverts and outer tail feathers, and a small white crescent just
below the eye. The mid-breast and upper belly are brilliant scarlet;
the lower belly and undertail coverts are white with dark flecks.

Adult male
1. *Yellow spectacles.*
2. *Black on side of head.*
3. *Black necklace on yellow breast.*
4. *Bluish-gray upperparts.*

Adult
1. *Red-and-black head pattern.*
2. *Gray upperparts.*
3. *Whitish underparts.*

Shows white rump in flight.

Adult
1. *Black head, breast, and upperparts.*
2. *Scarlet belly.*
3. *White wing patch.*
4. *White outer tail feathers.*

Juveniles resemble adults, but are sooty black above and dark gray to blackish below, with a whitish belly; often the breast has blackish streaks. The white patches on the wings and tail resemble those of adults, but the wing may be a bit more buff-colored.

Voice
Song usually opens with rapid, warbling, medium-pitched *weddle-weddle-weddle;* sometimes this phrase repeats several times, or song may terminate in a higher *weet-weet-weet.* Also a *weeta-weeta-weeta-aweeta-wee,* with last note higher pitched. Characteristic call a unique, loud, clearly whistled *wheoo,* with sharp, rising inflection in *he* portion, last *oo* down-slurred.

Range
Breeds from late March to September in northwestern Arizona (very casually to southeastern California), southwestern New Mexico, and locally and somewhat erratically in Trans-Pecos region of Texas; south through highlands to Nicaragua. Accidental in East. Usually winters from northwestern Mexico south; rarely in United States.   *Scott B. Terrill*

Rufous-capped Warbler

Basileuterus rufifrons
This rare visitor has a longish tail that is often held high or flipped about expressively. It mostly stays low in heavy undergrowth along ravines, canyon edges, or streams.

Description
5″ (12.5 cm). Short stout bill and rufous crown. Longer-tailed than most of our warblers. Narrow white eyebrow; broad black eyeline between eye and bill; rufous behind eye. Back, wings, and tail dull olive. Throat and small area on upper chest yellow; other underparts white with grayish-olive wash on flanks. Short white stripe between eyeline and yellow throat.

Voice
Song variable; usually an irregular ascending series of dry notes that become more rapid. Call note a light *tsit* or a stronger *tzzick.*

Range
Northern Mexico to Guatemala. Rare stray to western and southern Texas and in southeastern Arizona.   *Kenn Kaufman*

Yellow-breasted Chat

Icteria virens
The largest warbler in North America, this bird is common in thickets and forest edges. It is more often heard than seen.

Description
7½″ (19 cm). Large, dark, heavy bill and long tail. Upperparts olive-green. White spectacles, black lores, and bright yellow chin, throat, and breast. Belly and undertail coverts white.

Voice
Song of assorted clear, alternating scolds, whistles, mews, grunts, rattles, cackles, and squeaks. Single note a *kook* or *whoit.*

Range
S. British Columbia to Massachusetts; south to S. California, Gulf Coast, and N. Florida. Winters from Mexico to Panama; sparingly from Virginia to Florida and Se. Texas.   *Paul W. Sykes, Jr.*

Juvenile
1. *Sooty-black upperparts.*
2. *Gray breast.*
3. *Whitish belly.*
4. *White wing patch.*
5. *White outer tail feathers.*

Adult
1. *Rufous crown.*
2. *White eyebrow.*
3. *Rufous behind eye.*
4. *Yellow throat and breast.*
5. *Dull olive uperparts.*

Adult
1. *Heavy, dark bill.*
2. *White spectacles.*
3. *Bright yellow chin, throat, and breast.*
4. *Olive-green uperparts.*

   Large size.

Olive Warbler

Peucedramus taeniatus
The Olive Warbler lives in mountainous open pine, pine-oak, and fir forests. It often forages in the tops of coniferous trees, revealing its presence year-round with a loud, descending whistled call. Although they are common, Olive Warblers can be difficult to spot, especially in the breeding season, although they do react to spishing and imitations of pygmy-owl calls. They fly from the interior or top of one tree to another, only occasionally feeding from the outside or lower branches. In the nonbreeding season they often flock together and forage on the understory of deciduous trees or even on the ground. At least some Olive Warblers live at higher elevations in the winter—behavior that is unusual among warblers.

Description
4½–5″ (11.5–12.5 cm). These birds are rather large and bulky for warblers. They have large, flat heads with long, tapering, slightly decurved bills. Fully adult males have a unique bright burnt-orange head and upper breast, with a bold black mask. The rest of the upperparts are an unstreaked medium gray, which extends down onto the sides and flanks. The lower midbelly and undertail coverts are gray to white. The wings are blackish, with the edges of the flight feathers lighter, and there are 2 white wing bars. The outer tail feathers have white edges along most of their length. Adult females and immature males have the same characteristic shape, white wing bars, and white in the outer tail feathers, but they are drab, especially the females, with a yellowish head and upper breast. The facial pattern is distinctive, with a light eyebrow stripe accentuated by a darker greenish or grayish crown and a very noticeable dark ear patch. In their first fall and winter, immatures are very drab, often grayish and whitish, with occasional washes of buff. They lack streaking and wing bars, and have a dark smudge behind and, usually, below the eye. The edges of the flight feathers are buff-yellow. In the breeding season, immatures are drab yellowish or grayish-yellow to bright yellow or yellow-orange. The dark face patch varies from a smallish smudge behind the eye to a well-defined mask.

Voice
Songs variable. Usually a clear, loud warble like that of a titmouse: *peter-peter-peter-peter* or *weeta-weeta-weeta*, often becoming louder toward end. Also shorter, more diagnostic songs; *pit-cheer, pit-cheer, pit-cheer*, or *whit-er-a, whit-er-a*, with accent on *eer* portions and buzzy quality often in other portions. Common call a loud, clear, descending, whistled Evening Grosbeaklike or Tufted Titmouselike *sheu, peuw, whew*, or *chew*, sometimes sounding more like *peer*. Also a softer, more typical *chip* note.

Similar Species
Except for immature Hermit and Pine warblers, other similar warblers have streaking above or below and lack long, tapering, decurved bill and large, flat head. Pine Warbler lacks bold edgings to flight feathers; unrecorded within distribution of Olive in United States. Immature Hermit smaller, with shorter, straighter bill and greener back; usually has some streaking around throat and upper sides; call note different. Dark area behind eye lighter and smaller; yellow coloration duller when present.

Range
Central and southeastern Arizona and southwestern Mexico, south to Nicaragua. At least partially resident in United States range.
Scott B. Terrill

Adult male
1. *Burnt-orange head.*
2. *Black mask.*
3. *Burnt-orange breast.*
4. *Gray upperparts.*
5. *White wing bars.*

Adult female
1. *Greenish crown.*
2. *Yellowish face with dark ear patch.*
3. *White wing bars.*

Immature male
1. *Greenish crown.*
2. *Yellow-orange face and ear patch.*
3. *White wing bars.*
4. *Buff-yellow edgings to flight feathers in wing.*

Bananaquits

(Subfamily Coerebinae)
The subfamily Coerebinae, a neotropical group closely related to the wood warblers, has only a single representative, the Bananaquit. Like most of its close relatives, the Bananaquit is highly active and brightly colored. There are more than 20 North American records for the Bananaquit; all sightings have been in Florida, primarily in the southeastern coastal area of the Keys. The Coerebinae formerly included other birds that are now considered part of the tanagers and wood warblers. (World: 1 species. North America: 1 species.)
Scott B. Terrill

Bananaquit

Coereba flaveola
The Bananaquit is a common and widespread tropical honeycreeper that lives primarily in the West Indies and Central and South America; in our area it occurs irregularly in southern Florida. The Bananaquit is found in heavily landscaped gardens, dense shrubs and thickets, and West Indian hardwood hammocks. A nectar feeder, it is attracted to flowering trees and shrubs as well as sugar-water feeders; the Bananaquit also consumes small insects, spiders, and fruit. It is extremely active and sings in flight while foraging and from a perch. The Bananaquit appears to be closely related to the wood warblers. The birds that occur in Florida are wanderers from the Bahamas. This species is probably more regular in Florida than records indicate.

Description
4–5″ (10–12.5 cm). The Bananaquit is black above with a white spot on the edge of the wing at the base of the primaries and a white eyebrow stripe. The chin, throat, belly, and undertail coverts are white to ashy. The rump and breast are bright yellow, and the tail is black with white spots. The bill is short, pointed, and decurved.

Voice
Song a sweet, trilling *zee-e-e-e-swees-te*, becoming more rapid at end. Before and after song, the Bananaquit often makes various unmusical bubbling and reeling sounds. Call note a loud *quit;* alarm call a softer *chip.*

Range
Resident throughout West Indies, except Cuba; also in Central and South America. Occurs sparingly along southeastern coast of Florida and in Florida Keys.   *Paul W. Sykes, Jr.*

Bananaquit

Adult
1. *White eyebrow.*
2. *White throat.*
3. *Yellow breast.*
4. *White spots on tail.*

Small size.
Florida only.

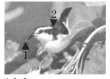

Adult
1. *Short, decurved, pointed bill.*
2. *Black upperparts.*

Shows yellow rump in flight.

Tanagers

(Subfamily Thraupinae)
This subfamily includes the tanagers, another primarily neotropical group. Most all tanagers are brilliantly colored, but several species (including all the breeding birds of temperate regions) have dull greenish and yellowish plumage. In this duller plumage they can be distinguished from similar orioles by the more conical, less tapered bill. Four tanagers normally reach North America. These all have distinctive vocalizations, including call notes that are given throughout the year. Dull-plumaged birds may require careful attention to bill structure and subtle plumage characteristics for identification. In general, our tanagers are secretive, very arboreal birds, and even the males in their brilliant breeding plumage can be hard to see, although they sing loudly and frequently. (World: 240 species. North America: 5 species.)   *Scott B. Terrill*

Stripe-headed Tanager

Spindalis zena
The Stripe-headed Tanager is a common West Indian species that occurs irregularly in our area only in southern Florida. This bird was first recorded in the United States in 1961 on the Florida Keys, and since that time has been one of the most prevalent of the West Indian species to occur in our area. Like the Bananaquit, the Stripe-headed Tanager is found in heavily landscaped gardens, dense shrubs and thickets, and West Indian hardwood hammocks; this species is highly coastal and generally does not range more than 3 miles from the ocean. Stripe-headed Tanagers feed mainly on small fruits, but will also eat tender leaf tips and new buds. They spend much of their time hidden in dense cover, usually remaining among the tree tops. Birds that occur in Florida belong to 2 Bahamian subspecies. The male of 1 race has a greenish back, while males of the other race have a black back; the females of these 2 forms, however, cannot be distinguished. In both subspecies, the sexes are strikingly different. Stripe-headed Tanagers are probably more regular in Florida than the records indicate, perhaps because of their skulking nature and the dense cover they inhabit.

Description
6–8″ (15–20.5 cm). The male has a black head with a white eyebrow and malar stripes. The nape and rump are chestnut, the back and tail black, and the wings black with white feather edgings. The chin, throat, and breast are bright yellow, with the central portion of the breast chestnut, becoming lighter outward and diffusing into the yellow; the central part of the chestnut patch may be almost black. The belly and undertail coverts are white. There is a broad white wing bar (secondary coverts) and a small square white spot on the edge of the wing at the base of the primaries. The female is plain olive-gray, darker above, with a small, square white spot on the edge of the wing as in the female Black-throated Blue Warbler.

Voice
Song a prolonged, weak warble and at close range sweet and melodious. Call note a loud, drawn-out, metallic *seeip*. Seldom sings in Florida.

Similar Species
Male unmistakable. Female Brown-headed Cowbird, Indigo and

Stripe-headed Tanager
Hepatic Tanager
Summer Tanager
Scarlet Tanager
Western Tanager

Adult male, black-backed race

1. *Black head with white eyebrow and malar stripe.*
2. *Chestnut nape.*
3. *Black back.*
4. *Chestnut rump.*
5. *Broad white wing bar.*

Adult male, olive-backed race

1. *Olive back.*

Painted buntings, and Summer and Scarlet tanagers have no white on wings. Female House Sparrow brown with streaks on back and buff eyebrow stripe.

Range
Resident of Bahamas, Greater Antilles, and Cozumel Island, Mexico. Occurs sparingly along southeastern coast of Florida and in Florida Keys.   *Paul W. Sykes, Jr.*

Hepatic Tanager

Piranga flava
Hepatic Tanagers are commonly found in pine-oak and oak woodlands; they are fairly common in more monotypic pine, oak, and piñon-juniper woodlands near streams. They are occasionally seen flycatching or singing from an exposed perch.

Description
7–8″ (18–20.5 cm). Older males are bright brick-red on the crown, throat, and underparts. The feather edgings give the upperparts a darker cast; the wings and tail also appear dark. The grayish ear patch does not occur in any other North American tanager. The dark gray bill is large; the upper mandible curves downward, extending beyond the tip of the lower mandible and ending in a slight hook. The females have a similar bill and facial pattern, but are gray to grayish-olive above; the underparts are yellow. In their first breeding plumage, males resemble females but are usually more richly colored; some have a reddish tinge below. In the second season, males are red, with areas of yellow or green, especially on the undertail coverts and lower belly.

Voice
Song a series of clear warblings, very similar to songs of *Pheucticus* grosbeaks, but often faster, more deliberate. Call, unique among tanagers, like Hermit Thrush's: a low, soft *chuck*.

Similar Species
Western Tanager has prominent short wing bar near shoulder and second, thinner whitish wing bar below; lacks dark ear patch and has smaller, paler, unhooked bill; yellow rump and dark back contrast strongly. Female and immature Scarlet Tanagers have smaller bills, much greener upperparts, lack dark cheek patch. Male Summer Tanager brighter, richer red all over; males and females lack dark ear patch, and usually have paler bill; song and call different.

Range
Breeds from southeastern California and northwestern Arizona (extremely local) through New Mexico and Trans-Pecos region of Texas, south through highlands to central Argentina. Rare in winter and as transient in coastal and southern California, lowland Arizona, and southern Texas.   *Scott B. Terrill*

Female
1. *Olive-gray upperparts.*
2. *Small white spot at base of primaries.*

Adult male
1. *Large dark bill.*
2. *Gray ear patch.*
3. *Brick-red plumage.*

Adult female
1. *Large dark bill.*
2. *Gray ear patch.*
3. *Olive-gray upperparts.*
4. *Yellowish underparts.*

Summer Tanager

Piranga rubra
The Summer Tanager is a common bird of oak and pine-oak woodlands and riparian forests, especially cottonwood-willow. These birds often remain concealed in higher vegetation, especially when breeding. They usually forage in a gleaning fashion, moving slowly and deliberately; they occasionally flurry suddenly.

Description
7–7¾" (18–19.5 cm). Adult males are a uniform bright red. Typical females and immatures are yellow with green tints to the wings and, to a lesser degree, the upperparts. Both sexes have large bills that are pale in the breeding season, but darker (especially in immatures) at other times of the year. Males in their first breeding plumage are similar to females, but are usually blotched or washed with a reddish tint. In their second breeding season, males resemble fully adult males but are duller, paler, and more yellowish. The upperparts of some females are grayish, and often the flight feathers or even the body feathers are reddish; the upperparts may be greenish. The race *P. r. cooperi* of the Southwest is larger and paler; its pale bill is larger than that of any other North American tanager.

Voice
Song resembles that of American Robin, with a series of sweet, clear phrases, but faster and often more deliberate. Call a dry, rattled *spit-a-chuck, pit-tuck* or *pit-a-chuck* or *pit, pit-a-tuck,* occasionally extended to *pik-i-tuck-i-tuck.*

Similar Species
See Hepatic, Scarlet, and Western tanagers. All North American tanagers except Summer Tanager have sharp, fairly conspicuous "tooth" midway along upper mandible.

Range
Southeastern California and southern Nevada to central Oklahoma; southeastern Nebraska to New Jersey, south to Gulf Coast and northern Mexico. Winters mainly from Mexico to Bolivia. Rare winter visitor to southern temperate areas, including southern and coastal California, southern Arizona, southern and central Texas, and Gulf Coast. Transient overshoots occur, especially during spring in Northeast.   *Scott B. Terrill*

Scarlet Tanager

Piranga olivacea
As the male's brilliant red and black plumage suggests, the Scarlet Tanager is a member of a large, colorful tropical family of almost 240 species that are found only in the Western Hemisphere. Of the 4 tanager species that occur regularly north of Mexico, the Scarlet Tanager undertakes the longest migration and has the northernmost breeding range. Scarlet Tanagers breed in mature deciduous and mixed pine forests as well as in extensive plantings of mature shade trees in suburbs and cemeteries. Despite their vivid plumage, these birds are often difficult to observe because they frequently perch motionless for long periods in the upper canopy. However, their hoarse caroling song and distinctive *chip-churrr* call reveal their presence. Scarlet Tanagers move slowly and deliberately, searching for insects, especially leaf-rolling caterpillars; they lack the constant energy displayed by most warblers. Spring migrants sometimes arrive before the foliage and associated insect life have fully developed; at this time, many can be seen in fields and on lawns foraging for food. In the fall the Scarlet Tanager's diet includes

Adult female
1. Large, pale bill.
2. Yellowish face.
3. Yellowish underparts.
4. Greenish tinge to wings and back.

Adult male
1. Large, pale bill.
2. Bright red plumage, including wings and tail.

Breeding male
1. Scarlet head, back, and underparts.
2. Black wings.
3. Black tail.

berries and fruit. During this season, molting males are oddly blotched with red, yellow, and green.

Description
6½–7½″ (16.5–19 cm). Adult males in breeding plumage are brilliant scarlet with shiny black wings and tail. In their first summer, males are duller orange-red; the flight feathers are brownish-black with some greenish edgings. Females typically have dull green backs and pale yellow underparts; their wings are dark gray-brown to blackish-brown. In fresh fall plumage, females are generally brighter and their wings are edged with olive-green. In the fall, males molt into a yellow-green plumage that resembles that of the females; however the back is brighter green, the crown has more yellow, and the underparts are a richer yellow. Juvenile birds resemble females but are more variable; they have bright yellow wing bars, which may cause them to be confused with the Western Tanager. The heavy, curved bill is normally blue-gray in males and dull olive-gray in females. A distinct "tooth" midway along the upper mandible is readily apparent at close range.

Voice
Hoarse caroling song of 4–5 phrases, similar to American Robin's but with a burr and less variation. Call *chip-churr* or *chip-burrrr*; also gives call somewhat like "Myrtle" Warbler's.

Similar Species
Summer Tanager's bill more massive, deeper, longer, usually paler; tooth on upper mandible less obvious. Female Summer Tanager has generally paler wings; body plumage, though variable, is typically warmer orange-yellow. Western Tanager has 2 obvious wing bars; median coverts form short, broad yellow bar and greater coverts form thinner, yellow-white wing bar.

Range
Breeds from southern Manitoba, southern Ontario, southern Quebec, and southern New Brunswick south to eastern North Dakota, central Nebraska, southern Kansas, eastern Oklahoma, central Arkansas, northern Alabama, and northern Georgia. Casual in West. Winters in Panama, Colombia, Ecuador, northern Bolivia, and Peru.   *Peter D. Vickery*

Western Tanager

Piranga ludoviciana
The Western Tanager's casual song is a characteristic sound of western forests. Despite the male's bright yellow-and-black plumage, this bird is not conspicuous. It can often be located by following its song, since it stays for some time on an exposed perch while singing. Western Tanagers feed quietly on the insects that they chance upon in the higher parts of trees; they will also fly out from their perch to take an insect on the wing. These birds are fairly common in open coniferous forests from the high isolated mountains of extreme western Texas and southern Arizona to the extensive forests of western Canada. They are also found in associated mixed deciduous forests, and less commonly in oak or piñon woodlands on higher mountain slopes. In migration they are common in western lowlands, where fruits and berries become a more important part of their diet. Although migrating birds may be seen in almost any type of vegetation, they always frequent trees when they can. While patiently gleaning insects from foliage, a quiet, slurred *pit-er-ick* call often reveals this bird's presence.

Molting male
1. *Red feathers scattered among yellowish feathers on head and underparts.*

Adult female
1. *Greenish upperparts.*
2. *Yellowish underparts.*
3. *Dark wings.*

Gray-phase female
1. *Two thin wing bars.*
2. *Grayish-white underparts with yellow undertail coverts.*

Description
7" (18 cm). The breeding male has a red face; the rest of the head, the underparts, and the rump are yellow. The wings, tail, and middle of the back are black. There are 2 wing bars, the upper one yellow and the lower one white. The bill is pale, blunt, and stout. Females are variable below. Most are yellow, palest on the belly, while others ("gray-phase" birds) range to distinctly grayish-white with the yellow restricted to the undertail coverts. They have an olive-yellow face and upperparts and a grayish back. Immatures are similar to females. The winter male is like the female Western, but has more conspicuous wing bars. The winter male is also brighter yellow on the underparts and may show a tinge of red to the face. The back is broadly edged with green.

Voice
Song a series of 2- and 3-syllable languid notes with alternating inflection. Call a slurred *pit-er-ick*.

Similar Species
Wing bars and contrasting grayish black distinguish Western Tanager from all other tanagers. Orioles may appear somewhat similar, but can be distinguished at a glance by long, pointed, conical bills.

Range
Breeds from extreme southeastern Alaska, southwestern Mackenzie, British Columbia, Alberta, and central Saskatchewan south to northern Baja California, southern Arizona, and extreme western Texas; also in Black Hills of South Dakota. Winters in Baja California and central Mexico south to Central America; small numbers winter in coastal southern California. Casual and widespread over much of United States and Canada.
Larry R. Ballard

Typical female
1. *Two thin wing bars.*
2. *Yellowish underparts.*

   Most females show gray saddle on back.

Breeding male
1. *Red face.*
2. *Yellow underparts and nape.*
3. *Black back and wings.*
4. *Two wing bars, 1 yellow and 1 white.*
5. *Black tail.*

Cardinals and Their Allies

(Subfamily Cardinalinae)
This subfamily includes the cardinals, the *Pheucticus* grosbeaks, the
New World buntings, and the Dickcissel. All species in the group
show marked sexual dimorphism: the males are often brightly
plumaged in red, yellow, and blue, and the females are more muted
in tone. All birds in the group have conical bills; this feature is
especially marked in the genera *Cardinalis* and *Pheucticus*, and in
the Blue Grosbeak. The buntings are the smallest members of the
subfamily, and they have very rounded proportions. Members of
each genus in the group have remarkably similar songs and calls.
(World: 39 species. North America: 12 species.)
Scott B. Terrill

Northern Cardinal

Cardinalis cardinalis
With their distinctive, brilliant red plumage, crest, and a large black
area surrounding a red bill, adult male Northern Cardinals are
unmistakable. The Northern Cardinal's song consists of clear,
whistled notes and phrases; the call is a distinctive, high, sharp
note. Cardinals are common in brushy undergrowth and are easily
drawn to feeders filled with sunflower seeds. They are conspicuous
in residential areas in the eastern United States. In the Southwest
they are found in brushy habitats in washes and riparian and
residential areas, as well as in denser desert thorn scrub. Northern
Cardinals are usually seen in pairs except during late summer and
early fall, when family groups are conspicuous as they call and
forage in the undergrowth. When they are excited, these birds erect
both their crests and tails; they often flick the tail as they call and
feed. Males sit at the top of an exposed perch, usually high above
the surrounding vegetation, to deliver their songs; the tail is often
held cocked at an angle toward the front of the body, and the crest is
held up straight. Cardinals fly in a somewhat jerky fashion, with
short gliding undulations that alternate with fast beats of their
rather rounded wings.

Description
7½–9″ (19–23 cm). Males are brilliant red with an erectile crest and
a red bill surrounded by a jet-black area that extends down the
throat and back to the eye. These rather long birds have rounded
underparts and a long tail that is somewhat wider at the slightly
rounded tip. Females are similarly shaped, but the crest and black
area around the bill are smaller. They have a pink bill and reddish
crest, wings, and tail; although older females can become
extensively red, the rest of the body is usually grayish or grayish-
olive on the upperparts and buff to pale greenish-gray on the
underparts. Immatures, especially females, often lack red and are
strongly gray, often with a brownish or buff-colored wash on the
underparts; the bill is dark.

Voice
Song a loud, clear, throaty whistle; female's song is softer and less
frequent than that of male. Variations include: *wheer wheer wheer
whoit whoit whoit whoit*, the first 3 notes descending in pitch, the
whoit notes rising sharply and delivered more rapidly; *hew hew heu*

Northern Cardinal
Pyrrhuloxia
Yellow Grosbeak
Rose-breasted Grosbeak
Black-headed Grosbeak
Blue Bunting
Blue Grosbeak
Lazuli Bunting
Indigo Bunting
Varied Bunting
Painted Bunting
Dickcissel

Adult male
1. *Red crest.*
2. *Red bill.*
3. *Black face.*
4. *Red plumage.*

Juvenile
1. *Dark bill.*
2. *Gray-brown plumage.*

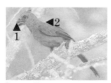

hew hew, each note descending; also *hew whoit whoit whoit* or *whit-chew, whit-chew, whit whit whit*. Call a sharp, loud, high *tsip*, *peep*, or slightly metallic *tsink*, all very similar in tone and pitch.

Similar Species
Male Pyrrhuloxia gray with bright pink patches on face, crown, underparts, wings, and tail; bill bright yellow. Adult female usually much grayer, less buff-brown, than female Cardinal, but color varies considerably. Juveniles and first-year birds of both species very similar; Pyrrhuloxia usually grayer, Cardinal usually browner; call notes and developing bill shape are best field marks. Immatures tend to associate with adults of same species.

Range
Resident in United States and southern Canada (locally) east of Rockies; common in southern Ontario, uncommon in southern Quebec; in Southwest from Colorado River Valley (rare and local) through central and southern Arizona to southwestern New Mexico and Texas; south throughout Mexican lowlands.   *Scott B. Terrill*

Pyrrhuloxia

Cardinalis sinuatus
Pyrrhuloxias are found primarily in dense thorn scrub in the arid southwestern interior near the Mexican border. They often flock in winter and occupy more diversified areas, including riparian forests, agricultural regions, and hedgerows. Pyrrhuloxias fly short distances with quick flaps on rounded wings, often landing in the middle of brushy areas. When alert, they often erect their crests and call loudly, flicking their tails with each note.

Description
7½–8½″ (19–21.5 cm). The distinctive adult male is grayish on the head, nape, and underparts, becoming whitish on the undertail coverts; the back is gray to brownish or brownish-gray. There are striking pink to scarlet-rose patches on the crest and around the eye and bill that extend in varying amounts down the middle of the breast. The thighs are also pink to rose, as are the flight feathers, especially on the underwing and the undertail coverts. Females are uniformly gray to brownish-gray above and buff to buff-gray below; they have varying amounts of pinkish or reddish, especially on the thighs. Like adult males, they have mostly pink wing linings. In all plumages, the shape of the bill is unique: the mandible has an abruptly curved culmen and a cutting edge that sharply angles up and then down; the lower mandible is very deep, ending abruptly. In adults, the bill is usually yellow, though it can be darkish in winter. Immatures are similar to females and have a dark bill.

Voice
Songs extremely varied and generally very similar to those of Northern Cardinal. Call note a *tsink*, like that of Cardinal but often more metallic and sharper.

Similar Species
See Northern Cardinal.

Range
Resident from Baja California, south-central (primarily) and southeastern Arizona, southern New Mexico, and southern and western Texas south to central Mexico. Range expands slightly and erratically in winter; very rarely includes southeastern California, where has bred once.   *Scott B. Terrill*

Adult female
1. *Pink bill.*
2. *Blackish face.*
3. *Reddish crest.*
4. *Grayish-olive upperparts.*
5. *Reddish wings.*
6. *Reddish tail.*

Adult female
1. *Stout yellow bill.*
2. *Long reddish crest.*
3. *Brownish-gray upperparts.*
4. *Buff-gray underparts.*

Adult male
1. *Stout yellow bill.*
2. *Long red crest.*
3. *Red throat and middle of breast.*
4. *Gray upperparts and flanks.*
5. *Red on wings.*
6. *Red on tail.*

Rose-breasted Grosbeak

Pheucticus ludovicianus
The Rose-breasted Grosbeak seems to require a combination of
large trees and open areas and thick shrubs or brush, a habitat that
occurs regularly along streams, ponds, marsh borders, and
roadsides, and in overgrown pastures or even residential areas. The
striking male is one of the forest's most fluent vocalists; his clear,
rich, rolling song rivals those of the thrushes in its beauty. Males
have the unusual habit of singing from the nest while incubating
eggs, and they sing while flying from perch to perch. Rose-breasted
Grosbeaks are frequently double-brooded; the female builds the
second nest while the male attends and feeds the fledglings from the
first. Rose-breasted Grosbeaks are closely related to Black-headed
Grosbeaks; the 2 species occasionally interbreed where their ranges
overlap.

Description
7–8½" (18–21.5 cm). Rose-breasted Grosbeaks have a very heavy,
arched bill. At least 5 different plumages can be identified. The adult
male in breeding plumage has a shiny black head, neck, throat, and
back. The wings are boldly patterned in black and white and the
black tail has white spots on the 3 outer tail feathers. The brilliant
carmine-red breast forms a triangular bib that extends down the
center to the belly. The wing linings are rose-red. The remaining
underparts and the rump are white. The first-spring male is similar
to the breeding adult male, but the red breast is less intense and the
flight feathers are brown. The female has a dark brown head and
upperparts, a broad gray-white eye stripe, a pale malar area, and a
buff-white stripe through the center of the crown. The brown wings
have 2 white wing bars and a small amount of white at the base of
the primaries. The wing linings are typically saffron-yellow but can
sometimes be pinkish-yellow. The underparts are mostly pale gray-
white, or sometimes buff-gray, with the breast, sides, and flanks
streaked dark brown. The adult male in winter plumage resembles
the female but has reddish wing linings, traces of red on the breast,
and bold black-and-white flight feathers. The immature male is
similar to the winter adult but usually has less red on the breast and
has brown flight feathers. Young birds just off the nest frequently
have buff breasts that can suggest the female Black-headed.

Voice
Rich, clear song similar to that of American Robin but with a fluid
quality and more rapidly delivered. Call note a high-pitched,
squeaky *ink*, *chink*, or *eek*.

Similar Species
Female Purple Finch much smaller and more heavily streaked
below; a plainer crown and wings. Female Black-headed Grosbeak
has warm buff to orange-buff breast; finer dark stripes generally
restricted to sides and flanks. Wing linings of female Black-headed
are lemon-yellow rather than saffron-yellow. Black-headed's call
note not as high or squeaky.

Range
Breeds from southern Mackenzie, across southern Canada to Nova
Scotia; south to eastern North Dakota and Kansas, northeastern
Oklahoma, southern Missouri, central Indiana, and Ohio to central
New Jersey; south along Appalachians to northern Georgia. Winters
from central Mexico to South America; rare but regular in
Southwest; rarely in Cuba.   *Peter D. Vickery*

Adult male
1. *Stout, pale bill.*
2. *Black head and upperparts.*
3. *Red breast.*
4. *White belly.*
5. *Black wings with white patches.*

Shows white rump in flight.

Female
1. *Stout, pale bill.*
2. *Pale eyebrow.*
3. *Dark crown with buff-white stripe through center.*
4. *Streaked breast and flanks.*

Has yellow wing linings.

Juvenile
1. *Buff breast like that of Black-headed Grosbeak, but with more extensive streaking.*

Black-headed Grosbeak

Pheucticus melanocephalus
The Black-headed Grosbeak breeds in a broad range of habitats with diverse vegetation and open edges. These common migrants have become a familiar sign of spring; their fall movement begins early, by late July, and continues through October.

Description
7–8½″ (18–21.5 cm). This large finch has a thick, stubby bill that is dark gray above and lighter below. Spring and summer males are bright orange-brown from the throat to the flanks with a tawny rump and collar. The midbelly is yellow, paling to white on the lower abdomen. The crown, cheeks, and chin are black, sometimes with orange stripes behind the eyes and at the rear of the crown. The black wings and tail are boldly patterned with white like those of the Rose-breasted. The back has broad tawny streaks. Females have a striped head pattern and a dark ear patch. The wings and tail are dark brown, without the male's bold white markings; instead there are 2 thin wing bars and a faint wing patch. The underparts are rich buff to orange-buff with fine streaks mostly restricted to the sides. The wing linings are lemon-yellow. Young birds in fall resemble the females, but have whiter stripes on the head and paler underparts, which are whiter below the breast.

Voice
Song composed of enthusiastic, fluty whistles, rising and falling, usually including a rolled note. Call most often heard a hard, sharp *spik;* also plaintive *whee,* which young birds draw out to *whee-you.* Young birds sometimes give squeaky *spik,* like call of Rose-breasted.

Similar Species
See Rose-breasted Grosbeak.

Range
Breeds from southwestern Canada east to southern Saskatchewan and central Kansas, then south to southern Mexico. Winters mainly in western Mexico from southern Baja California and southern Sonora south to Oaxaca. Casual fall visitor to East Coast and Gulf States, where occasionally seen in winter; very rare in winter in Southwest.   *Louis R. Bevier*

Blue Grosbeak

Guiraca caerulea
The Blue Grosbeak is a fairly common bird of the southern United States. It is found along hedgerows and roadsides, in thickets, shrubby areas, and farmlands, and near woodland borders and stream and ditch banks. It frequently perches on utility wires and fences; the male may sit motionless for long periods singing from a favorite perch. The plumage of the male and female are quite different. The Blue Grosbeak has a tendency to flick its tail occasionally. Its diet consists of a wide variety of insects and seeds, including grains.

Description
6–7½″ (15–19 cm). The Blue Grosbeak has a large, heavy conical bill. The male is deep blue with 2 rusty wing bars; the upper bar is broad and the lower one narrow. The female is a warm brown, darker above, with 2 rust- to buff-colored wing bars; the rump is tinged with blue. The immature male resembles the female but has a mixture of blue and brown plumage.

Adult male
1. Stout, pale bill.
2. Black head.
3. Orange-brown breast and flanks.
4. Black wings with white patches.

   Shows buff rump in flight.

Female
1. Stout, pale bill.
2. Striped head pattern.
3. Warm buff breast.
4. Fine streaks on flanks.
5. Pale wing bars.

Adult female
1. Stout, dark bill.
2. Brown upperparts.
3. Rust or buff wing bars.

Voice

Song a series of sweet warbled phrases that rise and fall, resembling song of Purple Finch but slower and more guttural. Note a sharp *spink* or *chink*.

Similar Species

Indigo Bunting found in the same types of habitats but smaller with smaller bill; lacks wing bars. Female and juvenile Brown-headed Cowbird paler brown, lack wing bars, have different call, do not flick tail.

Range

Breeds from central California, southern Nevada, southern and eastern Utah, southern Colorado, central South Dakota, western Iowa, central Illinois, southern Ohio, northern Kentucky, and southern Tennessee to southeastern Pennsylvania and extreme southern New York; south to Texas, Gulf Coast, and central Florida, south into Mexico. Wanders north to Great Lakes and Maritime Provinces. Winters from Mexico south to Panama, and in Bahamas and Cuba.   *Paul W. Sykes, Jr.*

Lazuli Bunting

Passerina amoena

The Lazuli Bunting nests in weedy areas with scattered shrubs near streams or springs. The Lazuli sings from exposed branches of bushes or low trees. It accompanies its nervous tail-flicking with a hard *pit* note. In fall, these migratory birds are often found with sparrows and finches.

Description

5–6″ (12.5–15 cm). The male has a sky-blue head, throat, back, and rump; the lores are black. The tail is black and edged with light blue, especially near the base. The 2 wing bars are white; the upper one is broader. The bird is a rich orange-brown across the breast and part way down the flanks; beneath these areas it is pure white. The female is grayish-brown above with a light blue rump, and patterned below like the male, but with a buff wash across the breast with white below that; there are 2 whitish wing bars. Juveniles resemble the female but may have faint streaking across the breast.

Voice

Song is loud, with sweet notes; toward end there are rapid, jumbled, rising and falling phrases, faster and more jumbled than that of Indigo Bunting. Calls a hard chip, *pit*, and a dry buzz, *zzzd*.

Similar Species

Female and immature Indigo Buntings are richer brown to cinnamon overall with underparts more uniformly buff to the belly and with faint streaks on sides; thinner wing bars usually cinnamon buff. Varied Bunting female lacks buff wash across breast, is grayish-brown overall, lacks wing bar, and has stubbier bill; upper mandible more convexly curved than Lazuli's (visible at close range).

Range

Breeds from southwestern Canada to northeastern South Dakota and east-central Nebraska, south to northwestern Baja California; in some riparian areas of southeastern California and in southern Nevada, central Arizona, and western Oklahoma. Winters from southern Baja California and southern Arizona to south-central Mexico. Casual to coast of British Columbia, east to Missouri, Illinois, and central Texas.   *Louis R. Bevier*

Adult male
1. *Stout bill.*
2. *Deep blue plumage.*
3. *Rust wing bars.*

Adult male
1. *Short, conical bill.*
2. *Bright blue head.*
3. *Orange-brown breast and flanks.*
4. *White belly.*
5. *Bold white wing bars.*

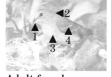

Adult female
1. *Short, conical bill.*
2. *Grayish-brown upperparts.*
3. *Buff underparts.*
4. *Pale wing bars.*

Indigo Bunting

Passerina cyanea

When April storms hit the Texas coast, thousands of migrant passerines flying north across the Gulf of Mexico are forced down to the nearest landfall. After such storms it is sometimes possible to see an unforgettably colorful sight as large flocks of brilliant male Indigo Buntings perch on low shrubs and feed in nearby fields or along roadways. Once they reach their breeding grounds, territorial males sing from the tops of trees or telephone lines where their bright colors are often difficult to see. Indigo Buntings nest in patches of dense, brushy ground cover where there are tall singing perches nearby. Old overgrown pastures, forest edges, and damp shrubs near water provide such a habitat. Indigo Buntings have more than 1 brood and this may partially explain the male's persistence in proclaiming his territory. Their strident, high-pitched song often continues unabated through the hottest days of summer and frequently can be heard until late August.

Description
5½" (14 cm). Indigo Buntings have stout conical bills with an obviously curved upper mandible. The male is deep, brilliant blue with a purplish head; the darker wing and tail feathers have blue edges. The brilliant plumage is best seen in good light; at a distance, males appear uniformly dark. Some young males in first spring plumage are mottled blue and olive-brown; others resemble full adults but are less intensely blue. All young spring males retain buff-brown wing bars and may be confused with the heavier-billed Blue Grosbeaks. Female Indigo Buntings have no readily apparent field marks. They have brown upper parts with obscure streaking to the back. The dusky wings and tail have bluish-green edges. The tertials and coverts have buff-brown edges, the latter forming inconspicuous wing bars. The underparts are dull buff-gray; the breast is faintly streaked gray-brown, the flanks are dull buff-olive, and the belly is paler gray. Immature birds closely resemble females but are usually more obviously streaked on the breast.

Voice
Song a wiry, high-pitched, strident series of couplets, each pair at a different pitch, with the second pair of notes especially harsh; *swee-swee zreet-zreet swee-swee zay-zay seeit-seeit*. Considerable variation from individual to individual. Also a jumbled flight song. Call note a sharp, distinctive *tsick*.

Similar Species
Blue Grosbeak is larger with much heavier bill. Female and immature Lazuli Buntings have unstreaked warm buff-colored breast and obvious buff-white wing bars. Female and immature Varied Buntings browner, unstreaked below, with stubbier, more sharply curved bill. See female Blue Bunting*.

Range
Breeds from southeastern Manitoba across southern Ontario, from southern Quebec to southern New Brunswick, south to eastern North Dakota, central South Dakota, central Nebraska; to central Arizona, Utah, and Colorado, and from south-central Texas to southern Louisiana, southern Mississippi, southern Alabama, and central Florida. Winters in southern Florida, infrequently in coastal Texas and along Gulf Coast; primarily in southern Mexico, Cuba, and West Indies south to Panama; rarely in Colombia and Venezuela.   *Peter D. Vickery*

Adult male
1. *Short, conical bill.*
2. *Blue plumage.*

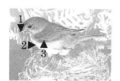

Female
1. *Short, conical bill.*
2. *Faint streaks on buff-gray breast.*
3. *Faint buff wing bars.*

Fall immature
1. *Heavier streaks on breast than in female.*

Varied Bunting

Passerina versicolor
This Mexican species breeds locally in the Southwest, where it is found in thorny scrub such as mesquite, in washes, and on hillsides in arid, often rocky areas. Varied Buntings are local and inconspicuous. The females are generally the only brownish, unstreaked buntings in the thorn scrub habitats in summer. Varied Buntings are late arrivals in Arizona, where they are most easily found in July and August.

Description
4½–5½″ (11.5–14 cm). Varied Buntings have rounded features and relatively short tails. The males appear uniformly black, but in good light the following bright, shimmering colors may be glimpsed: a round, bright red area on the nape; a red patch on the throat and upper breast; a blue collar or hindneck; a blue-violet rump; a blue-black tail; and varying degrees of plum, blue, and purple in the wings, on the back, and below. Females and immatures are dark brownish-gray with slightly darker wings and tail; they lack streaking or conspicuous wing bars. In all plumages, the bill is very conical, stubby even for a bunting, with a very curved upper mandible and a wide lower mandible.

Voice
Song a warbling of several distinct phrases, usually more abruptly delivered and shorter than other buntings. Call note metallic *pink* or *chink*, without buzz notes of Indigo and Lazuli buntings.

Similar Species
Male might be mistaken for Indigo Bunting in poor light as both look blackish. Females distinguished in breeding areas by bill shape; similar Indigo Bunting usually has streaking. Lazuli Bunting has wing bars and orange-brown wash on breast. Female and immature varied Buntings found outside of range probably not reliably identified in field. Extralimital birds should be documented.

Range
Breeds in south-central and southeastern Arizona, extreme southwestern New Mexico (Guadalupe Canyon), southeastern New Mexico (Carlsbad Caverns), and extreme southern Texas; south in Mexico to Guatemala. Winters south of United States, extremely rarely in our range.   *Scott B. Terrill*

Painted Bunting

Passerina ciris
The Painted Bunting is a locally common small finch of the southern United States. This brightly colored bird is found in gardens, weedy tangles, hedgerows, and old fields, and along roadsides, woodland edges, and stream banks. The male is a persistent singer and the most colorful of our songbirds. In the wild, Painted Buntings are shy and retiring, and can be difficult to locate except when the male is singing from an exposed perch.

Description
5–5½″ (12.5–14 cm). The male has a deep blue head, green back, brownish wings and tail; the lower back, rump, and underparts are bright red. The adult female is plain green, darker above and lighter yellow below. The immature female is lime-green above, dull grayish below, with a slight yellow wash to the sides and flanks.

Voice
Song a loud, clear, musical warble: *pew-eata, pew-eata, j-eaty-you-too*. Call note a sharp *chirp* or *chip*.

Female
1. *Stubby bill with curved upper mandible.*
2. *Uniform brownish-gray plumage.*

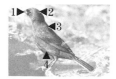

Adult male
1. *Short, conical bill.*
2. *Red nape.*
3. *Purplish-blue upperparts.*
4. *Purplish-blue underparts.*

Adult male
1. *Short, conical bill.*
2. *Blue head.*
3. *Red underparts.*
4. *Green back.*

Similar Species
Female Indigo and Lazuli buntings browner above than immature
Painted Bunting.

Range
Breeds from southeastern New Mexico and southern Missouri south
to southwestern Alabama and into Mexico; and in coastal regions
along Atlantic from southeastern North Carolina south to central
Florida. Winters from southeastern Texas, southern Louisiana,
central Florida, Bahamas, and Cuba south through Mexico to
Panama. Some extralimital records may be of escaped birds.
Paul W. Sykes, Jr.

Dickcissel

Spiza americana
This unique American finch is a common summer resident of the
prairie Midwest. It often nests in loose colonies in rank weedy
meadows and fields. Its summer distribution is erratic; it may be
common one year and rare the next, especially near the periphery of
its range. Migrants travel in huge, densely packed flocks; strays
sometimes turn up with flocks of House Sparrows.

Description
6–7″ (15–18 cm). The adult male has a gray head with a yellow
eyebrow, a pale crescent below the eye, and a white chin and
mustache setting off a small black V on the throat and chest. The
center of the breast is bright yellow, fading to grayish-white on the
sides and belly. The upperparts are warm brown, with black stripes
on the back and a rufous patch on the shoulder; the bill is blue-gray.
In autumn, the black chest mark may be obscured by pale feather
tips. The female is patterned like the male, but lacks the black chest
patch, has little yellow on the breast, is not so gray on the head, and
usually has fine streaking on the sides. The immature is more
nondescript, with fine streaking on the breast and little or no yellow
on the underparts; it has the adult's face pattern indicated in brown
and buff, and may have some rufous on the shoulder.

Voice
Song 1–3 (or more) sharp notes followed by buzzing or hissing notes:
tshk, tshk, tsszz-sszz-sszz. Call note a short, low *bzzt* or *prrt.*

Similar Species
Females and immatures resemble House Sparrows but have more
sharply defined ear patch, a blue-gray bill, and often some streaks
on flanks. They may have a rufous area on shoulder and some yellow
on face or breast. Female Bobolink has striped crown, spiky tail.

Range
Breeds from eastern Montana to Great Lakes area, south to Texas
and central Gulf States; locally farther east. Most common along
eastern edge of central Great Plains. Scarce regular fall migrant on
Atlantic Coast, vagrant west to Pacific Coast. Winters mostly from
Mexico to northern South America; a very few winter at feeders in
United States, mainly in Northeast.   *Kenn Kaufman*

Adult female
1. *Short, conical bill.*
2. *Dark green upperparts.*
3. *Yellow-green underparts.*

Breeding male
1. *Gray head.*
2. *Yellow eyebrow.*
3. *Black V on yellow breast.*
4. *Rufous shoulders.*
5. *Streaked upperparts.*

Female
1. *Dull gray bill.*
2. *Yellow stripes on face.*
3. *Streaked flanks.*
4. *Rufous shoulders.*

New World Sparrows and Their Allies

(Subfamily Emberizinae)
This large, diverse subfamily is represented in North America
primarily by the towhees, sparrows, and longspurs (Old World
buntings). Towhees are long-tailed, medium-size birds of the dense
underbrush. The eastern races of the Rufous-sided Towhee are the
only towhees that are sexually dimorphic; only it and the Green-
tailed Towhee are migratory. Sparrows are small, drab, brownish
birds with more or less streaked plumage; they feed primarily on the
ground. In general, the sexes are similar, but in many species the
immatures are distinctly different from adults. Most sparrows are
associated with grassy habitats. Adult juncos are primarily solid-
colored, or have plumage that is composed of patches of pastel
colors. They have pale bills and dark tails with extensive white in
the outer tail feathers. Juveniles have streaked plumage. The
longspurs are a distinctive group of 4 chunky, ground-dwelling
finches of open country. Males in breeding plumage all have bright
patterns. But when flocks come south in winter plumage, obscurely
marked in brown and gray, longspurs can be difficult to identify.
These birds often creep slowly over the ground. Winter longspurs
are best identified by habitat preference, diagnostic flight calls,
shape, and tail pattern, supplemented by other plumage
characteristics. The Old World buntings are represented in North
America by the genus *Plectrophenax*, whose members are primarily
white with black, white, brownish, or buff upperparts. Like the
longspurs and many species of sparrows (but not towhees), the Old
World buntings are highly gregarious in the nonbreeding seasons.
The other buntings in this subfamily that reach North America are
vagrants and occur primarily in Alaska. (World: 279 species. North
America: 52 species.)   *Scott B. Terrill and Kenn Kaufman*

Olive Sparrow

Arremonops rufivirgatus
The furtive Olive Sparrow haunts brushy thickets in southern
Texas. Its voice is often the best clue to its presence.

Description
5½–6″ (14–15 cm). Dull olive on back, brighter yellow-olive on wings
and tail. Head pale brownish gray with 2 bold brown crown stripes
and very narrow dark eyeline. Throat and belly whitish; chest and
flanks dull brownish-gray. Immature duller and browner above,
more buff-colored below, with faint wing bars.

Voice
Song a series of dry *chip* notes, widely spaced at first and speeding
up to a trill, all on 1 pitch. Call note a hard *tick*.

Similar Species
See Green-tailed Towhee.

Range
Southern Texas south locally to Costa Rica.   *Kenn Kaufman*

Olive Sparrow
Green-tailed Towhee
Rufous-sided Towhee
Brown Towhee
Abert's Towhee
White-collared Seedeater
Black-faced Grassquit
Bachman's Sparrow
Botteri's Sparrow
Cassin's Sparrow
Rufous-winged Sparrow
Rufous-crowned Sparrow
American Tree Sparrow
Chipping Sparrow
Clay-colored Sparrow
Brewer's Sparrow
Field Sparrow
Black-chinned Sparrow
Vesper Sparrow
Lark Sparrow
Black-throated Sparrow
Sage Sparrow
Five-striped Sparrow
Lark Bunting
Savannah Sparrow
Baird's Sparrow
Grasshopper Sparrow
Henslow's Sparrow
Le Conte's Sparrow
Sharp-tailed Sparrow
Seaside Sparrow
Fox Sparrow
Song Sparrow
Lincoln's Sparrow
Swamp Sparrow
White-throated Sparrow
Golden-crowned Sparrow
White-crowned Sparrow
Harris's Sparrow
Dark-eyed Junco
Yellow-eyed Junco

McCown's Longspur
Lapland Longspur
Smith's Longspur
Chestnut-collared Longspur
Little Bunting
Rustic Bunting
Gray Bunting
Pallas' Reed-Bunting
Common Reed-Bunting
Snow Bunting
McKay's Bunting

Adult
1. *Wide brown crown stripes.*
2. *Narrow line through eye.*
3. *Dull olive upperparts.*
4. *Brownish-gray flanks.*

Texas only.

Green-tailed Towhee

Pipilo chlorurus
The highly migratory Green-tailed Towhee breeds in relatively
unforested, dense shrub cover at higher elevations in the western
United States. In migration and winter, it may be found with White-
crowned Sparrows. This species is very secretive, often escaping
view by running swiftly under cover.

Description
6½–7″ (16.5–18 cm). The white throat, bordered first by black lines
and then by white lines, shows distinctly against a dark gray face
and breast. The crown is reddish-brown; the gray forehead has small
white borders. The long, rounded tail and longish wings have a
yellow-green cast. The bright yellow underwing coverts are
sometimes visible at the bend of the wing. Most of the upperparts
are gray tinged with green; the flanks are gray with a brown tone,
and the lower belly and undertail coverts are dull white. The legs
and conical bill are dark gray. Juveniles lack the crown patch, show
brown streaks above and below, and have 2 olive-buff wing bars (a
plumage not seen in migration).

Voice
Song often begins with 2 or 3 whistled notes, *swee-too*, followed by a
jumble of short, burry trills. Much like Fox Sparrow's song.
Infrequently includes songs and calls of neighboring species. Call a
catlike *puee*.

Similar Species
Olive Sparrow smaller, has shorter tail, dark eyeline, and striped
crown.

Range
Breeds from southeastern Washington and southwestern Montana
to southwestern Oregon and northern California, south through
interior mountains to southern California, central Arizona, and
southeastern New Mexico. Winters at lower elevations from
southern Arizona and southern and western Texas south to central
Mexico, casually north and west as far as central California. Casual
east of breeding range, usually in fall and winter, from
Saskatchewan to Nova Scotia south to Georgia and Louisiana.
Louis R. Bevier

Rufous-sided Towhee

Pipilo erythrophthalmus
This large, long-tailed, and brightly colored "sparrow" is common
and widespread, and frequents brushy habitats, including chaparral,
woodland edges, thickets, and even shrubs in cities and towns. Its
presence is often detected by the sound of scratching in leaf litter:
like other towhees, this bird rakes seeds and insects from the
ground by kicking both feet backward. At least 3 distinct forms
occur in North America: eastern birds show the greatest sexual
dimorphism; western birds, or "Spotted" Towhees, have distinct
white markings on the back and wings; and a race in the Southeast
has a white, rather than a red, eye. The "Spotted" and "Red-eyed"
forms were once believed to be separate species. However, they are
now known to interbreed where their ranges overlap. The well-
known song, *drink-your-tea*, is only given by most eastern birds.

Juvenile

Description
7¼–8¾″ (18.5–22 cm). The male has a black hood and black
upperparts that contrast with the rust-rufous sides and flanks, the

Juvenile
1. *Streaked crown and upperparts.*
2. *Whitish throat bordered by black line.*
3. *White line below eye.*
4. *Streaked underparts.*

Adult
1. *Reddish-brown crown.*
2. *White throat bordered with black line.*
3. *White line below eye.*
4. *Gray-green upperparts.*
5. *Greenish tail.*

Female, eastern form
1. *Brown head, breast, and upperparts.*
2. *Rufous sides and flanks.*
3. *White middle breast and belly.*

Juveniles have streaked underparts.

rich buff-colored undertail coverts, and the white midbreast and belly. The black tail has large white spots at the corners (reduced in females). In addition to the white edgings to the tertials and the small white patch at the base of the primaries present in eastern races, western birds show distinctive white spotting on the scapulars and wing coverts. Eastern females are like the males except that the black coloration is replaced throughout by brown. The western female is more similar to the male, with the black plumage appearing a somewhat washed-out grayish-black or brownish-black, not brown as in the eastern races. Juveniles lack a suggestion of the hood and have brownish upperparts and throat, with rusty tones to the crown, nape, and back; they have dark brown streaking to the throat, breast, and sides, and a buff-colored wash to the flanks and belly. The eye is closer to brown than red. Juveniles of the western races of the Rufous-sided Towhee show the pale spotting of the adults.

Voice
Song variable. Most eastern birds give a distinctive, musical *drink-your-tea* (last note trilled); western races a *chup-chup-zeeee* or a scratchy *chweee* or *ju-wee?* Call note a scratchy or slurred, ascending *to-whee?;* western birds typically utter a more monosyllabic *tweee* or *chweee*.

Range
Breeds from southern British Columbia to southern Maine south to southern Baja California, Guatemala, northern Oklahoma, eastern Louisiana, and southern Florida. Winters north to southern British Columbia, Utah, Colorado, southern Great Lakes area, and along Atlantic Coast north to Massachusetts. "Spotted" form casual in East.   *Paul Lehman*

Brown Towhee

Pipilo fuscus
Although superficially similar, the 2 races of the Brown Towhee, the "Pacific" Brown Towhee and the "interior western" Brown Towhee, are very different. In much of northern and coastal California, the "Pacific" Brown Towhee is abundant in parks, gardens, and woodlots, as well as in chaparral, open live-oak woodlands, riparian areas, and just about any brushy habitat within the range. The Pacific race is often cited as an example of a highly sedentary permanent resident. "Interior" Brown Towhees are found in scrubby, rocky hills and mountainous areas in the arid Southwest. The songs and calls of the 2 types are very different. Both often chase about, uttering a loud, scratchy *kwheek-kwheek-kwick, kwick-wik-wik-wik* ("duet squeals"). Both the "Pacific" Brown Towhee and the "Interior" Brown Towhee often twitch their long tails or hold them upward while foraging on the ground, where these birds are usually found. These birds generally fly for short distances in a straight direction with quick wingbeats broken as they glide with spread wings.

Male, eastern form
1. *Black head, breast, and upperparts.*
2. *Rufous sides and flanks.*
3. *White middle breast and belly.*

Shows white spots at corners of tail in flight.

Male, western form
1. *White spots on scapulars and wing coverts.*

Heavily streaked bird
1. *Black streaks on throat and upper breast.*
2. *Dark spot in middle of upper breast.*

Description
8–10″ (20.5–25.5 cm). California birds are a uniform, drab gray with brownish tints, darker on the upperparts and darkest on the tail. The undertail coverts are buff-rust or buff-brown. These birds have variable amounts of blackish around the bill (sometimes resembling Abert's Towhees) and streaking on the crown, the ear coverts, the throat, and below and in front of the eye. The throat and malar areas often have a pale brownish-gray to buff ground color and are the palest areas on the bird, except for a thin pale eye-ring. Interior birds are similar but have much more contrast and less brown in the plumage. They are paler below (very light gray in midbelly) and above, shading to darker on the wings and tail. They have a rust to buff-brown crown that contrasts sharply with the rest of the upperparts. The chin, throat, malar region, and upper breast are pale buff; blackish streaks on the malar region form a collar around the base of the buff bib where the buff and gray breast areas meet. The collar is terminated by a dark spot at the middle of the upper breast. Some birds are very pale.

Voice
In coastal birds song consists of a series of sharp, loud call notes: *pink-pink-pink-pink-pink-pink-pink-pink*, increasing in tempo and often changing a half step at acceleration point. Also, song with higher, less metallic notes: *cheep-cheep-cheep-chip-chip-cheep*, accelerating with *chip* notes, often a step lower in scale. Also variations of these songs. Interior towhees have more musical song of clear 2-syllable notes: *chili-chili-chili-chili, chili-chili-chewe-chew;* song variable. In coastal birds, call note a loud metallic *pink*. In interior birds, a loud, clear double call note: *chud-up* or *shed-up.*

Similar Species
Abert's Towhee has blackish area around bill, buff-cinnamon upper breast; lacks collar and malar stripes; does not show streaking on ear coverts; lighter brown above, more rufous below than Pacific race. Calls and songs very different from those of interior race; closer to those of coastal race. Abert's and interior race overlap only locally.

Range
Resident in southwestern Oregon, California (except higher mountains, desert regions, and extensive forests), Arizona, southeastern Colorado, to central western Texas, south into central and western Mexico.   *Scott B. Terrill*

Abert's Towhee

Pipilo aberti
These birds are abundant in desert valleys, especially around riparian areas with cottonwood, willow, mesquite, and salt cedar.

Description
9″ (23 cm). Brownish-gray above, darker on wings and especially on tail. Bill pale gray or brownish-gray, surrounded by blackish area that extends as narrow streaking onto throat. Cinnamon-buff below, brighter on upper breast and undertail coverts.

Voice
Call a sharp, varyingly metallic *peek*. Song often a staccato series of notes: *peek peek peek, peek peek peek*. Numerous variations.

Similar Species
See Brown Towhee.

Range
Se. California; S. Nevada and Utah through lower elevations in W., central, and S. Arizona and Sw. New Mexico.   *Scott B. Terrill*

Pacific Coast form
1. *Uniformly drab gray brown plumage.*
2. *Buff undertail coverts.*

Loud pink *call.*

Interior form
1. *Rust crown.*
2. *Gray-brown upperparts.*
3. *Pale buff throat and upper breast.*
4. *Buff undertail coverts.*

Clear chud-up *call.*

Adult
1. *Dark area around base of bill.*
2. *Brownish-gray upperparts.*
3. *Cinnamon-buff underparts.*

Sharp peek *call.*

White-collared Seedeater

Sporophila torqueola
Once fairly common in southern Texas, the tiny White-collared
Seedeater has become rare and irregular recently and in some years
it is not recorded north of the border at all. Singles and small flocks
still turn up unpredictably in rank weedy areas, brushy fields,
overgrown orchards, or clearings in the woods. In Mexico, where
Seedeaters are abundant in open country, even sizeable flocks can be
difficult to see in dense, low growth. However, they often pop into
view when lured by "spishing" or by imitations of Ferruginous
Pygmy-Owl calls. A peculiarity of the northernmost population,
including the Texas birds, is that the males rarely if ever develop
the clean-cut black-and-white adult pattern seen a little farther
south; consequently they are not really "white-collared" here.

Description
4″ (10 cm). In Texas, the White-collared Seedeater is variable, but
mostly quite drab. It is best identified by its very small size, stubby
rounded bill, and lack of any streaking. The basic pattern is olive-
brown above (often slightly paler on the rump) and buff-colored
below; the wings are dark with 2 white wing bars and a white patch
(sometimes absent) at the base of the primaries. In Texas, adult
males tend to be more grayish-brown above and whiter below; some
of them become fairly blackish on the crown, face, upper back, and
at the sides of the chest.

Voice
Song surprisingly loud for bird's small size; consists of clear whistles
with buntinglike quality: *twee twee twee, chew chew;* pattern varies.
Call notes include a metallic *tik-it* and a short *tewp.*

Similar Species
Goldfinches are slightly larger and do not have Seedeater's stubby,
rounded bill. Lesser Goldfinch always more yellow; American
Goldfinch has white rump and undertail coverts; both have shorter,
notched tails with some white on inner webs of tail feathers.

Range
Northern Mexico to Panama. Now a rare visitor (formerly resident)
in southern Texas.   *Kenn Kaufman*

Bachman's Sparrow

Aimophila aestivalis
This shy, solitary sparrow forages on the ground in open woods,
usually pine, and brushy fields. When disturbed, it runs over the
ground or flushes, dropping down out of sight many yards away or
occasionally flying up into the canopy and remaining still.

Description
5–5½″ (13–14 cm). Virtually identical to Botteri's Sparrow (not
found in same range) but usually more reddish above.

Voice
Song loud and ethereal; usually a clear, whistled note followed by a
slow, sweet trill, often repeated with variations.

Similar Species
See Botteri's, Grasshopper, and Swamp sparrows.

Range
Ne. Texas and Maryland south to Gulf Coast and central Florida.
Winters in southern part of breeding range.   *John Farrand, Jr.*

Adult male
1. *Stubby, rounded bill.*
2. *Blackish crown and face.*
3. *Whitish underparts.*
4. *Whitish wing bars.*

Female
1. *Stubby, rounded bill.*
2. *Brownish head and upperparts.*
3. *Buff underparts.*

Small size.

Adult
1. *Reddish eyeline.*
2. *Reddish-brown upperparts.*
3. *Unstreaked buff underparts.*

Secretive habits. Southeastern states.

Botteri's Sparrow

Aimophila botterii
This very secretive bird of the Southwest is always associated with
dense, tall grass. Usually heard before it is seen, it is perhaps the
archetypical *Aimophila*.

Description
5¼–6½" (13–16.5 cm). Primarily brownish above with streaked
upperparts; plain buff below. There is a buff eyebrow and a thin
dark eyeline. The brownish wings and tail are often tinted rust.

Voice
Song usually a series of musical *chips*, accelerating into a trill
("bouncing-ball" style). Call note a light, sharp *tsip*.

Similar Species
See Cassin's and Bachman's sparrows.

Range
Breeds from Se. Arizona and Se. Texas south to S. Mexico. Winter
distribution poorly understood.   *Scott B. Terrill*

Cassin's Sparrow

Aimophila cassinii
After summer rains finally drench the normally arid southwestern
grasslands, these areas may suddenly come alive with singing,
skylarking Cassin's Sparrows. The male often delivers its distinctive
song from a weak, fluttery, nearly hovering flight, then drops back
to an exposed perch. This species is relatively erratic in numbers
and distribution.

Description
5¼–6" (13.5–15 cm). Basically grayish, Cassin's Sparrow has a long,
rounded, dark gray tail with cross-hatchings on the central tail
feathers. The bill is fairly long and conical. Brownish spots form
streaking on the entire upperparts; there is a varyingly conspicuous
light eye-ring. The pale eyebrow is generally not conspicuous and
may be absent. The underparts are pale buff or whitish with limited
streaking on the flanks. Juveniles are similar, with streaks on the
underparts.

Voice
Song a long, single, musical trill that sounds like a long, drawn-out
note at a distance: *tseeeeeeee*, with closing notes *tee, tee* to *tay, tay*.
Call note a third *tseep;* also a louder *chip*.

Similar Species
Botteri's Sparrow somewhat less stocky, generally browner, and
less conspicuously streaked on upperparts; has more conspicuous
eyebrow and slightly less conical bill. Wings and tail often rust-
tinted; has more buff on eyebrow, face, and underparts. Botteri's
also lacks streaks on flanks and diagnostic heavy cross-barring on
central tail feathers. Song and skylarking behavior of Cassin's
distinctive.

Range
Breeds from southern Arizona (casual in southeastern California),
southeastern Colorado and southwestern Kansas south into southern
New Mexico, western and southern Texas, and northern Mexico.
Winters erratically and usually relatively sparingly in southern
portions of United States range to central Mexico.
Scott B. Terrill

Adult
1. *Long bill with rounded culmen.*
2. *Buff eyebrow.*
3. *Buff underparts.*
4. *Brownish streaked upperparts.*
5. *Long, rounded tail.*

Southwest only.

Adult
1. *Long bill with straight culmen.*
2. *Buff eyebrow.*
3. *Buff underparts.*
4. *Gray-brown, streaked upperparts.*

Sings in flight.

Juvenile
. *Streaks on underparts.*

Rufous-winged Sparrow

Aimophila carpalis
The Rufous-winged Sparrow favors thorny mesquite, bunch grass in washes, and more densely vegetated desert flats at lower elevations. No other similarly marked bird in the region has the Rufous-winged's type of song, which resembles that of Botteri's Sparrow. In summer, it is the only *Aimophila* in low-elevation arid habitats.

Description
5½" (14 cm). The Rufous-winged Sparrow has a light grayish head with rust crown stripes, a grayish-white median line, a thin, noticeably decurved, rust postocular eyeline, and a conspicuous pair of thin black whisker marks. The underparts are uniform pale gray or grayish-white with varying washes of buff on the flanks. The upper back is light gray with some rust tones, and has brownish-gray and buff streaking. The wings and tail are dark gray, with whitish edgings to the wing coverts that often form light wing bars. The rufous near the bend in the folded wing is not always visible. Juveniles are browner with streaks on the crown, breast, and flanks.

Voice
Songs variable; usually a short series of staccato, rather dry, but slightly musical notes, often in a "bouncing-ball" fashion; initiated with several plaintive notes and accelerating into a rapid series of *chips* or even a trill. Call a loud *seep*, given frequently.

Similar Species
Differs from *Spizella* sparrows in its characteristic *Aimophila* shape, with noticeably larger head and bill (often bicolored), longer but relatively heavy body, and long, wider, and more rounded tail. *Spizella* species have dark eyeline; immatures show marked contrast between ear covert region and rest of head and neck. Rufous-crowned Sparrow much darker, has darker gray on head and underparts, lacks light edgings to wings; has single, thicker, black whisker mark and conspicuous white eye-ring; found at higher elevations and has entirely different song.

Range
South-central Arizona (primarily Tucson region) west across Papago Indian Reservation and south to lower elevations of Santa Rita Mountains. Distribution fluctuates; populations more widely distributed in years with abundant rainfall.   *Scott B. Terrill*

Rufous-crowned Sparrow

Aimophila ruficeps
The Rufous-crowned Sparrow is a bird of rocky, brushy, relatively arid hillsides. Because it is a ground forager that seldom moves high in vegetation, it is fairly inconspicuous, but its feeble, jumbled song, which resembles that of a House Wren, makes its presence known. Rocky areas, especially boulders, are the best places to look for this bird. Like some other secretive sparrows, the Rufous-crowned Sparrow will often scurry from one bush to the cover of another instead of flying. It responds well to spishing, and in some areas, such as the mountains in southeastern Arizona, it has become quite tame and comes readily to feeders.

Description
5–6" (12.5–15 cm). The breast, sides, head, and nape are medium gray. The crown is rust-colored with varying conspicuous black striping on the extreme forehead and a pale median line. There is a buff-colored or whitish eyebrow bordered below by a rusty eyeline and dark lores. The black whisker mark contrasts sharply with the

Adult
1. *Rust crown stripes.*
2. *Two whiskers.*
3. *Pale gray*
   underparts.
4. *Long tail.*

Large-headed look.
Arizona only.

Juvenile
1. *Streaked crown.*
2. *Streaks on breast*
   and flanks.

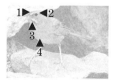

Adult
. *Rust crown.*
. *Light eyebrow and*
  eye-ring.
. *Black and white*
  whisker marks.
. *Plain, gray breast.*

Rocky habitat.

white above it and the white throat, and there is a fairly conspicuous white eye-ring. The back is streaked with dark brown, often with rusty tones, and the wings and tail are relatively uniform dark brown with slightly paler edgings. Juveniles are similar but more buff-colored, and with a less distinct facial pattern.

Voice
Song varies, but generally resembles weak *mumbo-jumbo* song of House Wren. Call a nasal *dear* or *churr* note, often repeated in doublets or triplets.

Similar Species
Chipping Sparrow is smaller, with thinner, notched *Spizella*like tail, and a black eyeline; adults lack conspicuous malar stripe. Adult Field Sparrow also has *Spizella* characteristics; lacks whisker mark, has pink bill and richly colored back. See Rufous-winged Sparrow.

Range
Central California east to southeastern Colorado and locally to western Arkansas, south into southern Mexico. Primarily resident, but with some movement occurring.   *Scott B. Terrill*

American Tree Sparrow

Spizella arborea
The first cold winds of October bring these birds south from their northern breeding grounds; by November, they are widespread in weedy fields, brushy pastures, and open country from the Canadian border to as far south as California and North Carolina. Studies indicate that males generally winter farther north than females. In the first warm days of March, these birds intimate the coming of spring with their full, beautiful song. Most migrate north in April and by late May reach the Canadian taiga.

Description
5½–6½" (14–16.5 cm). This handsome sparrow is easily identified by its chestnut crown and eyeline, dark breast spot, dark upper mandible, and yellowish lower mandible, which has a dusky tip. The cheek, throat, and upper breast are pale gray. A chestnut malar stripe is sometimes present. There is a bright deep chestnut patch on the side of the breast; the flanks are warm orange-buff and the lower breast and belly are pale gray-white. The colorful wings have a bright orange-chestnut wash and 2 obvious white wing bars. The black tertials have broad white edges and form 2 conspicuous dark rows along the plain gray-brown lower back. The upper back is warm brown with dark brown and buff-gray streaks. The long, dark tail feathers have thin white edges discernible at close range. Juveniles have a streaked breast, flanks, and crown. The western race has a paler back and a richer wash along the flanks.

Voice
Song clear, sweet, and sprightly; first 2 notes usually higher. Call an excited, musical triple note, *tseedle-eet;* note a soft *tseeep* or *teeeip.*

Similar Species
Field Sparrow smaller, has bright pink bill, conspicuous white eye-ring, and lacks dark breast spot. See Chipping Sparrow.

Range
Breeds from northern Alaska, Yukon, and northern British Columbia, across northern Canada to northern Quebec and Labrador, possibly to northern Newfoundland. Winters from southern Canada to northern California, central Arizona, central Texas, Arkansas, and South Carolina.   *Peter D. Vickery*

Juvenile
1. *Less distinct face pattern than adult.*
2. *Buff tinge to plumage.*

Adult, rear view
1. *Chestnut crown.*
2. *Dark upper mandible and yellow lower mandible.*
3. *White wing bars.*

Adult, side view
1. *Plain, grayish underparts.*
2. *Dark breast spot.*

Chipping Sparrow

Spizella passerina

The Chipping Sparrow is a familiar and common summer resident of gardens, woodlands, and forest edges in the East and open woodlands and mountain meadows in the West. It mixes loosely with other sparrows during migration and rarely occurs in pure flocks except in its favored wintering areas—weedy fields and dry scrubland in the South and Southwest. Somewhat more arboreal than most sparrows, the Chipping Sparrow typically sings from an elevated perch and often takes cover in trees. It generally forages on the ground in open meadows or lawnlike areas and is notably tame and unsuspecting.

Description
5–5¾" (12.5–14.5 cm). The adult Chipping Sparrow in breeding plumage is easily recognized by its bright rufous cap, which is sharply set off by a prominent white eyebrow and a distinct narrow black eyeline that continues through the lores to the dark bill. It has unmarked gray cheeks, underparts, and rump, and a warm brown back that has sharp blackish streaks. The nonbreeding adult is somewhat similar but its crown is less rufous, usually streaked with black, and often shows a faint median stripe. The eyebrow, underparts, and rump have a slight buff tinge, the bill is paler than that of the breeding adult, and it has a brownish cheek patch. The immature is similar but browner still. It lacks any trace of rufous in its distinctly streaked crown and has a stronger cheek patch (outlined above with a dark line) that contrasts with the grayish side of its neck. It has a buff eyebrow, a rather distinct median crown stripe, a faint whisker mark, and dark lores. Its bill is dull pinkish. Juveniles have finely but distinctly streaked underparts and brown, faintly streaked rumps. Unlike most passerines, young "Chippies" (at least in the West) keep their juvenal plumage well into the fall and sometimes throughout the fall migration.

Voice
Song a distinctive long, rapid, dry, rather unmusical, single-pitched trill. Sometimes virtually indistinguishable from song of Dark-eyed Junco but usually faster, dryer, and much less musical. Call a high, sweet *tseep* or *tsip*, generally shorter, higher, and sweeter than calls of most other sparrows; resembles the *tsit* of Savannah Sparrow but sweeter and less sibilant.

Similar Species
Breeding adults differ from all other "rufous-capped" sparrows and from Green-tailed Towhee by prominent white eyebrow and strong black eyeline. Nonbreeding adults and immatures easily identified as *Spizella* sparrows by small size, slim build, notched tail, and wing bars. Tree and Field sparrows have unstreaked crowns and rufous in back and crown. Brewer's Sparrow is smaller, relatively longer-tailed, paler, and more finely streaked; it has pale lores, a faint eye-ring, and a brownish rump (but juvenile Chipping has brown rump too). Juveniles best identified by characteristic *Spizella* shape; Savannah Sparrow most similar, but has shorter tail, heavier breast streaks, more distinct median crown stripe, yellowish about eyebrow and face, and brighter legs. See Clay-colored Sparrow.

Range
Breeds over much of North America, excluding Alaska, from near tree line in Canada south to Nicaragua and southeastern United States. Winters from southern United States to Nicaragua, rarely north to Oregon, lower Great Lakes, and Long Island.
David F. DeSante

Breeding adult
1. *Rufous cap.*
2. *White eyebrow.*
3. *Black eyeline and lores.*
4. *Plain underparts.*

Immature
1. *Streaked crown.*
2. *Brownish cheek patch bordered above by dark line.*
3. *Dark lores.*
4. *Gray rump.*

Juvenile
1. *Finely streaked underparts.*

   Brown, faintly streaked rump.

Clay-colored Sparrow

Spizella pallida
The Clay-colored Sparrow is locally common in the midcontinent, inhabiting open shrubland, brushy riparian and second-growth areas, and deciduous and coniferous forest edges and burns. In migration and winter, it associates with other sparrows, particularly other *Spizellas*, in weedy fields and dry scrublands.

Description
4¾–5¼" (12–13.5 cm). The breeding adult can be recognized by its small size, *Spizella* shape, unstreaked underparts, and contrasting head pattern. The head pattern consists of a prominent whitish median stripe on a very dark crown, a prominent whitish eyebrow and malar stripe, pale brownish lores, a contrasting brown cheek patch boldly outlined above and below with thin dark lines, and a distinct whisker mark. The distinctive medium gray of the nape and side of the neck contrasts with the rest of the plumage. The rich buff-brown back has sharp blackish streaking; the rump is brownish. Nonbreeding adults are slightly duller and more buff-colored. Immatures have much the same pattern as adults but are very buff-colored, especially across the breast, and show a somewhat less well-defined median crown stripe and a paler, more finely streaked crown. They still have medium gray on the nape and side of the neck that contrasts with the remainder of their brown and buff plumage, and they retain the malar stripe. Juveniles are like immatures but have finely streaked breasts and rumps; unlike young Chipping Sparrows, they molt out of juvenal plumage before they begin their fall migration. The bill is pinkish in all plumages but somewhat brighter in younger birds.

Voice
Song a distinctive series of 2–5 (usually 3–4) identical, slow, low-pitched, flat, unbirdlike buzzes. Call a soft *tsip*, thinner and less sweet than that of Chipping Sparrow.

Similar Species
Adults in breeding plumage fairly distinctive, but may be confused with Brewer's Sparrow. Immature Chipping and Brewer's sparrows very similar to fall adult and immature Clay-colored but generally less buff-colored with less contrast in head pattern and with grayer breast that contrasts less with malar stripe. Best mark is medium gray on side of neck and nape; though present to some extent on both Chipping and Brewer's, it does not contrast as strongly with rest of plumage as in Clay-colored. Chipping is also larger and has bold outline only above cheek patch, not above and below; has dark lores and grayish rump except in juvenal plumage. Brewer's has much less prominent (or absent) median crown stripe, faint eye-ring, longer tail, and paler grayish-brown, more finely streaked upperparts.

Range
Breeds in interior North America, primarily east of Rockies, from northeastern British Columbia and southern and western Ontario to southeastern Colorado and central Michigan. Territorial birds have occurred as far east as New York. Rare but regular transient to West in fall and spring; to Atlantic Coast in fall. Winters from northern Mexico and southern Texas to southern Mexico.
David F. DeSante

Breeding adult
1. *Strongly contrasting head pattern.*
2. *Gray sides of neck and nape.*
3. *Pale brownish lores.*
4. *Rich, buff-brown back with sharp blackish streaks.*

Immature
1. *Gray side of neck and nape.*
2. *Buff on breast.*

More buff overall than adult.

Immature
1. *Brown rump.*

Brewer's Sparrow

Spizella breweri
This common sparrow is the dominant summer land bird of the great
sagebrush flats and dry, brushy mountain meadows of the Great
Basin and northern Rocky Mountain region. In winter, it mixes with
other sparrows, particularly other *Spizellas*, in brushy desert scrub.

Description
5–5½" (12.5–14 cm). This small, nondescript, grayish-brown
Spizella has a notably long tail and shows a faint but characteristic
eye-ring in all plumages. The adult has a finely streaked grayish-
brown crown and back and a dull grayish-white eyebrow, malar
stripe, and underparts, with an occasional trace of vague streaking
on the sides of the breast. It has pale brownish lores, a pale
brownish cheek patch with a vague darker outline above and below,
and a faint whisker mark. The side of the neck and nape are dull
grayish, and the rump is grayish-brown, with faint, darker streaks.
Immatures are like adults but are slightly warmer brown above and
more buff-colored below. Their face pattern contrasts slightly more,
and they sometimes have a faint median crown stripe. Juveniles
have very finely streaked breasts and rumps but, like Clay-colored
Sparrows, molt into immature plumage before beginning their fall
migration. In all plumages, these birds have dull pinkish bills.

Voice
Song an astounding, elaborate, Canarylike series of long, sweet,
musical or buzzy trills that seem endlessly varied in speed, pitch,
and quality. A typical song may last 10 seconds or more. Call a soft
tsip or *chip*, similar to that of Clay-colored Sparrow.

Similar Species
See Chipping and Clay-colored sparrows. Can be distinguished from
other clear-breasted sparrows by characteristic *Spizella* shape, lack
of either rufous cap or strong head markings, and generally
nondescript plumage.

Range
Breeds in Great Basin and northern Rocky Mountain region from
southwestern Yukon and southern Alberta south (east of Cascades
and Sierra) to southern California and northern New Mexico.
Winters from Southwest to central Mexico.   *David F. DeSante*

Field Sparrow

Spizella pusilla
As their name suggests, Field Sparrows often inhabit neglected
pastures that have become overgrown with shrubs and weeds. As
agriculture declined during the last 100 years, farms and fields were
abandoned and the Field Sparrow's population increased. However,
more recently these open lands have reverted into forests, and
suburban areas were developed, reducing this habitat. Farther
south, these birds breed in lumbered pine forests and burned-over
woodlands wherever briars and brush have regenerated. The male is
a persistent singer and his sweet, clear song can be heard well into
July and August. As many as 3 broods are raised annually.

Description
5–6" (12.5–15 cm). Adults have bright pink bills. The crown is warm
rust-orange and the gray face is set off by a broad whitish eye-ring
and rust eyeline and ear coverts. The gray-white underparts have a
buff wash across the breast and flanks. The breast lacks a central
spot but the side of the breast is bright rust-orange. The rust-brown

Breeding adult
1. Grayish-brown, finely streaked upperparts.
2. No strongly contrasting head pattern.
3. Faint eye-ring.
4. Long tail.

Immature
1. Warmer brown upperparts than adult.
2. Faint eye-ring.
3. Less buff on breast than immature Clay-colored Sparrow.

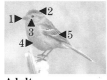

Adult
1. Pink bill.
2. Rust-orange crown.
3. White eye-ring.
4. Gray-white underparts.
5. White wing bars.

back has dark brown streaks. The wings have 2 white wing bars and the dark tail has gray edging. Immatures are duller and have thin streaks on the breast and flanks.

Voice
A sweet, plaintive song with long, clear introductory notes that accelerate to a trill: *seeeea-seeeea-seeee-seee-wee-wee-we-we-we-we.* Call note *tsip* or *tsee.*

Similar Species
Tree Sparrow larger, with dusky upper mandible, yellow lower mandible, and dark breast spot. Adult Chipping Sparrow has black bill, white eye stripe, black eyeline, plain gray underparts.

Range
Breeds from eastern Montana to southern Quebec, central and eastern Maine, and possibly southern New Brunswick; south to western Colorado and central Texas east to Georgia and rarely northern Florida. Winters from southern Nebraska to eastern Massachusetts, south to southern Texas, northeastern Mexico, Gulf States, and central Florida.   *Peter D. Vickery*

Black-chinned Sparrow

Spizella atrogularis
The unique Black-chinned Sparrow is confined to dense brushy slopes, especially during the breeding season, when its song carries a remarkable distance down the chaparral-covered hillsides. The Black-chinned Sparrow is seldom seen in groups, except occasionally in large winter flocks that consist of other species of sparrows and juncos. Although it is superficially more similar to a junco than a sparrow, in general size and shape it is a typical *Spizella:* it is small, with a small, conical bill and a relatively long, thin tail. They fly low and for short distances, and thus are seldom seen in flight. In a few local areas in the mountains of southern California and central Arizona, Black-chinned Sparrows are quite common and more easily seen, especially in the relatively open brush.

Description
5–5½″ (12.5–14 cm). The male is medium gray on the head, rump, and underparts, paling in the vent region. The pink bill is surrounded by a blackish area. The back is streaked with dark brown or blackish on a buff and light brown background. The wings are dark with brownish and buff edgings that often have rusty tones; the tail is dark with pale buff or whitish edgings. Females and winter-plumage birds are similar but lack the black area around the bill. First-winter birds are like winter adults but have streaks on the crown and nape.

Voice
Song introduced by several clear, plaintive notes, suddenly accelerating into increasingly rapid trill; trill may descend or rise a bit in pitch. Call a faint *tsip* or a louder *ship.*

Similar Species
Juncos stockier, more rotund, with relatively large heads and much more white in outer tail feathers; lack streaking on back.

Range
Breeds in central California, southern Nevada, southern Utah, Arizona, southern New Mexico, and Trans-Pecos region of Texas, south into western Mexico. Winters somewhat irregularly in southern deserts and brushy areas in interior border region, south into Mexico.   *Scott B. Terrill*

Immature
1. *Thin streaks on breast and flanks.*
2. *Dull upperparts.*

First-winter bird
1. *Pink bill.*
2. *Gray face and underparts.*
3. *Streaked crown, nape, and back.*

Adult male
1. *Pink bill.*
2. *Black face and chin.*
3. *Gray head.*
4. *Gray breast.*

Brushy desert hillsides.
Loud, trilling song.

Vesper Sparrow

Tail

◀3

Pooecetes gramineus
The Vesper Sparrow is named for its clear, musical song, which is
considered by some to be most impressive in the early evening.
However, these birds sing persistently, beginning in the early
morning, and frequently continue their sweet phrases through all but
the hottest summer days. They were originally, and more
appropriately, known as "Bay-winged Buntings," for the bright
chestnut wing patch frequently apparent on the lesser coverts.
Vesper Sparrows typically favor dry open fields and barrens with
sparse vegetation, but they will nest in a surprising variety of
habitats, including blueberry barrens, gravel pits, dry prairies,
coastal beachgrass, and, farther north, forest clearings and burned-
over areas. Unlike some sparrows, male Vespers require elevated
singing perches such as fence posts, shrubs, and scattered trees.
These birds seem inordinately fond of dust baths and it is common to
find several birds dusting themselves in bare patches on dirt roads.
When flushed from such occupations, their white outer tail feathers
are especially conspicuous. Except in the north, the first spring
migrants appear on breeding grounds in late March or April, where
2 broods are usually produced.

Description
5½–6½" (14–16.5 cm). The Vesper Sparrow has pale gray-brown
upperparts with dark brown streaks. The dull gray-white
underparts have thin dark brown stripes on the throat, breast,
sides, and flanks. The breast lacks a dark central spot and may be
tinged with a buff wash. The outer tail feathers are mostly white but
do not form a white terminal margin as in the Lark Sparrow.
Though this is the bird's most obvious feature in flight, on a
perching bird these white feathers can be obscured by the remaining
dark brown tail feathers. The chestnut wing patch on the lesser
coverts is variable, prominent on some individuals and much
diminished or absent on others. Buff edges to the greater and
median coverts form 2 vaguely defined wing bars. A conspicuous
white eye-ring stands out against the brown cheek patch and pale
side of the neck. The dusky upper mandible contrasts somewhat
with the flesh-colored lower mandible. Immature birds are similar to
adults. There is considerable variation in general coloration; the
widespread, slender-billed western race appears slightly larger and
paler gray with less distinct breast stripes than the eastern form.

Voice
Song with sweet, musical opening notes, usually 2 pairs of clear,
unhurried, slurred notes, second pair higher pitched, followed by a
descending series of rapid trills; sometimes described as *here-here
where-where all together down the hill.* Call note a sharp *chirp.*

Similar Species
Water Pipit and Sprague's Pipit have thin bills and walk rather than
hop. Savannah Sparrow usually has yellow lores and shorter tail
without obvious white feathers. Female Lark Bunting larger, has
obvious white wing patch and larger, silver-blue bill.

Range
Breeds from central British Columbia, southern Mackenzie,
northern Alberta, and central Saskatchewan to Nova Scotia and
south to central California, central Arizona, central Texas, central
Missouri, Tennessee, and western North Carolina. Winters from
central California, central Arizona, Oklahoma, southern Illinois,
coastal New Jersey, and Long Island to Gulf Coast, central Florida,
and southern Mexico.   *Peter D. Vickery*

Adult
1. *White eye-ring.*
2. *Pale gray-brown upperparts with dark brown streaks.*
3. *White outer tail feathers.*

Adult
. *Chestnut patch on lesser wing coverts.*

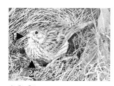

Adult
. *Dark upper mandible and pale lower mandible.*
. *Streaks on underparts without central dark spot.*

Lark Sparrow

Chondestes grammacus
The Lark Sparrow frequents open areas sparsely vegetated with scattered trees and shrubs. These birds are also found around agricultural areas, pastures, and ranchlands, and in adjacent open residential areas. They are often seen perched on fences or phone lines along roadsides in open country. Lark Sparrows are strongly territorial, and often sing from the ground or in flight. Large flocks may be formed in winter in areas where this species is a permanent resident. The strong flight is punctuated by long, shallow glides.

Description
6" (15 cm). Adults are alike in plumage, without seasonal changes. The head pattern consists of a white median head stripe bordered on either side by a wide chestnut band. Below this, there is a white line above the eye, followed by chestnut ear coverts, and a narrow white stripe separated from the white throat by a black mustache. The breast is white with a black splotch. The wings are brown with indistinct whitish wing bars; the back is brown with black streaks. The outer webs of the outermost tail feathers are white, with decreasing amounts of white in each feather inward to the 2 black central tail feathers. Juveniles have a streaked brown crown, a lightly streaked breast, and lack the black breast spot. The adult head pattern is present but less distinct. In flight, large amounts of white are visible in the tail, and the white breast and head pattern are evident, but the black blotch on the breast is less conspicuous.

Voice
Song consists of clear notes, buzzes, pauses, and trills given in various sequences. Call a metallic *tink*, given year-round.

Similar Species
Adults unmistakable. Vesper Sparrow also shows white in tail, but is more heavily streaked, lacks distinct head pattern.

Range
Breeds from parts of southern and central Canada south to northern Mexico, and from eastern Washington and California to Appalachians. Winters in central and southern California, southern Arizona, and south-central Texas south to Central America. Rare but regular in fall to East Coast.   *Larry R. Ballard*

Black-throated Sparrow

Amphispiza bilineata
This sparrow is common in arid regions of the southwestern interior in creosote habitats and desert scrub with cacti, north into Great Basin sage flats, and up into arid mountainous regions. These birds fly erratically, close to the ground, constantly calling, and often flicking the tail. Black-throated Sparrows are almost always found on or near the ground.

Description
4¾–5¼" (12–13.5 cm). Adults dark gray to brownish above, darker on crown and sides of head (or black anteriorly), becoming somewhat paler on sides and flanks. Wings and tail gray-brown to strongly brown; tail darker, even blackish. Bold white eyebrow often extends through eye; wide malar stripe also white. Middle of underparts varies from whitish to grayish. Outer tail feathers whitish. Juveniles similar but usually much browner, especially on back; more buff on wings and below; streaked below; lack black on throat; rest of adult face pattern present but often paler.

Adult

*1. Striking head
  pattern.*

*2. Brown upperparts
  with black streaks.*

Adult

*1. White underparts
  with black splotch on
  breast.*

*White on tail
feathers.*

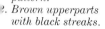

Adult

*1. Bold black-and-
  white facial pattern.*

2. Black throat.

3. Gray upperparts.

4. Whitish underparts.

Voice
Most songs and calls of high, soft, sharp, metallic, bell-like notes; songs vary from tinkling chatter to sweet, clear notes followed by a trill.

Similar Species
Juveniles similar to adult Sage Sparrow, but any dusky streaking below usually diffuse and confined to bib area, unlike well-defined streaking on Sage's sides (both can show central breast spot), or fine streaking on back. Sage has complete whitish eye-ring, much bolder than in Black-throated, and more conspicuous whitish wing bars. Sage Sparrows run on ground with tail carried high; frequent flicking of tail in perched birds more indicative of Sage. Calls nearly identical.

Range
Breeds from northeastern California to southwestern Wyoming and southeastern Colorado, south to central Mexico. Casual in Great Lakes and East. Winters in lower deserts in the southerly portion of United States range, south into Mexico.   *Scott B. Terrill*

Sage Sparrow

Amphispiza belli
Sage Sparrows are birds of open flatlands with scattered, low, sparse brush. They also occur in scrubby chaparral in California. Although they live where vegetation is minimal, Sage Sparrows can be inconspicuous. Their high, light call can be heard over a surprising distance, and is often the first clue to their presence. Sage Sparrows often run on the ground with the tail held cocked upward. While they perch they often flick the tail about conspicuously. These sparrows can disappear remarkably quickly into the sparse scrub. They will usually respond to spishing, however, flying from bush to bush until they are quite close to the observer. Males sing from exposed low perches.

Description
5–6″ (12.5–15 cm). The upperparts are gray with dark, fine streaking on the back, shading to brownish posteriorly. The white eyebrow and lower malar region contrast with the blackish lores and whisker mark. The sides and flanks are streaked with fine, very elongated spots, and there is a dark central spot on the whitish underparts that are often washed with brownish, buff, or gray, especially on the flanks. The tail is dark, contrasting sharply with the rest of the bird, with white in the outermost tail feathers, and tipped with white on the outer tail feathers. There are 2 varyingly conspicuous wing bars and a thin white eye-ring. Juveniles are heavily streaked above and below, with wings and tail like that of the adult; their facial pattern resembles that of the adult.

Voice
Song simple, clear, high-pitched, with 4–6 notes, the third note highest and accentuated. Call a high-pitched, sharp, musical, bell-like *tink* note, often rapidly repeated.

Similar Species
See immature Black-throated Sparrow.

Range
Breeds from southeastern Washington to northwestern Colorado; south to Baja California, northern Arizona, and northwestern New Mexico. Winters in southerly portions of range at low elevations. California coastal race resident.   *Scott B. Terrill*

Juvenile
1. *Bold facial pattern.*
2. *White throat.*
3. *Brownish upperparts.*
4. *Streaked underparts.*

Adult
1. *Gray-and-white face pattern.*
2. *White throat with dark whisker marks.*
3. *Streaked sides.*
4. *Whitish underparts with dark central spot on breast.*

Adult
1. *Dark lores and narrow white eye-ring.*
2. *Two wing bars.*

Five-striped Sparrow

Amphispiza quinquestriata
This infrequently seen bird is local in southeastern Arizona, where it is found on steep, arid, rocky hills with dense brush.

Description
5¾″ (14.5 cm). Very dark with white eyebrow, whisker, and throat stripes and triangular black whiskers. Rich, dark brownish-gray above, redder on back. Breast, sides, and flanks dark gray; midbelly whitish; breast has dark central spot. Juvenile like young Black-throated Sparrow but lacks bib streaking.

Voice
Songs extremely variable, but generally similar to those of Black-throated Sparrow. Call note a light, slightly metallic *tink*.

Similar Species
Black-throated Sparrow solidly black on throat, paler on breast, lacks central breast spot.

Range
Southeastern Arizona south into Mexico.   *Scott B. Terrill*

Lark Bunting

Calamospiza melanocorys
These striking black-and-white finches are found in prairies from south-central Canada to northern Texas. Sagebrush, grasslands, areas of predominantly low growth, and even areas of relatively barren earth characterize their habitat, much of which is shared with breeding Chestnut-collared and McCown's longspurs. The breeding male is a jet-black bird with a large white wing patch. Its song is a pleasant combination of clear notes, trills, and harsher notes. Often the song is given on the wing as the bird ascends rapidly to about 30 feet and circles slowly on splayed wings. Lark Buntings are gregarious and arrive on the breeding grounds in small flocks. Territory is not strongly developed, so that a number of males may be seen giving their flight song within a relatively small area. Female, juvenal, and winter male plumages are similar. Larger flocks, sometimes containing several hundred individuals, are formed in winter. Lark Buntings feed on the ground, taking seeds and insects, especially grasshoppers. They build their nests, which are fairly easy to find, in small depressions adjacent to short vegetation.

Description
7″ (18 cm). The breeding-plumage male is unmistakable: jet-black with a large white wing patch. Females have brownish upperparts with light, dusky streaking, a brownish cheek patch bordered above and below by a whitish line, and a hint of a wing patch. The underparts are whitish with conspicuous brownish streaks. The tail is distinctly rounded and has broad white corners. Immatures and males in winter plumage resemble the female, with indistinct buff or white wing patches, brownish cheek patches, and whitish underparts that show brown streaking. The rather large bill is usually dull silver-blue. Some males in winter have some blackish mottling on the underparts.

Voice
Varied series of spirited clear notes, trills, harsh notes; also a 2-note whistle.

Similar Species
Breeding-plumage male Bobolink has white patches on the back, a buff nape, and whitish rump. Females, juveniles, and winter males resemble streaked sparrows, but have brown cheek patch, larger

Adult
1. White eyebrow.
2. White whisker and throat.
3. Dark brown upperparts.
4. Dark gray underparts.

Southeastern Arizona only.

Female
1. Brownish cheek patch bordered by white.
2. Brownish streaked upperparts.
3. Whitish underparts with brown streaks.
4. Pale wing patch.

Winter male
1. Brownish cheek patch.
2. Brownish streaked upperparts.
3. Whitish underparts with brown streaks.
4. Bold white wing patch.

bill, hint of wing patch, and more rounded tail with white corners; are also larger.

Range
Breeds on Great Plains from south-central Canada to northern Texas; breeds sporadically on periphery of range. Winters in southern Arizona, New Mexico, and central Texas south to central Mexico. Very rare on West Coast; casual in East, primarily in fall.
Larry R. Ballard

Savannah Sparrow

Passerculus sandwichensis
The common Savannah Sparrow inhabits open, wet grasslands such as tundra, mountain meadows, marshes, streamsides, and grassy dunes. Dense cover is essential to this bird. It flies a short distance when flushed, quickly dropping out of sight into weedy cover. The Savannah Sparrow exhibits a fair degree of variation, especially between the different habitats it occupies, with 17 recognized races, many of which are migratory.

Description
5–6½" (12.5–16.5 cm). This small brown sparrow is streaked above and below, and has a short, slightly notched tail. The streaking on the underparts usually aggregates in the center of the breast to form a spot. There is a pale eyebrow, which is often yellow before the eye, and a pale median crown stripe. The legs are pinkish; the bill is dusky, and the lower mandible has a pale base. Races are distinguished on the basis of general coloration, bill and body size, and the coarseness and amount of streaking. The races most often seen closely fit the description above: some are grayer (e.g. *P. s. nevadensis* of the western interior) and some browner and darker. The darkest birds are resident in tidal marshes along the Pacific Coast from northern California south to Baja California; these have broader, blacker streaks, a longer bill, and are more noticeably yellow over the eye. Insular adaptation is seen in the large, pale race (*P. s. princeps*) that breeds on Cape Sable Island off Nova Scotia and winters in dunes along the Atlantic Coast. These birds have finer streaks, grayer upperparts, and a generally whitish eyebrow that shows pale yellow only after the anterior body molts in spring; the eyebrow wears to whitish in winter. The most distinctive forms are the marine littoral, large-billed races of the Gulf of California and Baja California; only 1 of these littoral races (*P. s. rostratus*) is known to occur in the United States. After breeding and in the winter it is a rare visitor to the Salton Sea. These birds are large, about the size of a House Finch, with rather plain backs and crowns; the yellow eyebrow is indistinct, and the large bill has a convexly curved culmen; they range from reddish-brown to grayish.

Voice
Song a buzzing trill preceded by a short series of high chips, sometimes ending with a few lower notes. Call a high thin *tsit*.

Breeding male
1. *Black head and body.*
2. *White wing patch.*

Often sings in flight.

Typical adult
1. *Yellow eyebrow.*
2. *Streaked upperparts.*
3. *Streaked underparts.*
4. *Short, notched tail.*

Thin tsit *call.*

Pacific Coast race
1. *Yellow above eye.*
2. *Broader streaks than typical form.*
3. *Longer bill than typical form.*

Similar Species
Vesper Sparrow has white outer tail feathers, evenly spaced stripes on underparts, dark cheek, thin white eye-ring, no pale median crown stripe. Song Sparrow longer with rounded tail, grayer about head, lacks yellow over eye. Lincoln's and Baird's sparrows are buff on breast or head.

Range
Found across North America. Breeds from Aleutian Islands, northern Alaska, to Labrador and Newfoundland; south to southern Baja California and northern Sinaloa, and in central Arizona, central Ohio, and southern New York. Resident from northern California south along Pacific Coast and Gulf of California. Winters from southwestern British Columbia (very casually as far north as central Alaska), central Arizona, across Gulf States, and Atlantic Coast from Nova Scotia (casually interiorly to Michigan) south to Honduras.   *Louis R. Bevier*

Baird's Sparrow

Ammodramus bairdii
Baird's Sparrow, relatively common in the northern plains, is probably more often sought by birders than any other sparrow. Males in the breeding season can be easily identified by their distinctive song despite their subtle plumage characteristics. Baird's lacks the flat-headed and short-tailed look characteristic of some sparrows. It is neither elusive nor secretive; it nests in lightly grazed pastures, undisturbed prairie, moist meadows, and drier rangeland.

Description
5–5½″ (12.5–14 cm). Aside from its unique song, this species' most distinctive attribute is the triangular area of dull orange or ocher on the crown and nape. Toward the forehead this area is narrow and difficult to see, but on the nape it is broader and more diffuse. The dull orange or ocher is pale and not always obvious; it is most easily seen from the back. Baird's also has 2 whisker marks and a spot on the back of the ear coverts behind the eye. The tail is of average length and is notched; the head has a rounded profile. A band or necklace of streaks across the breast is frequently mentioned in the literature, but is often entirely or largely absent in adults. Juveniles are similar to adults, but the crown stripe is paler and thinner, and there is more streaking on the sides.

Voice
Song a beautiful, musical, low-pitched trill preceded by 1–4 higher-pitched *zip* notes: *zip-zip-zip-zrr-r-r-r-r;* trill resembles end of House Wren's song. Call note a sharp *chip.*

Similar Species
Adult Henslow's and juvenile Grasshopper and Le Conte's sparrows have well-defined necklaces of streaks across breast; have shorter tail, flat-headed and larger-billed profile; lack ocher on crown.

Range
Breeds from southeastern Alberta, southern Saskatchewan, and southwestern Manitoba south to Montana and northern South Dakota. Winters from southeastern Arizona, southern New Mexico, and western and central Texas south to Mexico.   *Kim R. Eckert*

Cape Sable Island race
1. *Grayer upperparts than typical form.*
2. *Finer streaks than typical form.*
3. *Whitish eyebrow.*

Winters in coastal sand dunes.

Adult
1. *Dull ochre crown and nape.*
2. *Dark spot on ear coverts.*
3. *Two dark whisker marks.*
4. *Dark streaks on breast (often absent).*

Juvenile
1. *Ochre crown and nape less obvious than in adult.*
2. *More black on upperparts.*

Grasshopper Sparrow

Ammodramus savannarum
The Grasshopper Sparrow is a rather plain bird, with unstreaked underparts in the adult. It is found in grain fields, prairie grasslands, and weedy fields, usually in drier, upland grasses. During the breeding season, this species is normally cooperative for birders and is easily seen singing its insectlike buzz from a fence wire or weed stalk. It is also insectlike in its flight, which is usually short and weak, with rapid, buzzy wingbeats. In profile the Grasshopper Sparrow is flat-headed, large-billed, and short-tailed.

Description
4½–5¼" (11.5–13.5 cm). Grasshopper Sparrows have a conspicuously unmarked buff face, with plain buff ear coverts and no whisker marks; the "beady" black eye is prominent and obvious. The underparts are mostly buff-colored, without any streaking. The upperparts are streaked and buff-brown, with an overall buff tinge. At close range, the lores can be seen to be yellow, and there is a yellow spot at the bend of the wing. In immatures, the underparts are not as buff-colored, and there is diffuse streaking across the breast.

Voice
A thin, buzzy trill, sometimes preceded by an introductory note: *tic-zzzzzz*. Sometimes a trill followed by breezy, descending spiral of buzzes, similar to Sprague's Pipit's song: *tic-zzzzzz-zeeur-zeeur-zeer-zeer-zrr*.

Similar Species
Adult Henslow's similar to immature Grasshopper Sparrow but darker overall, with dark spot on ear coverts, whisker marks, olive head, and rust wings; breast streaks are more sharply defined. Clear-breasted immature Henslow's similar to adult Grasshopper Sparrow, but Grasshopper paler and more buff-colored overall; with unmarked face and lacks dingy olive head and rust-colored wings of Henslow's. Adult Le Conte's Sparrow has triangular gray patch on ear coverts, more extensive orange-buff on face, bluish-gray bill, and streaked sides and flanks; immature Le Conte's, like immature Grasshopper, also streaked on breast, but, like adult Le Conte's, has streaked sides and flanks and triangular gray ear patch. See Baird's Sparrow.

Range
Breeds from extreme southern Alberta, Saskatchewan, and Manitoba, and from Minnesota, Wisconsin, Michigan, and southern Ontario south to California, southeastern Arizona, Colorado, central Texas, Arkansas, central parts of Mississippi, Alabama, and Georgia, and Virginia and western Carolinas. Winters from central California (rare), southern Arizona, southern New Mexico, central Texas, southern Arkansas, Alabama, Georgia, and eastern North Carolina south to South America.   *Kim R. Eckert*

Adult, front view
1. *Unmarked buff face and underparts.*
2. *Prominent "beady" dark eye.*

Adult, side view
1. *Flat-headed profile.*
2. *Large bill.*
3. *Unstreaked underparts.*

Juvenile
1. *Less buff on underparts than in adult.*
2. *Diffuse streaking on breast.*

Henslow's Sparrow

Ammodramus henslowii
This bird has perhaps the most flat-headed profile of all sparrows, making its bill appear a few sizes too large. Henslow's is usually very difficult to find because of its local distribution and secretive nature. In addition, its habitat of fallow, weedy, often moist fields and meadows typically changes from year to year, and the bird's weak, ventriloqual song is easy to overlook and difficult to pinpoint.

Description
4¾–5¼″ (12–13.5 cm). In addition to its distinctive profile, Henslow's unique olive-colored head makes this bird relatively easy to identify. The wings are dull rust and there are sharply defined streaks on the buff breast and sides. Two whisker marks are present, as well as a dark smudge toward the back of the ear coverts. Juveniles are unstreaked, with extensive buff below, but they typically have an olive head and rust-colored wings like the adults.

Voice
A cricketlike, liquid, or metallic *tslit* or *tsi-lik;* audible only at relatively close range. Sometimes sings at night.

Similar Species
Immature Le Conte's has breast streaking and some rust in wing, like adult Henslow's, but is paler and more buff-colored like Grasshopper; lacks Henslow's olive head and has gray ear coverts. See Baird's Sparrow, which also has whisker marks and a smudge on ear coverts.

Range
Breeds from west-central and southeastern Minnesota, central Wisconsin, central Michigan, southern Ontario, and central New York south to northeastern Kansas, Missouri, Illinois, Indiana, central Ohio, and northern North Carolina. Very rare in New England, occurring primarily as transient. Winters in eastern Texas, Louisiana, southern parts of Mississippi, Alabama, and Georgia, and South Carolina and northern Florida.
Kim R. Eckert

Le Conte's Sparrow

Ammodramus leconteii
Although unfamiliar to most birders, Le Conte's Sparrows are relatively common and widespread in northern plains and bogs, where they breed in shallow prairie marshes, tall moist grasslands, and open fens in boreal forests. This short-tailed, flat-headed sparrow is not particularly elusive and is relatively easy to approach once its weak hissing song is learned. It sings erratically at any time of day or night, and is sometimes unpredictably silent, even at dawn.

Description
4½–5¼″ (11.5–13.5 cm). Le Conte's is a relatively colorful sparrow, with a buff or pale orange face and breast, gray ear coverts, a white median crown stripe, and a bluish bill. The sides are streaked; at close range dull pinkish streaks are visible on the nape. Juvenile Le Conte's also have a buff-and-gray face pattern, but are paler buff overall, with light streaking across the breast and a tinge of rust in the wings.

Adult
1. *Large bill.*
2. *Dull olive head with flat profile.*
3. *Dull rust wings.*
4. *Streaked breast and sides.*

Juvenile
1. *Unstreaked buff underparts.*
2. *Dull olive head.*
3. *Rust in wings.*

Adult
1. *Flat-headed profile.*
2. *Buff face and breast.*
3. *Gray ear coverts.*

Voice
A buzzy, 2-syllable hiss: *zzzz-zzt.* Often sings in early evening and at night.

Similar Species
Le Conte's face can be as orange as that of Sharp-tailed Sparrow, but Sharp-tailed lacks white median crown stripe. See Baird's and adult Henslow's sparrows. Grasshopper Sparrow lacks distinct dark streaks on flanks; immature has buff breast but lacks gray ear coverts of immature Le Conte's.

Range
Breeds from southern Mackenzie, central Manitoba, northern Ontario, and central Quebec south to northern Montana, North Dakota, northern parts of Minnesota, Wisconsin, and Michigan, and central Ontario. Casual in West and Northeast as migrant. Winters from eastern Oklahoma, southern Missouri, southern Illinois, Alabama, Georgia, and South Carolina south to Gulf Coast and central Florida.   *Kim R. Eckert*

Sharp-tailed Sparrow

Ammodramus caudacutus
Atlantic populations of the Sharp-tailed Sparrow are semicolonial inhabitants of extensive salt meadows along the seashore. Inland races occur in freshwater meadows and marshes. These birds run like mice, with their heads held low, periodically stopping and stretching their necks as they look around. When closely pursued, they flush and fly in a direct, buzzy fashion low over the grass, usually ending their flight with an ungraceful plunge into dense vegetation. As they fly, they seem to hold their heads high and their stubby tails low.

Description
5–5¾″ (12.5–14.5 cm). Although they can usually be recognized at species level, Sharp-tailed Sparrows show much racial variation. Inland birds are the richest buff below, with vague breast streaks and bold white streaks on the back. Atlantic coastal forms range in color from grayish above with indistinct breast streaking to dark above with sharply defined streaks both above and below. Typical adult Sharp-tailed Sparrows (*A. c. caudacutus*) have dark brown upperparts with conspicuous white or buff-white stripes on the back and no wing bars. The crown is dark brown (grayish in some races) and there is a broad, burnt-orange eyebrow stripe and face that contrasts with the gray ear coverts, making it appear as though a gray face is bordered with orange. Some races show a partial gray collar on the hindneck. The throat and underparts are white, except the upper breast, sides, and flanks, which are washed with buff and have blackish streaks. The extent of buff and streaking varies among the races. Juvenile Sharp-tailed Sparrows are very buff overall, resembling miniature female Bobolinks, but they generally show a semblance of the adult face pattern.

Voice
Song a short, raspy *te-sheeeeeeeee;* introductory note often inaudible at a distance. Resembles sound made as hot metal is plunged into water.

Similar Species
See Le Conte's and Seaside sparrows. Savannah Sparrow, which can occur in salt marshes, has white crown stripe, yellow lores, notched tail, and more zigzag flight.

Juvenile
1. Face and breast paler buff than in adult.
2. Streaked breast and sides.

Typical coastal form
1. Grayish crown.
2. Gray face bordered with orange.
3. Gray hindneck.
4. Distinct streaks on breast.

Inhabits salt marshes.

Inland form
1. Rich buff underparts with indistinct streaks on breast.
2. Gray collar on hindneck.
3. Bold white stripes on back.

Inhabits marshes.

Range
Breeds locally from southern Mackenzie, northeastern British
Columbia, central Saskatchewan, and central Manitoba south to
southern Alberta and North Dakota; James Bay; Atlantic Coast
from lower St. Lawrence Valley south to North Carolina. Winters
on Gulf Coast from southern Texas to Florida, and on the Atlantic
Coast from New York to southern Florida. Very small population
winters regularly on California coast. Casual elsewhere in
West.   *Wayne R. Petersen*

Seaside Sparrow

Ammodramus maritimus
The Seaside Sparrow is a dark, chunky bird with a large bill and a
short tail. It is found in Atlantic and Gulf Coast salt marshes. Its
weak, direct flight often terminates in a "crash landing" into dense
marsh grass or shrubbery near the edges of marshes, where it is
periodically forced to take refuge from high tides. It prefers rank
stands of *Spartina* grass along the borders of tidal creeks with
muddy bottoms. Several races of the Seaside Sparrow occur in
North America; 2 subspecies found in Florida, the "Cape Sable"
Seaside Sparrow and the "Dusky" Seaside Sparrow, were formerly
considered separate species. Bird watchers can often successfully
draw this species into view by making a squeaking noise on the back
of the hand.

Description
5¼–6½" (13.5–16.5 cm). Adults are olive-gray above with indistinct
light grayish stripes on the back. They lack wing bars and have a
bright yellow edge at the bend in the wing. There is a yellow patch
in front of the eye and a whitish jaw stripe that is bordered below by
a dusky whisker. The throat and underparts are whitish with blurry
grayish stripes on the breast, sides, and flanks. In late summer,
juveniles are browner above, with blackish streaks on the back; on
the breast, sides, and flanks, the streaked underparts have a buff
wash. There are several well-marked races of the Seaside Sparrow.
The most notable, the "Dusky" Seaside Sparrow (*A. m. nigrescens*)
of Merritt Island and the St. Johns River marshes in Florida, may
be nearly extinct. In this race the upperparts and ventral streaks
are nearly black. Another race is the "Cape Sable" Seaside Sparrow.
This olive-greenish subspecies occurs in the Cape Sable region of
extreme southern Florida. The population in this area, where the
"Cape Sable" is the only form of the Seaside Sparrow that occurs, is
very local and scarce.

Voice
Song a husky *tuptup zhe-eeeeeeee*, with strong emphasis on the *zhe*
and with pattern of Red-winged Blackbird's song; at a distance only
ending is audible. Frequently sings at dusk.

Similar Species
Sharp-tailed Sparrow smaller and browner, except for *subvirgatus*

Northern coastal form

1. Indistinct streaks on breast.

Typical adult

1. Yellow stripe in front of eye.
2. Pale jaw stripe.
3. Olive-gray upperparts.
4. Dusky streaks on underparts.

Found in salt marshes.

"Dusky" Seaside Sparrow

1. Blackish upperparts.
2. Blackish streaks on underparts:

Florida only.

race, which is grayish, with sharper back streaks and ocher face
pattern.

Range

Breeds along Atlantic Coast from Massachusetts south to northern
Florida and on Gulf Coast from southern Texas to central peninsular
Florida. Northern populations withdraw southward, wintering from
Virginia south to northern Florida and Gulf Coast; a few regularly
winter northward; very rare as far north as Nova Scotia.
Wayne R. Petersen

Fox Sparrow

Passerella iliaca
The Fox Sparrow is one of our largest sparrows and one of the most
varied geographically, in coloration, and in habitat. Eastern Fox
Sparrows have a bright rufous-red tail and a rusty head, back, and
wings. Those of the intermountain region have a less rufous tail and
show varying degrees of gray on the head and back. In some
intermountain races the head and back are nearly solid light gray.
West Coast birds tend to have a uniform dusky-brown tail, back,
and head. All races have dark breast streaking that is heavier than
that of most other sparrows. Close examination shows that many of
the individual blotches that form the streaks are shaped like
inverted Vs. The streaks usually converge on the upper breast,
forming a central spot. These birds are inconspicuous, except when
males deliver their song from exposed perches. They spend much of
their time digging through understory litter in towhee fashion,
kicking both feet backward simultaneously. In general, Fox
Sparrows do not stray far from the dense undergrowth associated
with hedgerows, ditches, and streamsides. However, many Fox
Sparrows in Canada, Alaska, and in areas with high-elevation
mountains associate with stunted coniferous, coniferous-edge,
parkland, and willow habitats.

Description

6¼–7½" (16–19 cm). The eastern race has a rufous-red tail and a
rust head, back, and wings. In the intermountain races, the tail is
less rufous and the head and upper back are gray in varying degrees
(some are nearly solid light gray). West Coast races are uniform
dusky-brown. All forms possess heavy breast streaking, heavier
than most other sparrows; the streaks consist of blotches shaped like
inverted Vs that usually converge, forming a central breast spot.
The wing bars are inconspicuous.

Voice

Song very melodious and musical; usually begins with introductory
whistle followed by series of sliding notes, whistles, and slurs; notes
are clearer and more whistled than those of Song Sparrow. Birds
with rufous-red tail usually have 1 song type that is repeated.
Western and Alaskan birds have 3 or more song types; they
alternate them in a fixed, sequential manner, presenting each once.
Calls are a variety of typical *clicks* and *chips*.

Juvenile
. *Brown upperparts
with black streaks.*
. *Streaked buff
underparts.*

Eastern race
. *Rust on head, back,
and wings.*
. *Rufous-red tail.*
. *Heavy streaks on
breast.*

Intermountain race
. *Grayish head and
upper back.*
. *Less rufous in tail
than eastern race.*
. *Heavy streaks on
breast.*

Similar Species
In East, Hermit Thrush is more olive-brown on back and has
thinner bill. In West, all brown thrushes are thin-billed and spotted
on breast, not streaked; most thrushes have eye-ring.

Range
Breeds from northern Alaska and Yukon across central Canada to
Newfoundland and south through Rockies into Colorado; throughout
intermountain region south to Nevada and through Cascades and
Sierra Nevada to southern California. Winters from southern
British Columbia along coast into Baja California. Inland and
eastern birds winter across southern Great Basin, southwestern
deserts, and from southern Kansas, Wisconsin, Michigan, Ontario,
and New Brunswick south to Gulf Coast and Florida.
Dennis J. Martin

Song Sparrow

Melospiza melodia
This common bird is a permanent resident in many areas, while in
others it arrives early in the spring and often departs late in the fall.
It usually prefers thickets, woodland edges, hedgerows, pond
margins, and weedy fields with adjacent brush for cover. It has a
peculiar way of pumping its longish, rounded tail as it flies.

Description
5¾–7″ (14.5–18 cm). Much regional variation: birds from the
Aleutians are the largest, with huge bills and olive to ash-gray
upperparts. Individuals from most populations exhibit the same
basic pattern: adults have brown upperparts and tail, with black and
grayish streaks and 2 vague whitish wing bars. The crown is brown
with a narrow gray stripe and buff or grayish ear coverts; there is a
broad grayish stripe over the eye. The underparts are whitish,
streaked on the breast, sides, and flanks with dark brown or black;
on the breast, the streaks form a dark spot. The white throat has a
heavy blackish mustache. Fall and winter birds are generally
washed with buff below and on the head; the ventral stripes are
more diffuse. Late summer and fall juveniles are yellowish-white
below with thin crisp breast streaks and usually no central spot.

Voice
Song begins with clear notes, *sweet sweet sweet*, then a trill,
dropping in pitch; highly variable. Call note a unique *chimp*.

Similar Species
Savannah Sparrow has short, notched tail, white crown stripe,
yellow in front of eye, sharp breast streaks that do not usually form
a spot, and pinker legs. See Lincoln's Sparrow. Swamp Sparrow has
grayish breast with finer streaks, grayer cheeks and collar, grayer
eyebrow; slightly smaller overall, with broad black streaks on back;
call different.

Range
Aleutian, southern Alaska, and southern Yukon to Newfoundland,
south to northern Mexico and New Mexico, northeastern Kansas,
northern Arkansas and Georgia, and northwestern South Carolina.
Winters from southern Alaska and southern Canada to southern
United States and northern Mexico.   *Wayne R. Petersen*

West Coast race
1. *Dusky head and back.*
2. *Heavy streaks on breast.*

Adult
1. *Brown streaks on upperparts.*
2. *Heavy streaks on underparts.*

   Dark spot on breast. Pumps tail in flight. Chimp call note.

Aleutian race
1. *Long, thin bill.*
2. *Olive or ash-gray upperparts.*

   Large size.

Lincoln's Sparrow

Melospiza lincolnii
In summer, this bird inhabits cool northern bogs and brushy wet meadows. But in migration, it can be found in weedy potato fields and brush piles, along tangled stream banks, and even in gardens. This skulker can sometimes be attracted by loudly kissing the back of one's hand; the bird then continually twitches and flits, and may elevate its crown feathers. In the West, Lincoln's is comparatively easy to see, especially in winter. It often pumps its tail, although without the energy of the Song Sparrow.

Description
5¼–6" (13.5–15 cm). Lincoln's resembles the Song Sparrow, but is slimmer, and its eyebrow stripe, ear coverts, and sides of the neck are lighter gray. The partial gray collar is broken only by the brown hindneck. There is usually a narrow, distinct white eye-ring. The light brown crown is streaked with black and has a gray median stripe; the upperparts are grayish-olive with 2 indistinct wing bars. The throat and underparts are white; a broad band of buff across the breast extends down to the sides and flanks. Within the buff areas there are thin black streaks that occasionally converge into a central spot. Juveniles in late summer resemble juvenile Song and Swamp sparrows but usually have a spotted chin and throat.

Voice
Song has gurgling quality and harmonics of Purple Finch's song: *kee kee kee, see see, see-dle see-dle see-dle, see-see-see-see;* starts low, rises, then drops. Call note a low, hard *tsup*, often repeated.

Similar Species
Immature Swamp Sparrow has unspotted throat, darker chestnut wings, and blacker crown; caution is advised. See Song Sparrow.

Range
Northwestern Alaska east to central Labrador and Newfoundland; south in mountains to southern California, central Arizona, and northern New Mexico, and from southern Manitoba to northern New England and Nova Scotia. Winters from Washington (uncommon), central Arizona, and central Missouri to Gulf Coast and Guatemala. Casual in North and Northeast.   *Wayne R. Petersen*

Swamp Sparrow

Melospiza georgiana
The dark, rust-colored Swamp Sparrow is common in open freshwater cattail marshes, brushy wet meadows, bogs, and swamps with tussock sedges (*Carex*). It delivers its ringing song from exposed perches, making it easy to find on the breeding grounds. But in migration it prefers dense cover and weedy growth, and it is more difficult to observe. In winter it frequents springs, seeps, and open brooks where it finds abundant nearby cover.

Description
5–5¾" (12.5–14.5 cm). Adults in breeding plumage have a chestnut crown, gray eyebrow stripe, dusky eyeline, and grayish face and sides of the neck. The upperparts are reddish-brown and broadly streaked with black. The wings are dark chestnut and lack wing bars, and the rump and shortish tail are brown. Below, the throat and belly are whitish and there is a broad gray breastband that extends to the sides and becomes a brownish wash on the flanks. The gray breast is sometimes finely streaked with black, the streaks

Adult
1. *Gray eyebrow, ear coverts, and sides of neck.*
2. *Grayish-olive upperparts.*

   Furtive behavior.

Adult
1. *Narrow white eye-ring.*
2. *Finely streaked breast and flanks with buff wash.*

Immature
. *Unspotted throat.*
. *Blackish crown stripes.*
. *Dark chestnut on wings.*

occasionally forming a vague dusky central spot. Winter adults and immatures have browner crowns with a slim, pale median stripe. Late summer juveniles resemble juvenile Lincoln's Sparrows, but have unspotted throats, darker chestnut wings, and blacker crowns.

Voice
Song a loud, metallic, even-pitched *weet-weet-weet-weet-weet.* Call note a sharp *chink;* resembles that of White-throated Sparrow.

Similar Species
Chipping Sparrow has longer tail, whiter eyebrow stripe, and different habitat. Tree and Field sparrows have conspicuous wing bars. See immature Song, Lincoln's, and White-throated sparrows.

Range
Breeds from Mackenzie and northeastern British Columbia east to Newfoundland, southeast from central Alberta to northern Missouri, central Ohio, Maryland, and Delaware. Winters from eastern Nebraska, Iowa, and southern Wisconsin through southern Great Lakes Basin to central New York and from Massachusetts to southern Texas, Gulf Coast, and Florida.   *Wayne R. Petersen*

White-throated Sparrow

Zonotrichia albicollis
The plaintive whistle of this sparrow is a familiar sound in northern coniferous forests, clearings, and bushy openings. Sluggish and abundant, this bird is often encountered in migration as it noisily scratches in dry leaves deep within dense cover; its presence is also revealed by the soft *tseet* notes given by a flock.

Description
6½–7¼" (16.5–18.5 cm). Adults have chestnut-brown upperparts that are streaked with black, a brown rump and tail, and 2 white wing bars. The tail is notched. These birds are polymorphic; thus their heads may have either broad black-and-white or tan-and-brown stripes, usually with obvious yellow lores. Also characteristic is a large, prominent white throat patch that contrasts with a gray breast, whitish belly, and obscurely streaked olive flanks. The bill is dark. In the fall, immatures have grayish throats that lack the sharp definition shown in adults; they often lack the yellow lores, and may have thin streaks of dark brown on the gray breast. Although most immatures have tan crown stripes, in some these are whitish.

Voice
Song a series of 2 clear notes followed by 3-note phrase repeated 3 times: *sow wheat peverly, peverly, peverly;* easily mimicked. Call note a loud *chink;* also a thin, high, drawn-out *tseet* or *tseep.*

Similar Species
See White-crowned Sparrow. Immature Swamp Sparrow similar to young White-throated Sparrow but smaller and darker, with rounded, not notched, tail; has gray collar and lacks head striping.

Range
Breeds from southern Yukon to southern Labrador and Newfoundland, south to central British Columbia, east to central Michigan, northeastern Pennsylvania, and Massachusetts. Winters from northern California, southern Arizona, southern New Mexico, eastern Kansas, Illinois, southern Ontario, Ohio, central New York, Massachusetts, and Nova Scotia south to southern Texas, Gulf Coast, and central Florida. Winters casually into southern Canada; regular in small numbers in West during fall and winter. Also winters in northern Mexico.   *Wayne R. Petersen*

Adult
1. *Chestnut crown.*
2. *Gray face.*
3. *White throat.*
4. *Gray breast.*
5. *Reddish-brown upperparts.*

Swampy habitats.

White-striped adult
1. *Black and white head stripes.*
2. *Yellow lores.*
3. *White throat patch.*
4. *Gray breast.*

Loud chink call.

Tan-striped adult
1. *Black and tan head stripes.*
2. *Yellow lores.*
3. *White throat patch.*
4. *Gray breast.*

Golden-crowned Sparrow

Zonotrichia atricapilla
The Golden-crowned Sparrow is a dark, handsome western bird that breeds at timberline in mountains and, in Alaska, in shrub thickets along the seacoast.

Description
6–7″ (15–18 cm). Adults in breeding plumage have a dark bill and a relatively long tail. They are fairly large, with a dull gold crown patch broadly bordered at the sides and forehead with jet black. The rest of the head and breast are dark gray, and there is a thin, inconspicuous white eye-ring. Adults in winter are similar, but have a slightly duller head pattern. Immatures also have a long tail and dark bill, but their finely streaked brown crown is suffused with dull yellow at the forehead.

Voice
Song distinctive, with 3 clear whistled descending notes: *gol-den-crown;* in some populations, middle note is lowest. Call a thin *seet,* also a sharp *chink.*

Similar Species
See White-crowned Sparrow.

Range
Breeds on coast from Seward Peninsula to Kenai Peninsula, Alaska; in mountains from central and southeastern Alaska and southern Yukon Territory south to southern British Columbia, western Alberta, and northernmost Washington. Winters from Kodiak Island, Alaska, east and south, primarily west of Coast and Cascade ranges and Sierra Nevada, through British Columbia and Pacific states to northern Baja California. Casual in East.
Daniel D. Gibson

White-crowned Sparrow

Zonotrichia leucophrys
The White-crowned Sparrow breeds in a variety of shrubby habitats. Common in much of the North, especially in western regions, it often nests in residential areas. There are several different races that have distinctive plumage differences and song dialects.

Description
5½–7″ (14–18 cm). Adults are fairly large, with a relatively long tail, a pale, dusky-tipped bill (ranging from pink to yellow, according to geographical variation), and a bold black-and-white head pattern. The rest of the head, neck, and breast are immaculate gray. Western birds tend to have dark lores, while populations from the Rockies and Great Basin area and eastern populations have pale lores. Juveniles also have a pale bill, but their head is patterned in cinnamon-brown and buff.

Voice
Song geographically variable. Call a high, thin *seet.*

Adult
1. *Dull gold crown.*
2. *Broad black eyebrow.*
3. *Long tail.*

Large size. Slender build.

Juvenile
1. *Dull yellow on forehead.*
2. *Finely streaked crown.*

Adult
1. *Pale bill.*
2. *Black-and-white head pattern.*
3. *Immaculate gray face, neck, and breast.*
4. *Long tail.*

Similar Species
Golden-crowned Sparrow larger with darker bill; duskier overall and
darker below; immature lacks well-defined head striping, has faint
tinge of yellow on forecrown.

Range
Breeds from northern and western Alaska east across subarctic
Canada to northern Quebec and Labrador, south to south-central
California, Nevada, central Arizona, northern New Mexico, central
Manitoba, and northern Ontario. Winters along Pacific Coast from
southern Alaska to Mexico, east to southeastern Washington,
southern Idaho, Wyoming, Kansas, Missouri, Kentucky, and
Maryland, and south to Gulf States and Mexico. Uncommon migrant
in Northeast.   *Daniel D. Gibson*

Harris' Sparrow

Zonotrichia querula
On the southern Great Plains in winter, the big, boldly patterned
Harris' Sparrow may be found in flocks of up to several dozen
individuals, feeding on the ground along woodlot borders and
hedgerows. When disturbed, the birds call sharply as they fly into
the bushes, often perching in the open to look back at the intruder.
Winter strays frequently turn up at feeders in the East and with
flocks of White-crowned Sparrows in the West. For the breeding
season, these birds retire to subarctic central Canada, where their
simple but haunting song is heard at clearings in the spruce woods.

Description
7½″ (19 cm). In all plumages, the large size, pink bill, striped brown
back, and bright white underparts with streaking on the flanks mark
the Harris' Sparrow. The adult has a black patch that surrounds the
bill, extends back to the eye and onto the crown, and forms a bib on
the throat and upper chest; the rest of the face is gray. The
immature's buff head often has traces of the adult's face pattern.

Voice
Song a series of 2–3 long, clear whistles in minor key; after long
pause, next song may be at same or different pitch. Call note *jeenk*
or *zheenk*, not as sharp as similar notes of White-crowned and
White-throated sparrows. In flocks, a rolling *chug-up, chug-up*. Like
other *Zonotrichia* sparrows, may sing in winter.

Similar Species
Winter Lapland Longspur resembles immature in pattern but has
shorter tail, sharply defined ear patch, and white on outer tail
feathers; lives in barren, open fields.

Range
Breeds in central Canada west of Hudson Bay (Northwest
Territories, northern Manitoba). Winters primarily along eastern
edge of Great Plains; center of abundance is in eastern Kansas, but
occurs north to South Dakota and southern Minnesota (sparsely to
North Dakota) and south to south-central Texas. Apparently
winters regularly in very small numbers in parts of interior West
and Southwest. Stragglers reach both Pacific and Atlantic seaboards
virtually every year.   *Kenn Kaufman*

Juvenile
. *Pale bill.*
. *Cinnamon-brown and buff head stripes.*

Adult
. *Pink bill.*
. *Black mask and throat.*
. *White underparts, with streaks on flanks.*

Large size.

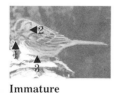

Immature
. *Pink bill.*
. *Buff head.*
. *White underparts, with streaks on flanks.*

Large size.

Dark-eyed Junco

Junco hyemalis
Juncos are conspicuous, unstreaked, and somewhat chunky
sparrows that forage on the ground. Unlike many other sparrows,
they do not scratch in the leaf litter, but pick exposed seeds and
insects from the surface. In spring and summer they are common to
abundant breeding birds in northern or mountain forests of conifers,
birches, and aspen, where they prefer edges and openings rather
than the deep interior of the forest. They hop among the leaves on
the forest floor, flying up into trees when disturbed, showing their
white outer tail feathers and giving alarm notes. On the breeding
grounds they become very agitated when an intruder is near a nest,
flying about close by and uttering alarm notes. During the autumn
and winter months, they gather in flocks and forage in fields, along
woodland edges, and in brushy areas, and are frequent and familiar
visitors to feeding stations throughout most of the United States
and southern Canada. The Dark-eyed Junco includes several rather
distinct races or groups of races that were formerly considered to be
separate species but which, because they interbreed freely where
their ranges come into contact, are all now treated as a single
species that is geographically highly variable. The English names of
these former species are still used to refer to these identifiable forms
of the Dark-eyed Junco. The most widespread form, the "Slate-
colored" Junco, is a common breeding bird in the boreal forest,
where its musical trill is one of the most frequently heard bird
songs. The "White-winged" Junco inhabits the ponderosa pine
forests of the Black Hills and neighboring parts of the northern
Great Plains. The "Oregon" Junco breeds in coniferous forests in the
far West, usually in the mountains, but reaching sea level in the
redwood forests as far south as Monterey, California. "Pink-sided"
Juncos breed in the northern Rockies, not only in coniferous forests
but also in extensive aspen groves. The "Gray-headed" Junco
inhabits the southern Rockies west to eastern California and breeds
readily in aspen groves as well as in coniferous forest.

4

Description
5–6½" (12.5–16.5 cm). Dark-eyed Juncos of all subspecies have pink
bills, white outer tail feathers, white bellies, and dark eyes. The rest
of the plumage varies geographically. The following are the 5 forms
of this species that may be distinguished in the field.
1. The "Slate-colored" Junco (*J. h. hyemalis, J. h. cismontanus,*
and *J. h. carolinensis*) has a dark gray head, back, breast, sides and
flanks. Some immatures, adult females, and adult males have buff on
the back, especially in the fall.
2. The "White-winged" Junco (*J. h. aikeni*) is similar to the "Slate-
colored," but has more extensive white in the tail; most birds have 2
white wing bars (hence the name "White-winged"), but the wing
bars are lacking in some individuals, and may appear in juncos of
other races (especially in the "Oregon" Junco).
3. The male of the "Oregon" Junco (*J. h. oreganus, J. h. thurberi,*
and other races) has a black hood, a sharply contrasting brown back,
and pink sides and flanks. Females of this group are similar but have
grayer hoods.
4. The "Pink-sided" Junco (*J. h. mearnsi*) has broad pink sides and
flanks, a pale gray head and breast, dark lores, and a dull, grayish-
brown back. There is no distinct contrast between the hood and
back, and in this race the sexes are alike.
5. "Gray-headed" Juncos (*J. h. caniceps* and *J. h. dorsalis*) have
bright reddish-brown backs, light gray heads, breasts, and sides,
and dark lores. The sexes are alike. In Arizona and New Mexico,
the breeding birds (*J. h. dorsalis*) have a dark upper mandible.

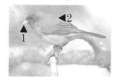

Female "Slate-colored" Junco
1. *Pink bill.*
2. *Buff tinge on gray back.*

Male "Slate-colored" Junco
1. *Pink bill.*
2. *Gray head, back, and breast.*
3. *White belly.*
4. *White outer tail feathers.*

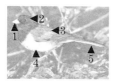

"Oregon" Junco
1. *Pink bill.*
2. *Black hood.*
3. *Brown back.*
4. *Pinkish sides.*
5. *White outer tail feathers.*

Because of interbreeding, intermediates between many of these
distinct forms of the Dark-eyed Junco are often seen in the field.
Such unusually plumaged individuals may be conspicuous in
wintering flocks in the West, when many populations mingle. These
puzzling birds are often impossible to assign with certainty to any of
the 5 well-marked forms of the species, and must simply be called
Dark-eyed Juncos. Juveniles of all races of the species have streaked
breasts.

Voice
A simple trill of constant pitch, more musical than that of the
Chipping Sparrow. Rarely, there is an abrupt change of pitch in the
middle of the trill. Call and alarm notes: *tic, ti-ti-tic; chek.*

Similar Species
Conical, pinkish-beige bill and white outer tail feathers make juncos
easy to distinguish from other birds of similar size. Yellow-eyed
Juncos have yellow eyes. Vesper and Lark sparrows also have white
outer tail feathers but have streaked backs and occur in more open
habitats.

Range
Breeds throughout boreal and mountainous coniferous forests of
North America. "Slate-colored" race breeds from Alaska to eastern
Canada, south to central prairie provinces, northeastern United
States, and south in Appalachians to Georgia. "White-winged"
Juncos breed in Black Hills of South Dakota and in adjacent
ponderosa pine forests of southeastern Montana, northeastern
Wyoming, and northwestern Nebraska. "Oregon" Juncos breed from
British Columbia east to northwestern Montana and south to
southern California. "Pink-sided" Juncos breed in mountains from
eastern Idaho to southeastern Alberta and southwestern
Saskatchewan (Cypress Hills) south to northern Utah and southern
Wyoming. "Gray-headed" Juncos breed in mountains of eastern
California (uncommonly) and Nevada east to Colorado and south to
central Arizona and New Mexico. "Slate-colored" Juncos winter
from southern Canada south to California (uncommonly), Texas, and
Florida. Western races form mixed wintering flocks from West
Coast east to western Great Plains; "Gray-headed" and "Pink-sided"
rare on West Coast north of Los Angeles.
George F. Barrowclough

Yellow-eyed Junco

Junco phaeonotus
This abundant, ground-dwelling junco is a resident of pine and
boreal forests at elevations above 7000 feet. These tame birds walk
as well as hop. In winter, they do not wander widely and are not
usually found in mixed flocks with other juncos.

Description
6½" (16.5 cm). Similar to "Gray-headed" Junco but with yellow eyes.
Upper mandible black; lower pale yellow. Upperwing coverts
reddish-brown. Juvenile has dark eye, streaked breast.

Voice
Song a combination of short trills and whistles; individual variation
makes identification difficult; important characteristic is
juxtaposition of trills and notes. Call notes similar to Dark-eyed
Junco's.

Range
Resident in pine-oak and coniferous forest from Se. Arizona and Sw.
New Mexico south to Guatemala.   *George F. Barrowclough*

"Pink-sided" Junco
1. *Pink bill.*
2. *Gray head and breast.*
3. *Broad pink sides.*
4. *White outer tail feathers.*

"Gray-headed" Junco
1. *Pink bill.*
2. *Dark eyes.*
3. *Gray head, breast, and sides.*
4. *Reddish-brown back.*

Hops on ground.

Adult
1. *Yellow eye.*
2. *Gray head.*
3. *Reddish-brown back.*

White outer tail feathers.
Walks on ground.

McCown's Longspur

Calcarius mccownii
The longspurs (genus *Calcarius*) form a distinctive group of 4
chunky, ground-dwelling finches of open country. Males in breeding
plumage all have bright patterns. But when flocks come south in
winter plumage, obscurely marked in brown and gray, longspurs can
be difficult to identify. For that matter, they can be difficult to see
well: the birds creep slowly over the ground, and it is a challenge to
spot them before approaching too closely and scaring them away.
Alarmed, the flocks make off in high, undulating flight. Winter
longspurs are best identified by habitat preference, diagnostic flight
calls, shape, and tail pattern, supplemented by other plumage
characteristics. McCown's is the longspur that haunts barren
ground. Breeding and wintering primarily on the Great Plains, its
range broadly overlaps that of the Chestnut-collared Longspur, but
everywhere McCown's favors more open ground: dry short-grass
prairies, overgrazed pastures, dry lake beds, and plowed fields. In
winter it often mixes with Horned Larks and sometimes with
Lapland Longspurs. Although winter concentrations may number in
the hundreds, overall McCown's is not a common bird.

Tail

5

Description
6″ (15 cm). McCown's Longspur has a large bill that looks swollen at
the base of the lower mandible. Its tail is short, with the central pair
of feathers brownish-black, the outermost pair mainly white, and
the remainder white with black tips, creating the effect of a black
inverted T on a white tail. In breeding plumage the male has a
silvery-gray head with a black cap and whisker. A black crescent
crossing the upper chest is variable in width, sometimes covering
the entire breast; the sides are gray and the belly is white. The back
is brown with black stripes, the rump is gray, and the wings are
brown with some paler edgings and with rufous lesser and median
coverts; these coverts are sometimes concealed by scapular feathers.
The bill is mostly black. Females are sandy-brown above with black
streaks, buff-gray on the chest and sides, with the center of the
lower breast and belly white; they usually are slightly rufous on the
shoulder, and their bills are pale with black tips. Winter males are
much like females but some of the black chest patch often shows
through the overlying pale feather edgings. Winter birds are
generally the plainest and palest of longspurs.

Voice
Song in display flight a rapid, twittering warble. Call notes: *poik* or
pwoik with odd ringing quality; a hard *kittip;* or a rattle, weaker
than that of Lapland Longspur. Flocks in alarm give harsh buzzing
note.

Similar Species
Lapland and Smith's longspurs have less white in tail. See Chestnut-
collared Longspur. All 3 have smaller bills.

Range
Breeds from southern Alberta east to North Dakota and south to
Colorado. Winters mainly from Arizona east to Oklahoma and Texas
and south into northern Mexico. Rare west to California, accidental
east to Atlantic Coast. *Kenn Kaufman*

Breeding male
1. *Black cap.*
2. *White throat.*
3. *Black breastband.*
4. *Rufous shoulders.*
5. *Black-and-white tail pattern.*

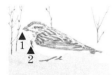

Female
1. *Large bill.*
2. *Sandy-brown upperparts with dark streaks.*
3. *Buff-gray chest and sides.*
4. *Rufous on shoulder.*
5. *Short tail with much white.*

Winter male
1. *Large bill.*
2. *Trace of black chest patch.*

Palest winter longspur.
Ringing pwoik *call.*
Dry kittip *call.*

Lapland Longspur

Tail

◄5

Calcarius lapponicus
By far the most numerous and widespread of the longspurs, this
bird breeds in tundra and coastal areas of the far North. In winter it
is found in open fields (either in short grass or on bare ground), and
on lakeshores and beaches, often in the company of Horned Larks or
Snow Buntings.

Description
6¼" (16 cm). In all plumages the tail pattern is distinctive, with less
white than other longspurs have; the white is not always apparent,
even when the bird flushes at close range. The outer 2 pairs of tail
feathers are white, but very dark at the base and on the outer
edges, and there is often some white toward the tip of the next pair
inward. In breeding plumage, the male has a black crown, face,
throat, and upper chest, with a white stripe behind the eye and
down behind the ear coverts, setting off the rufous-chestnut nape.
The underparts are white, with black streaking on the sides and
flanks; the back is buff with heavy black streaks, and the wings are
blackish with most of the feathers extensively edged with buff or
white. In summer, females have the crown streaked with buff and
black, a buff eyebrow, a brown ear patch with a blackish outline, a
partial rufous collar across the nape, and a variable amount of black
on the throat and neck; the upperparts and underparts are
otherwise patterned like those of the male. Winter males resemble
summer-plumage females. Females in winter and immatures may
lack the rufous on the nape and black smudging on the neck, and
may be slightly buff-colored on the chest with fine streaking, but
continue to have a sharply defined dark ear patch and white lower
underparts. Many winter birds of both sexes have extensive rufous
in the wings on the edges of the greater coverts, tertials, and
secondaries.

Voice
Song, often delivered in display flight, a slurring warble with rich
organlike quality. Flight calls (also delivered on ground) a rough 3-
syllabled rattle, *trididit*, and descending *teew;* these calls often given
in sequence.

Similar Species
Several other field birds have white in tail, but Horned Lark and
pipits are thin-billed, Vesper Sparrow heavily streaked below.
McCown's and Chestnut-collared longspurs have much more white
in tail. Smith's Longspur more buff-colored below, has more clean-
cut white outer tail feathers, often has white shoulder patch, never
has black smudging on neck nor obvious rufous on nape or wings;
flight call recognizably different.

Range
Breeds throughout tundra regions of Alaska and Canada, including
most islands. Winters from coast to coast and from extreme
southern Canada south to central Texas, but rare on most of Pacific
slope and in Southwest and casual in Southeast; most abundant on
southern Great Plains. Widespread in Eurasia.   *Kenn Kaufman*

Breeding male
1. *Black face and throat.*
2. *Chestnut nape.*
3. *White stripe on side of head and neck.*
4. *White underparts.*
5. *Reduced white in tail.*

Winter female
1. *Streaked, buff crown.*
2. *Dark ear patch.*
3. *Buff tinge to streaked breast.*
4. *Rufous in wing coverts.*

Rough trididit *and* teew *calls.*

Breeding female
1. *Buff eyebrow.*
2. *Brown ear patch with blackish outline.*
3. *Rufous on nape.*
4. *Blackish on throat and breast.*

Smith's Longspur

Tail

◀3

Calcarius pictus
This rather uncommon bird winters very locally on the eastern edge of the southern Great Plains in areas of short grass; in migration, flocks may feed in stubble fields. This species breeds near the tree line. It often sings from the tops of low, isolated spruce clumps on the tundra. Unlike other longspurs, Smith's does not typically sing in flight.

Description
6″ (15 cm). Bill proportionately longer, thinner, than those of other longspurs. In all plumages, 2 outer pairs of tail feathers mostly white. Breeding male has black crown, white eyebrow and lores, and bold black triangular ear patch with large white center. Throat, breast, and collar bright buff, paler on belly; flanks have some fine streaks. Back and wings blackish-brown with paler edgings. Lesser coverts white; dark centers of median coverts form small patch (sometimes concealed). Female has blackish crown and back with buff-olive feather edgings; pale face has vague dark outline around ear patch; buff below with fine brown streaks on chest; may have some white on shoulder. Immatures and winter males similar to female; winter males may be warmer buff below, more likely to have white on shoulder.

Voice
Song suggests Chestnut-sided Warbler but has wheezy undertone: *switoo-whideedeedew, whee-tew.* Call a fine dry rattle, lighter and more metallic than Lapland's and usually with more elements.

Similar Species
Other field birds have clean-cut white outer tail feathers, but pipits and Horned Lark have thin bills and Vesper Sparrow has strongly streaked breast. See Lapland and Chestnut-collared longspurs.

Range
Breeds locally near tree line from central Alaska east to northern Ontario. Winters mainly in Oklahoma, western Arkansas, northeastern Texas, and northwestern Louisiana; also sparsely north and east. In migration ranges a little farther east, at least to Indiana. Accidental east to Atlantic Coast.   *Kenn Kaufman*

Chestnut-collared Longspur

Tail

◀4

Calcarius ornatus
Of all the longspurs, the Chestnut-collared is the smallest and the one with the most distinctive flight call. It breeds and winters on the prairies of the interior, and favors areas of taller grasses than those chosen by other longspurs. Its winter flocks rarely mix with other species.

Description
5½″ (14 cm). The outermost pair of tail feathers is nearly all white; the next pair inward is dark at the tip, and the dark area increases with each pair inward to the central tail feathers, which are all dark. The effect produced is of a dark triangle on a white tail. In breeding plumage the male has a buff-white face with a black crown, a black line behind the eye and another below the ear patch, and a broad rufous-chestnut collar across the nape. The underparts are mostly black, sometimes with chestnut mixed in, and the lower belly and undertail coverts are white. The upperparts are brown, with black streaks on the back. The female is mostly buff-colored with fine dark

Breeding male
1. Black-and-white head pattern.
2. Buff-orange underparts.
3. White outer tail feathers.

Female
1. Streaked buff underparts.
2. White shoulders.

Rattling flight call.

Breeding male
1. Buff-white face.
2. Chestnut collar.
3. Black breast.
4. Black-and-white tail pattern.

streaking on the crown, heavy blackish-brown streaking on the
back, and some rufous-chestnut across the nape, which may be
obscured by buff feather tips in winter. Many females have some
black mottling on the underparts. Males in winter have the pattern
largely obscured by buff feather tips, but some of the chestnut collar
and black breast can usually be seen. The plainest winter immatures
lack any chestnut on the nape and are entirely buff below. Some
winter birds have white on the lesser wing coverts.

Voice
Song (often in display flight) a short, rich warble. Flight call a
musical *cheedup* or *cheedlup;* also a weak, rather sibilant rattle of
3–5 syllables.

Similar Species
Winter birds can be confused with Smith's Longspur (because of
buff underparts and occasional presence of white shoulder mark) but
Chestnut-collared paler above with much more white in tail.
McCown's Longspur sometimes claimed to be sighted among
Chestnut-collared flocks on basis of rattle calls and tail patterns,
which may be difficult to discern in field. McCown's noticeably larger
and paler; has much larger bill that appears somewhat swollen at
base of lower mandible. Most winter McCown's have at least a trace
of rufous or tawny on shoulder. In flight McCown's appears to have
broad-based wings, emphasizing short tail. Flight calls helpful in
distinguishing species.

Range
Breeds from southeastern Alberta east to Manitoba and western
Minnesota and south to northeastern Colorado and northern
Nebraska. Winters mainly in Southwest and southern Great Plains
from Arizona east to Oklahoma and Texas and south into Mexico.
Rare west to Pacific Coast, accidental east to Atlantic Coast.
Kenn Kaufman

Rustic Bunting

Emberiza rustica
The Rustic Bunting is a small Asiatic bird that is a rare or
uncommon spring and fall migrant in the western Aleutian Islands.
This visitor from the Old World is usually found singly or in pairs,
feeding on the ground in or near dense cover. It is often somewhat
shy.

Description
5½" (14 cm). The spring male has a distinctive black-and-white head
pattern: the crown, nape, ear coverts, and lores are black,
contrasting with the clear white throat, a white eyebrow from above
the eye to the back of the head, and a small white spot on the nape.
The underparts are white with a broad rust breastband, and there
are bold rust streaks on the flanks. The outer tail feathers are white,
and the rump is bright rust. The spring female is similar to the
male, but the black areas of the male's head pattern are brown.
Autumn immatures look much like adult females, but the white
areas of the head pattern are buff-colored, and the breastband is a

Winter male
1. *Trace of chestnut on nape.*
2. *Trace of black on underparts.*

   Smallest longspur. Musical cheedlup call.

Female
1. *Buff underparts.*
2. *Chestnut on nape.*

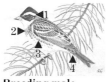

Breeding male
1. *Bold black-and-white head pattern.*
2. *Rust breastband.*
3. *Rust streaks on flanks.*
4. *White outer tail feathers.*

necklace of fine rust streaks, rather than the clean band of color that
the adults show.

Voice
Call note a sharp, rather metallic *tic;* call given at both rest and
during flight.

Range
Annual in North America in western Aleutian Islands, Alaska.
Casual farther east in Aleutians and on Alaska islands of Bering
Sea. Native to Northern Eurasia.   *Daniel D. Gibson*

Snow Bunting

Plectrophenax nivalis
This dooryard nesting bird is familiar in Arctic tundra and, during
the winter, in open country as far south as the northern United
States. The Snow Bunting is a fairly large bird, with very large
white wing patches and a mostly white body. It nests farther north
than any other passerine.

Description
6–7¼″ (15–18.5 cm). The summer male is largely white, with a black
back. Its 3 central pairs of tail feathers are black, as are the outer
half of the primaries, several of the primary coverts at the wrist,
and the tertials. The bill, eye, and legs are also black. The female is
similar but duller; there is mottled gray on the back and buff on the
crown and ear coverts. In the female, the jet-black areas of the male
are brownish-black. Immatures and winter adults are white with
varying amounts of bright buff on the head and rump; the back and
tertials are mottled beige and black, and the bill is straw-colored.

Voice
Song very musical, recalling that of Horned Lark but not given in
flight, a repeated *chi-chi-churee.* Call note a distinctive, whistled
teer or *tew.*

Similar Species
See McKay's Bunting.

Range
Breeds in Arctic tundra, south in Bering Sea and on Atlantic Coast
to central Canada; at high latitudes also breeds in high mountains.
Winters in open country on seacoasts and plains from Bering Sea
coast and southern Canada south to northern California (rare),
Utah, Kansas, and Carolinas; very irregularly farther to the
south.   *Daniel D. Gibson*

Female
1. *Brown-and-white head pattern.*
2. *Rust on breast.*
3. *Rust streaks on flanks.*
4. *White outer tail feathers.*

Winter plumage
1. *Buff on head.*
2. *Mottled beige-and-black upperparts.*
3. *Buff rump.*
4. *White underparts.*

In flight shows large white wing patches, white in tail.

Breeding male
1. *White head and underparts.*
2. *Black back.*

In flight shows large white wing patches, white rump, and white in tail.

McKay's Bunting

Plectrophenax hyperboreus
The only close relative of the Snow Bunting, McKay's Bunting is
endemic to islands of the Bering Sea. It may hybridize with the
Snow Bunting on St. Lawrence Island and the Pribilof Islands;
individuals with intermediate characteristics do occur and can be
difficult to identify.

Description
7" (18 cm). The summer male is white except for 1 or 2 pairs of
black-tipped tertials. The outer 1¼–2" of the wing tips are black; in
the Snow Bunting the outer 2½–2¾" are black. There are black
subterminal blotches on the central pair or central 2 pairs of tail
feathers, and the bill, eye, and legs are black. Infrequently there is
a single black primary covert at the wrist, where the Snow Bunting
has several. Females are similar to males, but have mottled backs.
Immatures and winter adults are similar to summer birds, but the
head, back, and rump are mottled with a highly variable amount of
rusty-beige feather edging, and the bill is straw-colored.

Voice
Similar to that of Snow Bunting.

Similar Species
Summer male Snow Bunting has black back; female has much more
extensive mottling in back than female McKay's. In all seasons, both
sexes of Snow Bunting have much more black in tail and in flight
feathers. Both species have black bill in summer, straw-colored bill
in winter.

Range
Breeds on St. Matthew and Hall islands in Bering Sea. Small
numbers have bred at St. Lawrence, St. Paul, and St. George
islands. Winters on mainland coast of western and southwestern
Alaska, from Norton Sound coast of Seward Peninsula south to tip
of Alaska Peninsula.   *Daniel D. Gibson*

Breeding male
. *Black bill.*
. *Largely white plumage.*
. *Black in tertials.*
. *Black wing tips.*
. *Black subterminal spots on central tail feathers.*

Winter plumage
. *Straw-colored bill.*
. *Rust-beige on head and breast.*
. *Rust-beige on rump.*

Amount of beige highly variable.

New World Blackbirds and Orioles

(Subfamily Icterinae)
This large subfamily includes several rather distinctive groups. Bobolinks are highly migratory, sexually dimorphic birds. All have tapered, spiked tails and utter a unique call note. The tribe Agelaiini includes the blackbirds, cowbirds, grackles, and meadowlarks. In the first 3 groups, the males are primarily black with glossy, iridescent metallic hues. Several species sport boldly contrasting shoulder patches, heads, or eyes. Blackbirds have somewhat conical bills; in some species, the bill is tapered, but in others it is uniformly slender. The males of many species are polygamous. The meadowlarks—especially the Western—are rather good singers, unlike the rest of the members of this subfamily. The orioles are primarily neotropical, and, like the wood warblers and tanagers, generally show more pronounced sexual dimorphism in the adults of more northerly breeding species. The brighter plumages often show brilliant orange, yellow, or red, with black-and-white wings and tails. Many species are loud singers capable of complex vocalizations. (World: 95 species. North America: 23 species.)   *Scott B. Terrill*

Bobolink

Dolichonyx oryzivorus
The male Bobolink is a familiar sight as it flutters over hay fields, delivering its bubbling song. Like the Red-winged Blackbird, the male uses its song to attract several females to its territory. Bobolinks prefer lush fields with tall grasses, alfalfa, clover, and grain crops. In the Southwest, they have extended their range as cropland has been irrigated, but their numbers seem to have decreased in the Northeast as agriculture has declined. These long-distance migrants sometimes fly from Canada to Argentina.

Description
6–8″ (15–20.5 cm). Bobolinks have a conical bill, long wings, and a stiff tail with sharply pointed tips. The breeding male has a black head and underparts; the flanks, abdomen, and undertail coverts may be edged with buff. The nape has a prominent golden-buff patch, while the lower back, rump, uppertail coverts, and scapulars are a pale gray-white. The tail and wings are black. Adult females have buff-olive upperparts with heavy dark brown streaks and dusky wings with broad buff-white edges. The nape is paler buff-olive with thin brown stripes, the dark brown crown has a broad buff central stripe, and the face is yellow-olive with a pronounced dark brown eyeline. The dull buff-white underparts are warmer buff across the breast and paler on the belly; there are thin dark stripes on the sides, flanks, and undertail coverts. In the fall, immature birds resemble females but have decidedly yellow underparts. Males in winter plumage resemble females but may have a darker back and a more obviously yellow face.

Voice
Bubbling flight song with a banjolike quality: *Bobolink-bobolink-bobolink-bobolink-bobolink-bobolink*. Flight note a sharp *pink*.

Similar Species
Savannah Sparrow has streaks across breast.

Range
Breeds from southeastern British Columbia and central Alberta to Nova Scotia, infrequently to Newfoundland, then south to northern California, northern Utah, central Colorado, northern Kansas, and central Illinois, Ohio, West Virginia, and New Jersey. Winters in South America.   *Peter D. Vickery*

Bobolink
Red-winged Blackbird
Tricolored Blackbird
Tawny-shouldered Blackbird
Eastern Meadowlark
Western Meadowlark
Yellow-headed Blackbird
Rusty Blackbird
Brewer's Blackbird
Great-tailed Grackle
Boat-tailed Grackle
Common Grackle
Bronzed Cowbird
Brown-headed Cowbird
Black-vented Oriole
Orchard Oriole
Hooded Oriole
Streak-backed Oriole
Spot-breasted Oriole
Altamira Oriole

Audubon's Oriole
Northern Oriole
Scott's Oriole

Breeding male
1. *Black head.*
2. *Golden-buff nape.*
3. *Black underparts.*
4. *Whitish scapulars.*
5. *Whitish rump.*

Female
1. *Striped crown.*
2. *Buff-white underparts.*
3. *Striped flanks.*
4. *Streaked upperparts.*

Red-winged Blackbird

Agelaius phoeniceus
This widespread species is one of the best known birds in North America. Returning early in the spring to many areas, the males set up breeding territories in freshwater marshes, moist thickets, and wet fields. Their black plumage, red shoulders, and distinctive *conk-ka-ree* song are familiar throughout much of the continent. The streaked females and immatures are more cryptically colored. During the nonbreeding season, Red-winged Blackbirds form large flocks—sometimes immense ones—often mixed with other blackbird species. They forage in open country, particularly in agricultural areas.

Description
7½–9½″ (19–24 cm). The adult male is entirely black except for a bright reddish or reddish-orange shoulder patch on the lesser wing coverts. The patch has a buff-whitish border; when the Red-winged is at rest, the red is sometimes hidden so that only the buff border is visible. The female is dark brown above, tinged with black and gray, and has a light or buff eyebrow; its pale underparts are heavily streaked with blackish-brown. The first-winter and spring male is similar to the adult but is more mottled overall; it is duller black with pale feather edgings and the shoulder is more orange with some dark flecking. Immatures are similar to adult females but have the upperparts edged with buff and the underparts washed with pale buff.

Voice
Song a liquid *conk-ka-ree* or *ok-a-lee*. Call note a low *chuck;* also gives a higher-pitched *tee-ay*, slurring downward, as well as a metallic *kink*.

Similar Species
Females and immatures distinguished from other blackbirds (except Tricolored) by streaking below. Juvenile Brown-headed Cowbirds also streaked below but slightly smaller overall, stockier, and paler, with shorter, more conical bills. Tricolored Blackbird similar; restricted in range to California and southern Oregon. Male Tricolored is slightly slimmer than Red-winged and glossier blue-black overall; bill also slimmer; Tricolored has deeper red shoulder patch with white border; gives more raspy and nasal calls and songs. Female Tricolored closely resembles female Red-winged but is darker overall, particularly on the belly, which shows little distinct streaking.

Range
Breeds from central Alaska, southern Yukon, northern Manitoba, and southern Newfoundland south to Baja California, Central America, and West Indies. Winters throughout much of southern breeding range, north as far as southern British Columbia, Colorado, southern Great Lakes, and coastal New England.
Paul Lehman

Adult male
1. *Black plumage.*
2. *Red shoulder with buff border.*

Female
1. *Light eyebrow.*
2. *Dark brown upperparts.*
3. *Heavy streaks on underparts.*

Immature male
. *Light eyebrow.*
. *Dark brown upperparts.*
. *Orange-red shoulder.*
. *Heavy streaks on underparts.*

Tricolored Blackbird

Agelaius tricolor
This close relative of the Red-winged Blackbird is largely restricted
to California west of the Sierra Nevada. It is one of the most
gregarious of North American birds; individual birds are only rarely
seen. The Tricolored Blackbird breeds in large, very localized
colonies among cattails and bulrushes in freshwater marshes; it
forages in marshes, fields, and livestock pens. During the
nonbreeding season, flocks are often segregated by sex. Taking
advantage of favorable local conditions, they are somewhat nomadic
and occur irregularly, especially in the nonbreeding season.

Description
7½–9″ (19–23 cm). The male is somewhat slimmer in shape and a
glossier blue-black overall than the Red-winged Blackbird. It has a
slightly slimmer bill and the shoulder is a deeper red with a white
border that may appear tinged with buff in fresh fall plumage. The
red shoulder is often hidden when the bird is at rest so that only the
white border is visible. The females are similar to female Red-
winged Blackbirds but are darker brown overall; the dark belly is
not streaked. First-winter males are similar to females but have dull
red shoulders.

Voice
Song much more nasal and raspy than Red-winged's; has been
likened to sound of brawling cats. Call a nasal *kaap*, also a soft
chuck.

Similar Species
Male Red-winged Blackbird stouter, not as glossy, has slightly
thicker bill, more orange-red shoulder patch; female has lighter
brown belly. Song also differs.

Range
Breeds from southern Oregon (Klamath Lake) south to
northwestern Baja California. Winters north to northern
California.   *Paul Lehman*

Eastern Meadowlark

Tail

Sturnella magna
The Eastern Meadowlark is a chunky, relatively long-billed, short-
tailed bird of open country, fields, and meadows. It is common and
conspicuous along roadsides, where it frequently sings from utility
wires and poles and from fenceposts. Like the Western Meadowlark,
it has a bright yellow breast marked with a bold black V and a long,
pointed bill that is diagnostic. In flight, it alternates a series of rapid
wingbeats, each with a noticeable downward thrust, with short
glides as the wings are held stiffly downward. When flushed or
alarmed, these birds prominently and rapidly open and shut their
tails, displaying the white outer tail feathers. In fall and winter,
meadowlarks are gregarious and often forage in large flocks.

Description
7–10″ (18–25.5 cm). The upperparts and flanks of the Eastern
Meadowlark are cryptically patterned with buff, brown, and black,
making it difficult to spot birds on the ground. The head is broadly
striped with buff and dark brown. The wings and tail are barred

Adult male
1. *Black plumage.*
2. *Red shoulder with white border.*

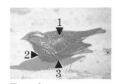

Female
1. *Dark brown upperparts.*
2. *Dark streaks on breast.*
3. *Dark belly.*

Adult, side view
1. *Long, pointed bill.*
2. *Streaked upperparts.*
3. *Streaked flanks.*
4. *White outer tail feathers.*

with dark brown, while the outer tail feathers are almost entirely
white. The throat, breast, and abdomen are bright yellow, with a
broad black V on the upper breast. The straight, pointed bill is
about as long as the head, and the tail is relatively short.
Populations from the Southwest are significantly duller than those
from the East, and more closely resemble the Western Meadowlark.

Voice
Song a series of 2–8 (usually 3–5) loud, plaintive, whistled notes,
often slurred and usually descending in pitch; quite homogeneous
throughout. Call note a harsh, rasping *dzert* or a longer, buzzy *zeree*.

Similar Species
See Western Meadowlark.

Range
Breeds from southeastern Canada south through eastern United
States, west to Nebraska, Texas, and Arizona; also in Cuba, Central
America, and northern South America. Extreme northern
populations migrate; winters sparsely north to Minnesota, southern
Great Lakes, and New England.   *Wesley E. Lanyon*

Western Meadowlark

Sturnella neglecta
This bird is virtually identical to the Eastern Meadowlark in both
appearance and habits. Where the ranges of the 2 species overlap in
the north-central states, Western Meadowlarks prefer drier
grasslands in uplands, while Eastern Meadowlarks favor wetter,
more poorly drained meadows in river valleys. In the desert
grasslands of the Southwest, these habitat preferences are more
variable and sometimes curiously reversed. The 2 species are among
the most difficult of North American birds to distinguish by plumage
alone.

Description
8–10″ (20.5–25.5 cm). Like the Eastern Meadowlark, the Western
Meadowlark has buff, brown, and black upperparts and flanks, and a
buff and brown head. The wings and tail are barred with brown, and
the outer tail feathers are white. The throat, breast, and abdomen
are bright yellow, with a broad black V on the upper breast.

Voice
Song more melodious, richer, and lower-pitched than that of
Eastern Meadowlark. Generally has 2 distinct phases: 1–6 pure
whistled notes, followed by more complex, liquid, consonantlike
notes. Call note a sharp *chupp* or *chuck*, lower than Eastern's.

Similar Species
Eastern Meadowlark slightly darker; yellow on throat does not
extend as far on cheek; tends to have more white in tail feathers (at
least in birds of Southwest); more eastern populations of Eastern
have blacker crown than Western. Differences subtle; identification
difficult if not impossible without recourse to voice.

Range
Breeds from southwestern and south-central Canada through
western United States and central Mexico, to eastern Great Lakes
region (locally), northwestern Missouri, and central Oklahoma;
overlaps range of Eastern Meadowlark along southwest-northeast
zone from southern Arizona through central Oklahoma and southern
Great Lakes to southeastern Ontario. Extreme northern populations
winter from southern British Columbia very sparsely north to
southern Canada and southern Wisconsin, south to southern Texas
where it overlaps with Eastern.   *Wesley E. Lanyon*

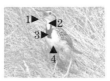

Adult, front view
1. Long, pointed bill.
2. Yellow on throat, not extending to cheek.
3. Black V on breast.
4. Yellow breast and belly.

Adult
1. Long, pointed bill.
2. Yellow on throat, extending to cheek.
3. Black V on breast.
4. Yellow underparts.
5. Pale streaked upperparts.
6. White outer tail feathers.

Adult in fresh fall plumage
Pale feather edges obscure markings.

Yellow-headed Blackbird

Xanthocephalus xanthocephalus
This big, marsh-nesting blackbird, larger than the Red-winged, is
common over the western two-thirds of North America. It is
gregarious year-round; some of its nesting colonies are huge, and
the marshes may throb with the awful din of "singing" males. As
they sing, they perch in the open with their feathers fluffed out,
quivering with apparent effort. Outside the breeding season Yellow-
heads mix with other blackbirds in pastures and agricultural fields
and around feedlots. In winter they are quite local, but in the
Southwest some concentrations may number in the thousands or
tens of thousands. These flocks are made up mostly of males,
because females tend to winter farther south, in central Mexico.

Description
8–11" (20.5–28 cm). The adult male is mostly black, with a bright
golden-yellow or orange-yellow head and breast; a small black mask
connects the eyes and the bill. A white patch on and near the
primary coverts appears small on the folded wing but is striking in
flight. The female is noticeably smaller than the male and much
duller, mostly dusky-brown on the crown, back, wings, tail, and
lower underparts. Its breast and face are golden-yellow, with a
poorly defined dark ear patch; the lower breast is streaked with
white. Immatures resemble adult females, but the yellow areas are
paler and more restricted.

Voice
"Song" a cacophonous scraping or strangling noise, usually preceded
by a few warning notes. Other nesting season noises include liquid
clucks and low quacking sounds. Call note a deep *ktuk*, lower-
pitched than similar note of Red-winged Blackbird.

Range
Breeds from central British Columbia and northern Saskatchewan
east to Wisconsin (locally farther east in Great Lakes region) and
south to southern California, northern New Mexico, and central
Illinois. Locally abundant in winter in central Arizona; fairly
common in California, southern New Mexico, and western Texas;
east regularly in small numbers to Florida. Autumn strays turn up
east as far as Atlantic Coast.   *Kenn Kaufman*

Rusty Blackbird

Euphagus carolinus
The Rusty Blackbird is almost always found near water. It breeds in
boggy spruce woods in the far North and winters around swamps,
riversides, and lakes. Typically it forages by wading in shallow
water, but it also ventures into pastures and agricultural fields.
Migrating north early in the spring, the Rusty Blackbird has mostly
disappeared from its wintering grounds by mid-April.

Description
9¼" (24 cm). Sharply pointed bill sometimes appears slightly
decurved. Tail medium-long, proportionately slightly longer than
Red-winged's. Eyes yellow. Breeding-plumage male entirely dull
black with faint green iridescence on head, breast, back, wings, and
tail; iridescence rarely evident. Breeding female may be as dark as
male or dull slate-gray, often with some brownish edgings on wings.
In fall, all plumages rust-brown on crown, back, and chest; eyebrow
and throat buff; wings edged with brown. Face shows dark gray
patch, and rump and lower underparts dark gray. All brown areas

Adult male
1. *Bright yellow head and breast.*
2. *Black body, wings, and tail.*
3. *White patches on wings.*

Female
1. *Yellow face and breast.*
2. *Dusky-brown body, wings, and tail.*

Fall plumage
1. *Yellow eyes.*
2. *Rust crown and buff eyebrow.*
3. *Rufous edgings on breast.*
4. *Rufous edgings on back and wings.*

formed by feather tips that wear away and disappear by spring,
leaving only underlying gray or black of breeding plumage.
Juveniles in summer may have dark eyes.

Voice
Song a creaking *tk-tsheeeik* or *ksshleeah.* Call note a metallic *check.*
Flocks make clear whistles, clucks, and other notes.

Similar Species
Common Grackle larger, more iridescent, with longer, wedge-
shaped tail. Some Brewer's in winter plumage may have pale bars
on back and chest as well as pale eyebrow, but these areas dull gray
or brownish-gray rather than rust-brown and buff.

Range
Alaska east to Newfoundland and south to central British Columbia,
southern Ontario, New England, and northern New York. Winters
mainly from Great Plains to Atlantic Coast and from Great Lakes
and New England to Gulf Coast and central Florida. Sparse in fall to
western states, sometimes wintering.   *Kenn Kaufman*

Brewer's Blackbird

Euphagus cyanocephalus
Common in open country in the West, Brewer's Blackbird breeds
practically anywhere there are trees and open ground, including
towns, ranches, riversides, and mountain meadows. It tends to
avoid the hottest desert regions.

Description
8–10″ (20.5–25.5 cm). Brewer's has a conical, sharply pointed bill and
a medium-long tail, which is proportionately a little longer than that
of the Red-winged Blackbird. The adult male is entirely black; in
good light, a purple iridescence on the head and a green iridescence
on the body are visible. The eyes are creamy white or very pale
yellow. The female is mostly smooth dusty-gray, but blackish,
sometimes with a greenish gloss, on the lower back, wings, and tail.
The eyebrow and throat are paler gray, but do not contrast sharply
with the darker crown and face. The eyes are dark brown. Juveniles
resemble adult females. Young males in winter may be blackish,
with gray eyebrows and some gray barring on the back and chest.

Voice
Song a creaking *ksheeik,* similar to Rusty's but usually hoarser. Call
note a metallic *check.* Various other notes heard from flocks.

Similar Species
See Common Grackle. In flight overhead, Red-winged Blackbird has
discernibly shorter tail. Rusty Blackbird very similar in some
plumages; with comparative experience, shape differences apparent:
Brewer's looks noticeably small-headed with straight conical bill;
Rusty more bulky-headed with bill usually longer, more acutely
pointed at tip, and sometimes appearing slightly decurved. Rusty
slightly bulkier overall and has slightly shorter tail; breeding male
usually dull black without noticeable iridescence, but rarely has
conspicuous green gloss on wings and tail. Rusty's eyes usually dull
medium-yellow (Brewer's usually more whitish).

Range
Central British Columbia to Michigan and southern Ontario
(expanding eastward); south to southern California, New Mexico,
and rarely western Texas. Winters from southern British Columbia
across western and southern states east to Carolinas, Florida, and
central Mexico. Rare in Northeast.   *Kenn Kaufman*

Breeding male
1. *Sharply pointed bill.*
2. *Yellow eye.*
3. *Dull black plumage faintly glossed with greenish.*

Breeding male
1. *Sharply pointed bill.*
2. *Whitish eye.*
3. *Black head glossed with purple.*
4. *Black body glossed with greenish.*

Female
1. *Sharply pointed bill.*
2. *Dark brown eye.*
3. *Dusty-gray plumage.*

Great-tailed Grackle

Quiscalus mexicanus
These noisy and conspicuous birds are familiar residents of city
parks, towns, ranch lands, and occasionally marshes, where they
form huge nesting colonies in isolated groves. With their long keel-
shaped tails, piercing yellow eyes, and distinctly odd songs and calls,
the males are among our more spectacular native birds. At all
seasons these grackles have a sleek, thin-headed profile.

Description
Male: 18″ (45.5 cm); female: 14″ (35.5 cm). Adult males are shiny
black with a purple gloss on the head, neck, and back and a blue
gloss on the breast. The tail is disproportionately long and folded
down the middle, forming a scoop or keel shape. The eye is a clear
golden-yellow. First-year males are dull black; in the fall their eyes
are brown, changing to yellow over the winter; their tails are flat,
not folded down the middle. Adult females are mostly warm olive-
brown, darker above with a slight metallic sheen and pale yellow
eyes. First-year females are much paler and grayer and may show a
strong face pattern with a dusty white eyebrow and dark streak
through the eye. Their eyes change color from brown to pale yellow
over the first winter. Great-tails of southeastern California and
southwestern Arizona are noticeably smaller than those of other
populations; the females are very pale, almost white, on the breast.

Voice
Highly varied. Long, upslurred whistle and a ratchet-like series of
clacks or *clocks* especially diagnostic. Also other cackles, hissing and
crashing sounds, and unearthly whistles.

Similar Species
Crows have heavier bills and proportionately shorter, fan-shaped
tails. Other blackbirds much smaller, also with fan-shaped tails. See
Common and Boat-tailed grackles (in Florida, yellow-eyed birds are
wintering Boat-tailed Grackles from Atlantic Coast).

Range
Rapidly expanding northward. Presently resident from southern
interior California to south-central Louisiana, north to southern
Colorado and central Kansas, south into central Mexico. Vagrants to
northern California and Midwest.   *H. Douglas Pratt*

Boat-tailed Grackle

Quiscalus major
Closely resembling the Great-tailed Grackle, the somewhat smaller
Boat-tailed Grackle is common along the Atlantic and Gulf coasts,
where it is found mainly in marshes, farmland, and city parks. Male
Boat-tailed Grackles often fluff their head feathers during spring and
summer, and thus appear thick-headed compared to the sleek Great-
tail. The Boat-tail's calls are much less varied and not as "weird" as
the Great-tail's. Both sexes exhibit slight but noticeable differences
in plumage color as compared to the Great-tail. Where the 2 birds
overlap in Texas and Louisiana, the best identifying mark is eye
color.

Description
Male: 16½″ (42 cm); female: 13″ (33 cm). Adult males are very similar
to Great-tailed Grackles but show more blue and blue-green
reflections on the back and breast. Eye color varies: it is bright
yellow in Atlantic Coast birds, dark brown in peninsular Florida and
along the northwestern Gulf Coast, and medium brown with a

Adult male
1. *Yellow eye.*
2. *Black plumage glossed with purple.*
3. *Long, keeled tail.*

Large size. Whistled and clack *calls.*

Female
1. *Pale yellow eye.*
2. *Olive-brown breast.*
3. *Dark brown glossy upperparts.*

Large size.

Female
1. *Brown eye.*
2. *Buff breast.*
3. *Dark brown upperparts with no gloss.*

Large size.

yellow periphery along the central Gulf Coast. Adult females are also like their Great-tailed counterparts, but they have much more buff on the breast and no glossy or metallic reflections on the back. First-year birds are indistinguishable from Great-tailed Grackles of the same age until the latter acquire their yellow irises.

Voice
A harsh, vibrating *jibe-jibe-jibe* or *jeeb-jeeb-jeeb*, a sharp *keet* or *keet-keet*, and a chuckling sound like that of a coot pattering its feet.

Similar Species
Great-tailed larger, with clear yellow eyes; if eye not absolutely clear yellow, bird probably a paler-eyed variant of Boat-tailed. Male Great-tailed has thin-headed profile. Voice different.

Range
Resident in tidewater areas from New York to central Texas and throughout peninsular Florida, occasionally inland along rivers. Some Alantic Coast and central Gulf Coast birds wander to South and West in winter.   *H. Douglas Pratt*

Common Grackle

Quiscalus quiscula
The Common Grackle is a common and familiar blackbird in eastern North America, where it frequents parks, residential areas, woods and groves of trees along rivers, and croplands. It nests in small, loose colonies, usually in conifers. A social bird throughout the year, in the winter it joins huge roosts of blackbirds and starlings; these roosts have recently become a nuisance in many areas. In these mixed flocks, Common Grackles can be easily distinguished from other birds by their lankier proportions and in particular by their long, somewhat spoon-shaped tails, which look thicker at the trailing end in profile, especially in males. In bright sunlight, adults are very handsome, with an iridescent or metallic sheen to the plumage and bright yellow eyes. Two color types occur, one purple and the other bronze. The purple birds are found only in the Southeast, north along the coast to southern New England, while the bronze type occupies the rest of the range of the species. In areas where the breeding ranges of these 2 color types come together, intermediate birds, impossible to assign to one color type or the other, may be found.

Description
11–13½″ (28–34.5 cm). Smaller than either the Great-tailed or Boat-tailed grackle, this species is similar in shape to its relatives but has a proportionately shorter tail. Adults are entirely black with a strong metallic sheen. The purple color type has a relatively uniform violet gloss, but in the bronze type the somewhat brassy reflections of the back and breast contrast sharply with the glossy blue head and neck. The eyes of both forms are yellow. Juvenile Common Grackles are sooty brown without any gloss; at first they have dark eyes.

Voice
A loud *tchack* or *tchuck;* also a wheezy, upslurred *tssh-shkleet.*

Similar Species
Blackbirds, cowbirds, and starlings smaller, stockier, with shorter, fanlike tails and proportionately shorter bills. All have more rounded head in profile. Great-tailed Grackle and Boat-tailed Grackle larger, with longer tails, less metallic gloss, and very different voices.

Adult male
1. *Glossy black plumage.*
2. *Long, keeled tail.*
3. *Pale eyes.*

Florida birds have brown eyes.

Male, purple type
1. *Black plumage with uniform purple gloss.*
2. *Yellow eyes.*
3. *Long, keeled tail.*

Smaller than Great-tailed and Boat-tailed grackles.

Male, bronze type
1. *Yellow eyes.*
2. *Blue gloss on head and neck.*
3. *Brassy gloss on back and breast.*
4. *Long, keeled tail.*

Range
Breeds east of Rockies from northeastern British Columbia and
southern Mackenzie across boreal Canada to southwestern
Newfoundland; south to central Colorado, southern Texas, Gulf
Coast, and southern Florida. In winter, withdraws entirely from
boreal Canada (except for strays at feeders), and from much of
northern United States; winters uncommonly as far north as
southern Minnesota, Wisconsin, southern Great Lakes, and coastal
southern New England.   *H. Douglas Pratt*

Bronzed Cowbird

Molothrus aeneus
In their limited range in the United States, Bronzed or "Red-eyed"
Cowbirds are found in a variety of relatively open areas at lower
elevations. There they are common on lawns in well-watered
residential areas, in agricultural areas, and at feedlots. At moderate
montane elevations, they occur in open riparian areas. They flock—
often in very large numbers—in the early spring, then erratically
until early summer, when they are most often seen singly, in pairs,
or in small groups. More frequently they flock in late summer and
fall. In winter, they occur locally, often around livestock and in
parks with other blackbirds. The male performs a bizarre strutting
display and hovering flight to win a female's attention.

Description
7–8¾" (18–22 cm). Both sexes are rather rotund, with flat heads,
short tails, and deep red eyes. They have a long bill that often
appears slightly decurved in the field; the gonys, or angle on the
lower mandible, curves strongly upward, and the lower mandible
has a wide base. Males are glossy black with iridescent greenish and
bronze shades on the body and blue and purple shades on the wings,
tail, and rump. The feathers around the back of the neck are
elongated, making the bird appear ruffled, especially in profile.
Females are similar but are flat black or gray, and smaller overall
with a reduced ruff. In winter, the eye color may be dull, even
brownish. Juveniles are shaped like adults but are paler.

Voice
Squeaky, creaky sounds, like rusty hinges. Also a low, guttural,
blackbirdlike *chuck*.

Similar Species
Deep red eye diagnostic. Brown-headed Cowbird less elongated; has
shorter, more conical bill, rounder head; lacks ruff.

Range
Breeds from lower Colorado River (very rare elsewhere in
southeastern California) through central and southern Arizona,
extreme southwestern New Mexico, and Texas; south throughout
Mexico to Panama. May withdraw from north in winter. Range
appears to be expanding. Rare but almost annual in East.
Scott B. Terrill

Juvenile
1. *Sooty-brown plumage.*
2. *Dark eye.*

Adult male
1. *Long, conical bill.*
2. *Flat forehead.*
3. *Red eye.*
4. *Ruffled neck feathers.*
5. *Glossy black plumage.*

Female
1. *Long, conical bill.*
2. *Flat forehead.*
3. *Red eye.*
4. *Dull gray plumage.*

Brown-headed Cowbird

Molothrus ater

The Brown-headed Cowbird can be distinguished from similar blackbirds by its relatively conical bill and short, squared tail. Cowbirds often flock with blackbirds around livestock in agricultural and residential areas. Both the Bronzed and Brown-headed seem to be expanding their ranges as a result of cattle domestication and major alterations of habitat that have been imposed by man. In flight, cowbirds can be distinguished from blackbirds by their short wings and tail and by their swifter, more continuous wingbeats. As they feed in flocks, cowbirds hold their hind ends up, with the tail sticking straight up, higher than that of any other icterid. Although no pair bonds are formed, both species of cowbird perform courtship displays, which are elaborate in the case of the Bronzed Cowbird. Male Brown-headed Cowbirds perch in trees near the female, throwing their heads back so that the bill points straight up; the body feathers are fluffed up, and the bird swells while giving bubbling notes and fanning its wings and tail. This swelling is culminated by a loud *squeek* note. There are variations on this theme: Brown-headed Cowbirds also display on the ground, and occasionally indulge in short display flights. However, none is as impressive as the dramatic strutting and "helicopter" flight of the displaying male Bronzed Cowbird. Like Bronzed Cowbirds, Brown-headeds are brood parasites, primarily of passerines. During the breeding season, female cowbirds often sit motionless, awaiting an opportunity to slip their eggs into an unsuspecting bird's nest. This parasitism has reduced the population of many species, such as orioles, tanagers, warblers, and vireos.

Description
6–8" (15–20 cm). The Brown-headed Cowbird is relatively small, with rotund proportions and a short, wide, almost conical bill. The tail is short and squared at the tip. Males are glossy, iridescent black with a rich brown head. Females are uniform brownish-gray. Juveniles are pale gray, varyingly streaked with darker gray.

Voice
Song high-pitched, squeaky, and bubbly. Calls high-pitched and squeaky. Female has chattering call.

Similar Species
All other blackbirds have longer, more pointed bills. Bronzed Cowbird similar to female Brown-headed but has longer, upward curved bill, more elongated, slightly ruffled appearance, and diagnostic deep red eye.

Range
Breeds from northeastern British Columbia and southern Mackenzie east to northern Ontario and southern Nova Scotia, south to northern Mexico. Winters in central and southern portions of breeding range, from Minnesota and southern Ontario, becoming more common in more southerly regions; to southern Mexico.
Scott B. Terrill

Juvenile

. *Conical bill.*
. *Pale plumage with dark streaks.*

Female

. *Short, conical bill.*
. *Gray-brown plumage.*
. *Short tail.*

Adult male

. *Short, conical bill.*
. *Brown head.*
. *Glossy black body.*
. *Short tail.*

Orchard Oriole

Icterus spurius
The Orchard Oriole is a widespread, locally common songbird of
eastern North America. It is found in orchards, shade trees, and
woodland edges, and prefers open country with a few scattered
trees. The sexes are strikingly different. Like other orioles, these
birds have a loud, musical song; the male often sings in flight and
from favorite perches. Orchard Orioles eat insects and small fruits.
The nest is a tightly woven, shallow suspended cup constructed
mostly of grasses. This species migrates in the early autumn.

Description
6–7″ (15–18 cm). The Orchard Oriole has a short straight bill and
often twitches its tail sideways. The male has a black head, throat,
and back, a dark tail and wings, and a deep chestnut rump and
underparts. The female and immature are olive-green above and dull
yellow to bright yellow below, with 2 indistinct white wing bars.
Some birds may have a paler belly with the yellow confined to the
rest of the underparts. The first-year male resembles the female but
has a black chin and throat.

Voice
Song a rich, quick, varied series of notes, somewhat like song of
Purple Finch, often with a distinctive downslurred note at end. Call
a soft *chuck*, unlike calls of other orioles.

Similar Species
Female and immature male Northern Orioles have larger, longer bill
and darker upperparts; do not appear greenish, and have orange-
yellow underparts. See female Hooded Oriole. Female Scarlet and
Summer tanagers lack wing bars; have different bill shape and
different overall profile.

Range
Breeds from southern Manitoba, central Wisconsin, south-central
Michigan, southern Ontario, central Pennsylvania, and central New
England south to northern Florida; west across Gulf Coast to
eastern New Mexico, south into Mexico. Winters from Mexico south
to northern South America. Rare but regular in fall and winter in
California; very rare transient in fall and spring elsewhere in
Southwest.   *Paul W. Sykes, Jr.*

Hooded Oriole

Icterus cucullatus
This bird's long, thin, slightly decurved bill, slender body, and long,
thin tail distinguish it from other North American orioles. Its call
note—a high, nasal, slightly metallic *wheenk* or *wheet*—is also
distinctive. Because these birds frequently nest in dense palm
fronds, often in very tall trees, their calls may be the only indication
of their presence. In some areas, however, especially in desert oases
with palms, cottonwoods, and willows, Hooded Orioles can be
abundant and quite conspicuous; they fly about, calling and
chattering repeatedly throughout the day, even when it is hot.
These birds are also common in riparian areas at lower to moderate
elevations and in residential areas with ornamental plantings
(especially Washington fan palms, which have helped to expand the
breeding range as far north as extreme northern California).
Ornamental plantings and hummingbird feeders have also enabled
small numbers of these birds to winter somewhat regularly north of
Mexico, especially in coastal California. As is true of some other
oriole species, the distinctively plumaged second-year males

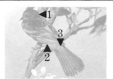

Adult male
1. *Black head and upperparts.*
2. *Deep chestnut underparts.*
3. *Deep chestnut rump.*

Female
1. *Straight, pointed bill.*
2. *Olive-green upperparts.*
3. *Dull yellow underparts.*
4. *White wing bars.*

Immature male
1. *Slender, decurved bill.*
2. *Black chin and throat.*
3. *Greenish-yellow upperparts.*
4. *Dull yellow underparts, including belly.*
5. *White wing bars.*

sometimes associate with a mated pair of adults during the breeding season.

Description
7–7¾″ (18–19.5 cm). Adult males are bright orange-yellow; they are paler and more yellowish in the western portion of their range. There is a black area around the eye and bill that extends into a bib on the middle of the upper breast. The back and wings are black; there are 2 white wing bars and white edgings to the flight feathers. The tail is solid black. Females are greenish-yellow, darker greenish-gray on the upperparts, and have 2 whitish wing bars. Through the first breeding season, immature males are similar to females but are more richly colored and have a smaller black bib. Except for very young birds, all Hooded Orioles have a long, thin, slightly decurved bill.

Voice
Song variable; usually a clear, rapid series of warbles, thinner and less whistled than songs of other orioles; Hooded sings less often than other orioles. Rattle drier and faster than that of Northern Oriole, with more staccato notes. Also various scolds. Call diagnostic; a high, often thin, usually slightly metallic *sheenk*, *wheenk*, *wheet*, or *eet*. Also gives other calls and a soft chatter.

Similar Species
Altamira Oriole much larger and heavier, with relatively large, deep bill. Female and immature Northern Orioles stockier, with contrasting paler bellies; Hooded Orioles have uniformly colored underparts. Females and immature Orchard Orioles difficult to distinguish from Hooded, especially young birds. Orchard Oriole has very short tail, often flicked sideways in quick, jerky manner; has shorter, less decurved bill than most Hoodeds (except for very young Hooded). Orchard gives diagnostic low *chuck* note. Also see Scott's and Streak-backed orioles.

Range
Breeds from northern California (local) south and east to southern California, southern Nevada, and extreme southern Utah; south through central and southern Arizona, southern New Mexico, southern Texas, and lowland Mexico. Winters primarily in Mexico; rare but annual in coastal California and rare in arid interior Southwest (primarily around hummingbird feeders) and southern Texas.   *Scott B. Terrill*

Streak-backed Oriole

Icterus pustulatus
This species is a rare but increasingly frequent visitor to southeastern Arizona. It is common just south of the border in brushy thorn forests and in riparian areas in north-central Sonora, Mexico. Additionally, it is an erratic straggler into southern California. Most recent sightings in the United States have been in the vicinity of Tucson, Arizona. Females and immatures of this species are difficult to identify.

Description
8½″ (21.5 cm). The unmistakable adult males have scarlet-red heads, brilliant orange underparts, heavily streaked backs, and extensive white areas in the wings. The tail is mostly black, with white-tipped outer tail feathers. Females and immature males, except for very young birds, have a greenish back with dark, elongated blotches; these blotches are arranged in longitudinal streaks but are less conspicuous than in the male. Very young birds lack this streaking and are extremely difficult to identify.

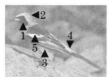

Adult male
1. *Black face and throat.*
2. *Orange-yellow head.*
3. *Orange-yellow underparts.*
4. *Orange-yellow rump.*
5. *White wing bars.*

Small size.

Female
1. *Slender, decurved bill.*
2. *Greenish-yellow upperparts.*
3. *Dull yellow underparts, including belly.*
4. *White wing bars.*

Adult female
1. *Back with less obvious streaks than in male.*
2. *White areas in wings.*

Voice

Song similar to Northern "Bullock's" Oriole's but louder, with more clear whistled notes. Call a thin *reep;* also gives a dry rattle. Combination of these songs and calls unique to Streak-backed.

Similar Species

Northern "Bullock's" Orioles very similar to immature and female Streak-backed but lack streaking on back and have more curved upper mandible. Hooded Oriole much slimmer; in fresh winter plumage, can show black scalloping or spotting on olive-tinted back (back becomes entirely black by breeding season); shows more contrast between back and paler head; has narrow, slightly decurved bill. Streak-backed has very straight upper mandible and black lower mandible with deep, contrasting bluish base. Young and females of other orioles do not show bright forehead contrasting sharply with rest of head; lack bright malar areas; calls also differ.

Range

Rare but increasingly frequent visitor to southeastern Arizona; casual to southern California. Native to Mexico.   *Scott B. Terrill*

Spot-breasted Oriole

Icterus pectoralis

The Spot-breasted Oriole is native to Central America. In the early 1950s, it was either introduced in southern Florida or escaped. Since 1976 its population has decreased dramatically. This bird is locally common in heavily landscaped gardens and parks and on the edges of West Indian hardwood hammocks, where it feeds on nectar, small fruits, and insects. The sexes are similar, but the female is duller. The Spot-breasted Oriole frequently perches in exposed places, singing loudly. During the nonbreeding season it can be found in small groups. It is the only oriole in southeastern Florida during the summer.

Description

8–9″ (20.5–23 cm). The adult is orange with a black face, bib, back, wings, and tail; there are black spots on the sides of the bib. The base of the primaries is white, and the secondaries are edged with white. The immature is similar to the adult but duller; it lacks the black spots and has a grayish-green back and tail. The juvenile is yellow instead of orange, lacks the black bib and spots, and has a dingy olive-green back, wings, and tail.

Voice

Song a series of loud, flutelike whistles that vary in pitch; more continuous than that of most other orioles. Call a loud, harsh, grating note.

Range

Resident from southern Mexico to Costa Rica. Introduced and established on southeastern coast of Florida from Stuart south to Homestead.   *Paul W. Sykes, Jr.*

Adult male
1. *Orange-red head.*
2. *Streaked back.*
3. *Extensive white patches in wings.*
4. *Black tail with white tip.*

Immature
1. *Grayish-green back.*
2. *Breast has black bib without spots.*

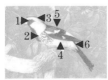

Adult male
1. *Black face.*
2. *Black throat and spots on breast.*
3. *Orange head.*
4. *Orange underparts.*
5. *Black back.*
6. *Orange rump.*

Florida only.

Altamira Oriole

Icterus gularis
Formerly rare in the United States, the Altamira Oriole is now the most common oriole resident along the Rio Grande in extreme southern Texas. It is fairly conspicuous because of its large size, bright colors, and rasping call notes, and because it forages in open areas in the woods.

Description
8½–10″ (21.5–25.5 cm). In both sexes of the adult Altamira Oriole the head, underparts, and rump are bright orange, except for a black mask that extends from the bill back to the eyes and trails down onto the breast in a broad black bib. The tail and upper back are black. The wings are black, with yellow-orange lesser coverts, 1 white wing bar on the tips of the greater coverts, and conspicuous white edgings to the tertials and the bases of the primaries. The bill is heavy and blue-gray at the base. Immatures are olive-drab on the back and yellow on the head, rump, and underparts; they have dark lores, and there is often an orange tinge to the face. Their wings are brownish with yellow edgings on the coverts and white edgings on the flight feathers; these edgings are particularly noticeable on the tertials and at the bases of the primaries.

Voice
Song a fairly rapid series of short whistles interspersed with low, harsh notes. Call notes nasal and rasping.

Similar Species
Adults resemble adult male Hooded Oriole (now much less common in southern Texas) but are larger, with proportionately thicker bill. Wing patterns differ: Hooded has 2 white wing bars, with upper bar very broad and conspicuous; Altamira lacks upper wing bar, has yellow-orange lesser coverts and more conspicuous white crescent formed by broad white edgings at bases of outer primaries. Immature Altamira larger than other Texas orioles, has traces of adult wing pattern; brighter yellow than immature Audubon's.

Range
Permanent resident from Lower Rio Grande Valley of southern Texas (upriver at least to San Ignacio) south to Nicaragua.
Kenn Kaufman

Audubon's Oriole

Icterus graduacauda
These uncommon birds occur in pairs, foraging at midlevels in trees in dense woods. Slow, shy, and quiet, they are easily overlooked.

Description
9″ (23 cm). Ragged black hood extends onto chest in front, reaches base of nape in back. Back greenish-yellow (darker and duller in females); rump and underparts dull lemon-yellow. Wings mostly black with yellow lesser coverts and some white edgings; tail black. Base of the lower mandible pale. Immature lacks black hood; wings and tail more brownish; sides washed with grayish.

Voice
Song a hesitant series of mellow whistles with human quality.

Similar Species
No other oriole has yellow back and black head. Immature distinguished by size, greenish-yellow cast, dark wings and tail.

Range
S. Texas (locally to Laredo) and Mexico.   *Kenn Kaufman*

Immature
1. *Olive-drab back.*
2. *Yellow head and underparts.*
3. *Yellow wing bars.*
4. *White edgings on tertials and at base of primaries.*

Large size.

Adult
1. *Thick-based bill.*
2. *Black face and throat.*
3. *Orange head.*
4. *Orange underparts.*
5. *Yellow-orange lesser wing coverts.*
6. *White wing bar.*

Texas only.

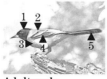

Adult male
1. *Black head.*
2. *Greenish-yellow back.*
3. *Yellow underparts.*
4. *Black wings with yellow lesser wing coverts.*
5. *Black tail.*

Texas only.

Northern "Baltimore" Oriole

Icterus galbula galbula
The brightly colored, orange-and-black male Northern "Baltimore"
Oriole is a well-known bird in the East, where it inhabits a variety
of shade trees in open deciduous woodland and residential
neighborhoods. Until recently it was thought to be a separate
species from the western "Bullock's" Oriole; although the 2 birds
are now considered to be conspecific, some researchers believe the
2 are indeed distinct species.

Description
7–8" (18–20.5 cm). The adult male is brilliantly colored, with a solid
black hood and back, bright orange lower back and rump, orange
and black tail, orange shoulder bar, single white wing bar, and a
bright orange lower breast, belly, and undertail coverts. Females
are somewhat variable in plumage. The upperparts vary from olive-
brown to brownish-gray, with the back the grayest, and they have a
variable amount of dark spotting. The crown, nape, and rump are
more golden-brown; there are 2 distinct white wing bars. The
underparts are also somewhat variable. Most females have a strong
yellowish-orange wash that is strongest across the breast and on the
undertail coverts, paling on the lower breast and belly; paler
individuals are mostly yellow below, with only a tinge of orange and
a more extensive area of white or grayish-white on the belly and
lower breast. Some females have black on the throat and a small
amount of dark flecking on the head. The first-winter male looks like
a brightly colored female. The first-spring male is a slightly duller
orange than the adult; its black hood is duller and more splotchy,
and the back may be golden-brown.

Voice
Song a rich, flute-like series of notes, somewhat disjointed. Some
individual variation. Call a 1- or 2-syllable flutelike whistle; also a
chatter.

Similar Species
Male "Bullock's" Oriole has orange cheek, eyebrow, and large white
wing patch. Female "Bullock's" resembles paler female "Baltimore"
but always paler yellow overall; paler gray above; with less bold
wing bars, usually more extensive whitish belly, and yellowish
eyebrow. Chatter calls given by the 2 subspecies distinguishable
with practice. Orchard Oriole smaller, shorter-billed, gives *chuck*
call; male is chestnut-brown and black; most females and first-winter
males are bright yellow below and have green backs. Female
Hooded Oriole slimmer, longer-tailed, has decurved bill; mostly
yellow below; call an ascending, whistled *wheet* and chatter notes. In
southern Florida, see Spot-breasted Oriole.

Range
Breeds from central Alberta, central Ontario, and Nova Scotia south
to Oklahoma, Louisiana, and northern Georgia. Winters primarily
from Mexico to northern South America; rare along Gulf Coast and
Atlantic Coast north to Virginia, also in coastal California; very rare
elsewhere in East, north to southern Great Lakes and coastal
Massachusetts (primarily at feeders). Rare migrant in West.
Paul Lehman

Adult male
1. Black head.
2. Black back.
3. Orange underparts.
4. Orange rump.
5. Black wings with
   white wing bars.
6. Orange on tail.

Female
1. Olive-brown
   upperparts.
2. Orange-yellow
   underparts.
3. White wing bars.

Immature male
1. Splotchy black hood.
2. Dull orange
   underparts.

Northern "Bullock's" Oriole

Icterus galbula bullockii
The Northern "Bullock's" Oriole is widespread in the West, where it frequents a variety of deciduous trees. In California, wintering birds are found almost exclusively in blooming eucalyptus trees.

Description
7–8½" (18–21.5 cm). Adult males have a uniform black crown, nape, and back; a thin black line runs from the lores through the eye and to the nape. This line contrasts with a bright orange eyebrow and cheek. The wings are mostly black, with a broad white wing patch formed by white greater and middle wing coverts. The rump is orange-yellow, and the tail is black with orange-yellow outer tail feathers. A thick black stripe runs from the chin down the middle of the throat to the center of the upper breast; the remainder of the underparts are orange, paling to yellow-orange below the breast. Females are paler than the female "Baltimore"; the back is pale gray and mostly unmarked; they have a yellowish eyebrow, a pale yellow rump, and thin white wing bars. The yellow on the underparts (rarely an orange-yellow) is restricted to the throat, breast, and undertail coverts, with the belly and flanks a dirty white or grayish-white. On some pale individuals, the yellow is restricted to the throat and upper breast. Some females show a variable amount of black on the chin and throat. The immature male is similar to the female but the yellow of the underparts is more orange; there is a black eyeline, a broad black stripe down the chin and throat, and some dark spotting or streaking on the back. First-spring males are somewhat like adults but have pale bellies, duskier upperparts, and lack the white wing patch.

Voice
Song a rich, whistled series of notes, faster and less varied than that of the "Baltimore," with guttural notes and rattles interspersed. Call a grating chatter; also a clear, sweet *kleek*.

Similar Species
See "Baltimore" Oriole. Hooded Oriole slimmer, with longer tail, slimmer and more decurved bill; gives whistled *wheet* call in addition to a chatter. Male has orange crown, lacks white wing patch; female and first-winter male have more uniform and deeper yellow underparts. Female and first-winter male Orchard Oriole smaller, shorter-billed, brighter yellow below, more greenish above; give *chuck* call. Female Scott's Oriole deeper greenish-yellow below, including the belly, has gray back with distinct dark streaking, and broader-based bill; gives *shack* call. See Streak-backed Oriole.

Range
Breeds from southern British Columbia, southern Saskatchewan, and western North Dakota south to Baja California, central Mexico, and southern Texas. Winters primarily from Mexico to Costa Rica; small numbers remain in coastal California; very rare along western Gulf Coast. Casual migrant and winter visitor in remainder of East, often at feeders.   *Paul Lehman*

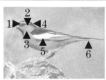

Adult male
1. *Orange eyebrow.*
2. *Black eyeline.*
3. *Orange cheek and underparts.*
4. *Black crown and upperparts.*
5. *White wing patch.*
6. *Yellow outer tail feathers.*

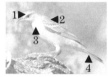

Female
1. *Yellow eyebrow.*
2. *Pale gray back.*
3. *Yellow throat and upper breast.*
4. *Yellow undertail coverts.*

Immature male
1. *Bright yellow-orange underparts.*
2. *Black throat.*

Scott's Oriole

Icterus parisorum
Male Scott's Orioles are unmistakable. They have a black head,
back, breast, and wings, bright yellow underparts and rump, and a
black-and-yellow tail. Females and immature males are greenish-
gray, with a long, heavy bill, a streaked back, and—except for
young females—varying amounts of black on the throat. These birds
are found in higher deserts where yucca plants are abundant; in
pine-live oak, piñon-juniper, and scrub oak areas, especially places
with yuccas; and near Joshua trees in the arid Southwest. Scott's
Orioles are tremendous singers. In the canyons that they frequent,
their loud, clear songs can be heard for long distances; between
songs, the birds often fly from one side of the canyon to another. In
wider, open areas, territories are quite large; here birds fly long
distances as well, in a style more undulating than that of other
orioles. These orioles can be observed closely and for prolonged
periods around hummingbird feeders in southern canyons and at
flowering yucca and agave plants. During the breeding season,
Scott's Orioles are often seen in trios that include an immature male.
All plumages and both sexes sing.

Description
7¼–8½" (18.5–21.5 cm). This fairly large, stocky oriole has long
wings and a long tail. The bill is long, often slightly decurved, and
relatively broad at the base, especially the lower mandible. Adult
males have a deep black head, back, upper breast, and tail that
contrast sharply with the yellow underparts, bend of the wing,
rump, and outer tail feathers, except for the basal portions. There is
1 white wing bar and a shorter yellow bar on the upper wing; the
flight feathers have white edgings, especially on the secondaries.
Immature males are dark gray-green above, with rather indistinct
streaking on the back; they are light gray-green below, palest on the
belly, with varying amounts of black blotching on the throat and
upper breast. Most females are very similar to immature males;
younger females, however, lack the black areas. Both have 2
relatively narrow whitish wing bars.

Voice
Song loud clear whistles, superficially resembling song of Western
Meadowlark, but less bubbly. Numerous variations, but usually with
the same clear quality. Call note a harsh *shack*.

Similar Species
Black-headed Oriole larger, with green back and solid black tail.
Similar female orioles, except for Streak-backed, lack vertical
streaking on back; bills usually thinner and shorter and less bulky.
Other orioles lighter, more yellow or orange, and have different call
notes.

Range
Breeds in southern California, southern Nevada, Utah, Arizona,
New Mexico, and western Texas, south into Oaxaca. Very rare in
Colorado; casual elsewhere to west and north. Winters primarily in
Mexico; very rarely in United States, usually at feeders.
Scott B. Terrill

Adult male
1. *Black head, throat, breast, and back.*
2. *Yellow underparts and rump.*
3. *Yellow bend of wing.*
4. *White wing bar.*
5. *Yellow on tail.*

Female
1. *Gray-green upperparts with streaks.*
2. *Greenish-gray underparts.*

Immature male
1. *Black blotches on throat and upper breast.*

Finches

(Family Fringillidae)
This is a family of small to medium-size robust birds that fit the classic definition of finches. Most species are sexually dimorphic. The Pine Grosbeak and the smaller *Carpodacus* finches have rose-red to orange adult male plumage; the females and immatures are dull brown to gray and usually streaked. The parrotlike crossbills live primarily in boreal coniferous forests. They open cones by a sideways movement of the lower mandible, over which the upper mandible crosses in a unique manner. The redpolls are rather like tiny, robust *Carpodacus* finches. The Pine Siskin is shaped much like the redpolls, but is uniformly streaked with dark and light brown and buff. Goldfinches are small, sexually dimorphic birds that commonly feed on weedy material. The Evening Grosbeak, a very robust bird of coniferous forests, occurs regularly in lowlands in winter. Almost all finches are known for their irruptive movements, which in some species are cyclical. All species give characteristic flight calls that are indispensable in identification. (World: 145 species. North America: 19 species.)   *Scott B. Terrill*

Brambling

Fringilla montifringilla
The Brambling, a small, distinctive Eurasian finch, is slightly smaller than the Lapland Longspur. In spring and fall, it is an uncommon annual migrant through the western Aleutian Islands. There it occurs singly or in small flocks; in exceptional years, flocks comprise as many as 50 birds. The Brambling feeds on thistle-head seeds and cow parsnip umbels or forages on the ground.

Description
5¾″ (14.5 cm). Male Bramblings in spring cannot be confused with any other Alaska bird. They are boldly marked in black, white, and orange. The head and back are shiny black, often with some buff feather edging, a remnant of the winter plumage. The wings are mainly black, with orange shoulders, bold orange-and-white wing bars, and a white or orange wing stripe. The throat and upper breast are bright orange, and the rump, lower back, lower breast, belly, and undertail coverts are white. The flanks are spotted with black. Unlike spring males, spring females and autumn birds of both sexes are colored in pastel shades of gray, orange, and buff, with an orange-buff wash on the breast, sides, shoulders, and the broad edging of the wing and back feathers. They also have a distinctive head pattern: 2 broad, parallel black lines begin at the sides of the crown and end at the nape, where they are separated by a pale gray-buff patch. All Bramblings have pale yellow or pale blue, dark-tipped bills, and all have the distinctive white rump and lower back.

Voice
On ground or perched, a soft, single *chup* or *chuk;* in flight, repeated rapidly.

Range
Migrant in western Aleutian Islands, Alaska. Casual visitor as far east as Alaska mainland in spring, fall, and winter. Accidental elsewhere in North America. Native to northern Eurasia.
Daniel D. Gibson

Breeding male
1. *Pale bill.*
2. *Black head and upper back.*
3. *Bright orange throat, upper breast, and shoulders.*
4. *White rump and lower back.*

Fall plumage
1. *Pale yellow, dark-tipped bill.*
2. *Broad line on back of head from crown to nape.*
3. *Orange-buff breast, sides, and shoulders.*
4. *White rump and lower back.*

Rosy Finch

Leucosticte arctoa
The Rosy Finch is a medium-size, stocky finch that breeds near or above timberline in the highest mountain ranges. It is commonly seen feeding on moist meadows at the edge of the retreating snow or hopping across snowbanks, picking up insects frozen on the surface. It usually nests in cracks in the cliffs of surrounding peaks, making long flights to the meadows and snow to feed. It is readily distinguished in flight by its undulating pattern of rapid wingbeats and glides, and by the contrast of its dark body with the light undersurface of its wings, which appear almost transparent. In late fall, it moves to lower altitudes and often south to open parks, intermountain basins, and plains, where it winters in large flocks. Rosy Finches often visit bird feeders and cattle-feeding troughs, and after a sudden, heavy snowstorm congregate in large numbers along the edges of major highways. At night, they escape the cold by roosting in barns, caves, Cliff Swallow nests, and mine shafts.

Description
5½–6½″ (14–16.5 cm). Adult male Rosy Finches have brown or black bodies with pink to red on the rump, bend of the wing, belly, and flanks; short, white feathers cover the nostrils. The bill is black in summer and yellow in winter. Adult females look similar but duller. Eight subspecies are recognized in North America (A.O.U. Checklist 1957), and these can be grouped into 5 easily identified patterns. Four of these, all but No. 2 below, have been considered separate species at one time or another, and although they are currently considered 1 species, there is evidence that several species are represented.
1. The "Gray-cheeked" or "Hepburn's" Rosy Finch (*L.a. littoralis*) has a cinnamon-brown body, black forehead and forecrown, gray hindcrown and cheeks, and, often, a gray throat.
2. The "Aleutian" Rosy Finch (*L.a. griseonucha* and *L.a. umbrina*) is similar to *littoralis*, but the body is much darker brown, more than an inch longer (about 7½″) and about twice as heavy.
3. The "Gray-crowned" Rosy Finch (restricted definition: *L.a. dawsoni*, *L.a. tephrocotis*, and *L.a. wallowa*) resembles the "Gray-cheeked" form except that the head is gray only on the crown. Some females in worn plumage (summer) may show only a trace of gray on the head, thus resembling the "Brown-capped" (see No. 5 below).
4. The "Black" Rosy Finch (*L.a. atrata*) resembles the "Gray-cheeked" form, but the gray is limited to the crown, and the body is black. In some females, the red may not be visible, and only a trace of gray may show on the head.
5. The "Brown-capped" Rosy Finch (*L.a. australis*) looks like the "Gray-cheeked," but the body is lighter brown, the red extends higher on the belly, and there is no gray on the head. Some females lack red markings.
Immature birds of all forms are completely gray-brown; they lack the head markings of adults and any trace of red.

Voice
Song a series of short, descending *chew* notes. Call notes a low, hoarse *pert*, a high-pitched *chirp*, and a single *chew* note.

Similar Species
Other red finches have red or pink breasts.

Range
Breeding ranges of North American forms: Gray-cheeked—from Alaska to California in Alaska Range, Coast Mountains, and Cascades; Aleutian form—Pribilof and Aleutian islands and Alaska Peninsula north along Bering Sea Coast; Gray-crowned—Rocky

"Gray-crowned" Rosy Finch

1. _Black forehead._
2. _Gray crown._
3. _Cinnamon-brown body and cheeks._
4. _Reddish on belly and flanks._

Red on rump and shoulder.

"Aleutian" Rosy Finch

1. _Black forehead._
2. _Gray crown and cheeks._
3. _Dark brown body._
4. _Reddish on belly, flanks, and shoulder._

Larger than other races.

"Black" Rosy Finch

1. _Gray crown._
2. _Black body._
3. _Reddish on belly._

Mountains from northern Alaska to central Idaho and Montana, also
Wallowa Mountains, Oregon, and Sierra Nevada and White
Mountains, California; Black form—central Montana and Idaho,
western Wyoming, south to southeastern Oregon, eastern Nevada,
and southern Utah; Brown-capped form—Rocky Mountains from
southern Wyoming to northern New Mexico. Winters on islands and
coast of Alaska and British Columbia east to Saskatchewan and
Dakotas and south to northern Arizona and New Mexico. Flocks of 2
or more forms increasingly common toward south. Also in mountains
of Asia.   *Richard E. Johnson*

Pine Grosbeak

Pinicola enucleator
The Pine Grosbeak is a large northern finch with a conspicuously
stubby bill. During the nesting season, it is confined to the
coniferous forests of Alaska, Canada, and the mountainous areas of
the western part of the United States. In winter, however, it may
be found south of its breeding range, where it visits bird feeders,
deciduous forest, and fruit trees. The Pine Grosbeak forages on the
fruits of crabapple, red cedar, bittersweet, sumac, and mountain
ash. In western areas it is often associated with Bohemian
Waxwings, another grayish species that occurs in large flocks at
mountain ash trees; a flock of large, grayish birds foraging in
mountain ash could be either species. The Pine Grosbeak also feeds
on the buds of a variety of trees, including maples, elms, and
birches, and takes the seeds of many plants. At bird feeders, it often
shows a preference for sunflower seeds. Like other winter finches,
Pine Grosbeaks are more common in some years than in others. The
colorful adult males generally form only a minority of winter flocks.

Description
8–10″ (20.5–25.5 cm). Adult male Pine Grosbeaks are unmistakable:
they have pinkish-red body plumage, black wings with white wing
bars, and contrasting, pale gray sides and belly. Females lack the
pink plumage and are grayish overall, with olive on the head and
rump. Immature males closely resemble the grayish females, but
have maroon heads and rumps. All ages have small, stubby bills.

Voice
Song a varied and musical warble similar to Purple Finch's, but
shorter, less varied, and weaker. Call note a loud 2- or 3-syllable
whistle, second note higher in pitch than others. Also a short,
muffled, whistled trill given in flight and quiet chattering while
feeding in flocks.

Similar Species
Male White-winged Crossbill also bright pinkish with dark wings
and white wing bars, but is smaller and has distinctive bill shape.
Bohemian Waxwing (also found in flocks in mountain ash) has
different shape, with crest and thinner bill, and has shorter, yellow-
tipped tail. Bill of Pine Grosbeak stubbier than that of any other
winter finch.

**"Brown-capped"
Rosy Finch**
1. *Brown head without
   gray on crown.*
2. *Red extends high
   on belly.*

Female
1. *Stubby bill.*
2. *Gray plumage.*
3. *Olive head.*
4. *Olive rump.*

   Large size.

Adult male
1. *Stubby bill.*
2. *Pinkish-red
   plumage.*
3. *White wing bars.*

   Large size.

Range

Boreal forests of Northern Hemisphere. In North America, resident from Alaska, Yukon, western Mackenzie, northern parts of Manitoba, Ontario, Quebec, Labrador, and Newfoundland south in higher mountains to central California and eastern Arizona (local), southern Quebec, and Nova Scotia. Winters in breeding range mountains of Great Basin, and regularly south to North Dakota, northern Minnesota, northern Wisconsin, northern Michigan, New York, and northern New England; in invasion years occurs farther south.   *Kim R. Eckert*

Purple Finch

Carpodacus purpureus

The Purple Finch is usually detected when its call note is heard as the bird flies high overhead. It is generally seen in small flocks among treetops. Rather sluggish for a bird of its size, the Purple Finch feeds less frequently on the ground than the House or Cassin's finches, and it is usually less gregarious. It is found outside of wooded areas less often than the House Finch but is much less restricted to conifers than Cassin's. In winter, the Purple Finch is a characteristic visitor to feeding stations in the East, less so in the West.

Description

5¼–5¾″ (13.5–14.5 cm). The male has a burgundy-red crown, nape, throat, breast,upper belly, and flanks, and a whitish lower belly and undertail coverts. The cheeks are reddish-brown, outlined in red. The streaked back is dark brown, suffused with burgundy-red, and the rump is bright red. The wings are dusky brown with reddish-edged coverts. The female's upperparts are dark brown with indistinct streaks; the underparts are whitish mixed with buff-yellowish tones, and conspicuously streaked with dark brown. The dark brown cheeks and mustache are emphasized by a whitish eyebrow and face. In both sexes, the tail is brownish, notched, and unmarked. Birds of the Pacific Coast are more buff-colored than eastern birds. The first-year male is similar to the female, but may sing like the adult male.

Voice

Song an outburst of rich, bubbly, rapidly delivered notes on various pitches. Most notes given in pairs or triplets; in contrast, House Finch's consecutive notes are seldom alike. In flight, gives a dry, soft *pick* call.

Similar Species

Male Cassin's Finch has much greater contrast between red crown and brown nape and back, which have only trace of reddish color; throat and breast of male Cassin's also paler and rosier. Female Cassin's Finch lacks strongly contrasting cheeks and mustache; has narrower, sharper breast streaks; pure whitish below without buff-yellowish tones; undertail coverts almost always streaked. In both sexes of Purple Finch, overall body size smaller than that of Cassin's

Immature male
1. *Stubby bill.*
2. *Gray plumage.*
3. *Maroon head.*
4. *Maroon rump.*

Large size.

Immature male
1. *Heavily streaked
   underparts.*
2. *Whitish eyebrow.*
3. *Dark brown cheeks
   and mustache.*

*Sings like adult
male.*

Female
1. *Heavily streaked
   underparts.*
2. *Whitish eyebrow.*
3. *Dark brown cheeks
   and mustache.*
4. *Notched tail.*

Finch, bill shorter and stubbier-looking, and flight calls very
different. See House Finch and Pine Siskin.

Range
Breeds in humid coastal forests from British Columbia to southern
California, western slopes of Cascades and Sierras, and across
boreal Canada and north-central and northeastern United States to
Atlantic Coast; south in Appalachians to West Virginia and Virginia.
Winters from southern edge of Canada erratically south to Mexico
and Gulf Coast; very scarce or absent from Great Basin-Rocky
Mountain region.   *J. V. Remsen, Jr.*

Cassin's Finch

Carpodacus cassinii
Cassin's Finch is found in montane, coniferous forests of the West
that are higher and drier than those favored by the Purple Finch.
This species' behavior is very similar to that of the Purple Finch,
but Cassin's is much more restricted to conifers, primarily pines.
The shiny, red crown of the male Cassin's Finch is often slightly
elevated, making the bird appear short-crested.

Description
5¾–6″ (14.5–15 cm). The male Cassin's Finch looks like the male
Purple Finch, but the back and nape are paler and only faintly
tinged with red. The female Cassin's Finch resembles the female
Purple Finch, but the face pattern is not as distinct nor the breast
streaks as broad; it also has streaked undertail coverts. Cassin's has
a longer bill than either the House or Purple finch.

Voice
Song similar to that of Purple Finch but more variable and less
organized. Both species incorporate other species' notes in songs,
but Cassin's Finch does so more frequently. Flight call a double or
triple note, *soo-leep* or *cheedly-up*, very different from that of
Purple Finch.

Similar Species
See Purple Finch, House Finch, and Pine Siskin. Female House,
Purple, and Cassin's finches differ from streaked sparrows in being
less conspicuously marked on face and back; are less terrestrial, and
have richer, more variable call notes; their flight is slower and more
undulating.

Range
Breeds from southwestern Canada south to southern California and
east into northern Arizona and New Mexico. Somewhat more
widespread in winter, especially in lowlands of Great Basin.
J. V. Remsen, Jr.

Adult male
1. *Burgundy-red head, throat, and breast.*
2. *Burgundy-red back with streaks.*
3. *Notched tail.*

Soft pick *flight call.*

Adult male
1. *Pale streaked back with little red.*

Double- or triple-note flight call, soo-leep *or* cheedly-up.

Female
1. *Less distinct face pattern than female Purple Finch.*
2. *Narrower streaks on breast than female Purple Finch.*

House Finch

Carpodacus mexicanus
The House Finch is abundant in areas inhabited by humans and is
often the commonest bird in suburban areas of the West. It feeds
from the tree tops to the ground but avoids heavy undergrowth and
tall grass. It is very gregarious; a flock of 25 or more House Finches
perched in the top of a cottonwood is a characteristic sight. At
feeding stations, the House Finch lands hesitatingly, jerking its tail,
and departs twittering.

Description
5–5½″ (12.5–14 cm). The male's forehead, throat, and long eyebrow
are orange to deep red, blending raggedly into the pale buff-gray
belly and flanks, which are streaked with brown. The cheeks,
hindcrown, nape, and back are brownish, suffused with reddish-
orange. The wings are dull brown, and the wing coverts are edged
in buff-white, forming wing bars in birds with fresh plumage. The
female is dull grayish-brown throughout, streaked indistinctly above
and strongly below. The head lacks a conspicuous pattern. In both
sexes, the tail is brown, squarish, and unmarked.

Voice
Song a scrambled series of rhythmic notes usually lasting 3 or more
seconds. Song slower, less monotonic, less fluid, and higher than
that of Cassin's or Purple finch; often ends on distinctive ascending
note. Flight call a sweet *cheeet*, often given in series, especially
when bird takes flight. Perched birds often give drawn-out,
ascending note similar to last note of song.

Similar Species
See Purple and Cassin's finches, Pine Siskin, and Common Redpoll.

Range
Resident from southern British Columbia, Idaho, Wyoming, and
western Nebraska south throughout West to Mexican border,
except in heavily forested areas or high elevations. Introduced in
East on Long Island, New York; has spread north to southern
Ontario, west to Illinois, and south to Alabama; range apparently
still expanding.   *J. V. Remsen, Jr.*

Red Crossbill

Loxia curvirostra
These birds are partial to pines, and are usually absent from areas of
the boreal forest that are dominated by spruce and lacking in pines.
They are quite vocal in flight, but usually silent while feeding, when
the cracking of the cone seeds reveals their presence. The Red
Crossbill is the more widespread of the 2 crossbills, breeding not
only in northern forests, but also throughout most of the mountains
in the West. In migration and winter, these birds can turn up in
suitable habitats almost anywhere; however, they are unlikely to
remain in the same area for an entire season. There are several
subspecies in North America that show differences in size and color.

Description
5¼–6½″ (13.5–16.5 cm). In addition to having crossed mandibles,
which are not obvious at a distance, the male Red Crossbill has dull
red plumage and a black tail and wings; it lacks wing bars. Adult
females are grayish-olive instead of red, especially on the
underparts; they have a greenish-yellow rump and sometimes have

Adult male
1. *Red forehead and eyebrow.*
2. *Red throat.*
3. *Streaked belly and flanks.*

   Sweet cheet *flight call.*

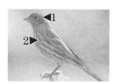

Female
1. *Unpatterned head.*
2. *Strong streaks on underparts.*

Female
1. *Crossed mandibles.*
2. *Grayish-olive plumage.*
3. *Plain wings.*

diffuse streaking on the back and breast. Both sexes show some variability in plumage color. Juveniles are duller, browner, and more heavily streaked than adults.

Voice
Song a variable series of whistles, trills, or warbles, often in groups of 2 or 3 notes: *chip-chip-chip, jeea-jeea,* or *jib-jib-jib-jee-jee-jee.* Call note a hard, flat *jib-jib-jib* or *kip-kip-kip.*

Similar Species
See White-winged Crossbill. Pine Siskin somewhat similar to immature Red Crossbill, but smaller and has thinner bill.

Range
Resident from southeastern Alaska, southern Yukon, southwestern Mackenzie, central Manitoba, central Ontario, southern Quebec, and Newfoundland south to central Saskatchewan, southern Manitoba, northern Minnesota, Wisconsin, and Michigan, southern Ontario, northern New York, and northern New England; south in mountains to Central America. Winters in northern and central United States. Also in Old World.   *Kim R. Eckert*

White-winged Crossbill

Loxia leucoptera
Like the Red Crossbill, the White-winged Crossbill is unpredictable in its wanderings, fond of spruce and pine cones, has crossed mandibles (obvious only at close range), and lives in northern coniferous forests. Unlike the Red, the White-winged is found in the western United States only in winter and is less apt to wander beyond the northeastern United States. These birds are sometimes found on roadways picking up salt and grit.

Description
6–6¾″ (15–17 cm). The most colorful winter finch, the adult male White-winged Crossbill is mostly bright pink with a black tail and wings, and conspicuous white wing bars. Adult females and juveniles are similar in color to the olive-colored female Red Crossbill, but have prominent white wing bars.

Voice
Song a long and varied series of trills, the notes like those of canaries or juncos; often given in flight. Call notes: *wink-wink-wink,* with upward, questioning inflection. Also a dry, soft chatter or trill, somewhat resembling that of a distant kingfisher.

Similar Species
In all plumages, Red Crossbill can be distinguished from White-winged by lack of wing bars. Red Crossbill's call harder, flatter, with downward inflection. See Pine Grosbeak.

Range
Resident from northern Alaska, Yukon, central Mackenzie, northern Manitoba, Ontario, Quebec, Labrador, and Newfoundland south to southern British Columbia, central Alberta, Saskatchewan, and Manitoba, northern Minnesota, northern Michigan, central Ontario, southern Quebec, and Maine. Winters south to Washington, Idaho, Colorado, and northern states; less regularly to Long Island. Irregular in winter in central states; casually south to Oregon, southern Utah, and northern New Mexico. Also in Old World.
Kim R. Eckert

Adult male
1. *Crossed mandibles.*
2. *Dull red plumage.*
3. *Plain wings.*

Adult male
1. *Crossed mandibles.*
2. *Bright pink plumage.*
3. *White wing bars.*

Female
1. *Crossed mandibles.*
2. *Grayish-olive plumage with dark streaks.*
3. *White wing bars.*

Common Redpoll

Carduelis flammea

Redpolls nest in Arctic and subarctic tundra, but in winter they move south to the northern half of the United States, where they occur in flocks at bird feeders, along roadsides, in weedy fields, and in mixed woods. They feed on the seeds of many trees, including birch, alder, and willow, both foraging in the trees and taking fallen seeds from the ground; they also eat the seeds of a variety of weeds. During invasion years, the Common Redpoll is sometimes the most widespread bird in an area, but in other years they may be scarce and hard to find, especially in the southern part of the species' range. Like other winter finches, Common Redpolls are often noisy, particularly in flight.

Description

5–5½″ (12.5–14 cm). The Common Redpoll is a small winter finch easily recognized by its red cap and black chin. Adult males have a conspicuous pink breast, with the pink often spreading down the flanks and onto the rump. This redpoll usually has brown and grayish-buff upperparts, a heavily streaked rump, and distinctly streaked sides and undertail coverts. However, some Commons are more gray and whitish above and have whitish rumps and less streaking on the rump and sides. The length of the bill is normally greater than the thickness of its base; however, their bill shape and undertail coverts may be impossible to see clearly. Juvenile Commons are heavily streaked and lack the red cap and black chin of the adult.

Voice

Song a rapid jumble of whistles, trills, and buzzes; similar to siskin's song, but not as nasal or burry. Call note a *chit-chit* or *chit-chit-chit;* also gives a note like that of goldfinch, rising in pitch: *sweeeet.*

Similar Species

Hoary Redpoll probably conspecific with Common. Paler Common Redpolls look much like Hoary Redpolls and may be impossible to distinguish in field. Commons tend to look frostier when perched in a tree and seen from below, but on ground appear distinctly darker. Male Commons often look frostier than females, but bird with extensive pink on breast is nevertheless a Common, since male Hoaries normally have only pale pinkish cast to breast. House Finch may be unfamiliar to beginning birders in East; has been misidentified as Common Redpoll. In West, see also Cassin's Finch, which has similar red cap.

Range

In North America, breeds in Alaska, Yukon, Mackenzie, Keewatin, northern Saskatchewan, Manitoba, Ontario, Quebec, Labrador, and Newfoundland. Winters irregularly south to Oregon, northern Nevada, Utah, and Colorado, Nebraska, Iowa, northern Illinois and Indiana, Ohio, West Virginia, and Virginia. Also in northern parts of Old World.   *Kim R. Eckert*

Adult male
1. Red cap.
2. Black chin.
3. Pink breast.

Adult
1. Heavily streaked
   rump.

Pale adult
1. Long, conical bill.
2. Heavily streaked
   flanks.

Hoary Redpoll

Carduelis hornemanni
Possibly conspecific with the Common Redpoll, the Hoary Redpoll barely reaches the northern United States in winter, where it is usually outnumbered by Commons by almost 100 to 1. A typically frosty Hoary is easily identified, but marginally pale redpolls are more often encountered, and identification can be very difficult.

Description
5–5½" (12.5–14 cm). A classic Hoary Redpoll is so pale that it clearly stands out even from pale Common Redpolls. Its overall color above is pale grayish, its underparts are white with little or no streaking on the sides, and its rump is pure white, also without streaking. Hoaries often droop their wings down to their sides, making the white rump easy to see. The male Hoary normally has only an indistinct tinge of pink on the breast. A typical Hoary also has a stubby, "pushed-in" bill, the length of which equals the thickness of the base; however, the bill shape may either be intermediate or difficult to see. The unstreaked undertail coverts are also usually difficult to see; what appears to be a streak may be only a shadow or a crease. Hoaries also seem to have a smaller, more sharply defined red cap than Common Redpoll.

Voice
Song similar if not identical to Common Redpoll's. Call note a *chit-chit;* seems higher in pitch than Common's.

Similar Species
Paler Commons and darker Hoaries not always distinguishable; both have whitish rumps, but Common's is completely or mostly streaked, while Hoary's is at least partly unstreaked. Can be equally frosty above; however, male Common has deeper pink breast. Presence or absence of streaking on undertail coverts usually difficult to discern. Darker Hoaries can be heavily streaked on the sides. Bill of Hoary does not always appear stubbier.

Range
Breeds along Arctic slope and Bering Coast of Alaska, northern parts of Yukon east to Manitoba and Ellesmere and northern Baffin islands. Winters irregularly south to southern British Columbia and northern states; casual to northern mid-Atlantic.   *Kim R. Eckert*

Pine Siskin

Carduelis pinus
Pine Siskins are small, nondescript, noisy finches whose diagnostic yellow markings can be quite inconspicuous. Like other winter finches, they typically occur in erratic flocks. They prefer feeders and coniferous trees and can be found in a variety of habitats.

Description
4½–5¼" (11.5–13.5 cm). The smallest of the winter finches, the Pine Siskin is usually heavily and uniformly streaked with brown and has diagnostic yellow patches along the base of the flight feathers and on the sides of the base of the tail. However, the yellow may be invisible or inconspicuous when the bird is perched, and, even in flight, the yellow wing stripe can be difficult to see. The Pine Siskin's distinctive bill is longer and thinner than that of any other finch. Plumages are quite variable; some individuals have little streaking on the underparts, an obvious greenish tinge above, and brighter and more extensive yellow wing and tail patches. Such birds resemble Eurasian Siskins and can be misidentified.

Adult
*Stubby bill.
Sparse streaks on
flanks.*

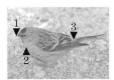

Adult male
*Stubby bill.
Indistinct tinge of
pink on breast.
White rump without
streaks.*

Pale adult
*Lightly streaked
underparts.
Extensive yellow in
wing.
Yellow at sides of
base of tail.*

Voice
Song a long, rapid jumble of notes with overall nasal quality; loud, forceful, rising *zzzhrreeee* note usually included. Call note a *sweeeet*, similar to that of goldfinch or redpoll; also more nasal and chattering than that of a redpoll.

Similar Species
See immature Red Crossbill. Also resembles juvenile redpolls and female House Finch; these have thicker bills and lack Siskin's yellow wing and tail patches (but these are often concealed and difficult to see).

Range
Breeds from southern Alaska, central Yukon, southern Mackenzie, northern Saskatchewan, central Manitoba, northern Ontario, central Quebec, and southern Labrador south in mountains to California, Arizona, New Mexico, and Texas, and to southern Saskatchewan, southern Manitoba, northern Minnesota, Wisconsin, and Michigan, and to southeastern Ontario and northern New England. Winters from southern Alaska and southern Canada south.

Kim R. Eckert

Lesser Goldfinch

Carduelis psaltria
At lower elevations, small flocks of Lesser Goldfinches can be found in open, brushy country with scattered trees and weedy stream borders. The flocks remain together when flushed, flying around the grassy ditches or hillsides, then gradually reassembling to feed on dry seeds. Plaintive calls, white wing patches, yellow underparts, and undulating flight distinguish a flock of Lesser Goldfinches. This bird appropriates the songs and calls of other birds. As William Dawson wrote in 1923, "It deftly seizes the notes of all its associates. There is no time for leisurely choice. Song of Flicker, Wren, or Pewee—everything goes."

Description
4–4½″ (10–11.5 cm). Goldfinches are small, short-tailed finches that remind most people of canaries. A flock of Lesser Goldfinches consists of many green-and-yellow birds that show white wing patches in flight. There are 2 forms of males. Throughout most of their range in the United States, adult males have a black crown, green back, yellow underparts, and black wings and tail; the wings have white edgings on the tertials and a white patch at the base of the primaries, which is visible in flight. The tail has white at the base, but this is visible only when the tail is spread. Unlike the adult males in the western part of the range (California, Arizona, and Sonora, Mexico), which have greenish backs, those from Colorado and farther south usually have entirely black upperparts year-round. Populations in Mexico and farther south appear to be exclusively of the black type, while in Colorado and west Texas some of the green type are found. These are not likely to be 1-year-old males, because in all other finches, 1-year-olds are virtually identical to adults; these northern populations may exhibit simple polymorphism. Females of all populations are greenish-yellow overall, and yellowest on the throat and undertail coverts; they have a dull version of the male's wing and tail pattern. Immatures are generally all greenish, sometimes with faint streaks on the breast.

Voice
Song a sweet twittering with interspersed upslurred notes. Typical calls: questioning, plaintive *tee-yee* or *choo-i*, and *cheeo;* also plainer *jee* or *ee-ee*, often heard when flushed and uttered in glides between wingbeats. Song not as extended and clear as song of Lawrence's.

Dark adult
. Heavy streaks on
  underparts.
. Little yellow visible
  in wing.

Green-backed male
. Black cap.
. Dark green back.
. Yellow underparts.
. White wing patch.

Usually in flocks.

Female
. Greenish-yellow
  upperparts,
  including rump.

White at base of tail
visible in flight.

Similar Species
American Goldfinch not greenish, either all bright yellow (spring male) or brownish-yellow; lacks white wing patch, has concealed white spots to tip of tail but not to base, and white to buff crissum.

Range
Breeds from southwestern Washington, western Oregon, and northern Nevada east to northern Colorado and central Texas, south to northwestern Peru and northern Venezuela. Largely resident, although eastern form is partially migratory. Casual outside of breeding areas to British Columbia, Louisiana, and Kentucky.
Louis R. Bevier

Lawrence's Goldfinch

Carduelis lawrencei
Lawrence's Goldfinch has a soft gray body washed in places with gold. Its movements are unpredictable; one often only hears its bell-like call overhead. They breed almost exclusviely in California, where they prefer the drier, interior valleys and lower mountains.

Description
4–4½" (10–11.5 cm). Both male and female Lawrence's Goldfinches are gray with a yellow wash on the breast, wings, and rump. Males are brighter yellow, and may show a tinge of green on the back; they also have black around the front of the face on the forehead, lores, and chin. This pattern is acquired fresh each fall since there is no spring molt. There are white spots on the center of the inner webs of the tail feathers. These spots can be seen from below and sometimes in flight. Immatures are grayish-brown with only traces of the yellow; they sometimes have faint breast streaks.

Voice
Call a *tink-oo* or *tink-l*, frequently given, mostly in flight; harsh *kee-yerr* sometimes given when perched. Song has tinkling quality of call with typical goldfinch twittering. Like Lesser Goldfinch, Lawrence's appropriates much of song from other birds, but Lawrence's song more extended and clearer than Lesser's.

Similar Species
Lucy's, Virginia's, and Colima warblers are gray and similar in size, but lack white tail spots and yellow on wings; bills not conical; calls differ. Nondescript immature Lawrence's might be confused with other warblers or vireos except for bill shape and tail spots.

Range
Local and discontinuous distribution; numbers variable from one year to next. Primarily summer resident (March to September) in arid interior foothills and valleys from northern California west of Sierra Nevada south to northern Baja California; most common from Los Angeles County south occasionally to southern Arizona. Winters very irregularly over much of this area, mostly in south, but also in southern Arizona, New Mexico, west Texas, and adjacent northern Mexico. Casual migrant to deserts southeast of Sierra Nevada to Nevada.   *Louis R. Bevier*

Black-backed male
1. *Black crown and upperparts.*
2. *Yellow underparts.*
3. *White wing patch.*

Adult male
1. *Black face and chin.*
2. *Yellow breast.*
3. *Gray back.*
4. *Yellow wing bars.*

Female
1. *Grayish head.*
2. *Yellow on breast.*
3. *Gray back.*
4. *Yellow wing bars.*

American Goldfinch

Carduelis tristis
The American Goldfinch is a widespread and relatively common bird with a lively, cheerful disposition. This species prefers to feed on plants bearing many seeds, like thistles; deciduous trees and weedy fields are also used, especially by wintering flocks. American Goldfinches need trees for nesting and, except in winter, avoid treeless plains and thick forests. In California and the Southwest, these birds are associated with riparian areas, particularly where there are willows along streams and ditches. Over most of its breeding range, this species is a very late nester (July through August); however birds of California and the Southwest have an early nesting period (April through May) that is carefully timed to avoid the summer drought. The spring molt of the race in California is prolonged and irregular; some individuals apparently never attain the bright plumage of other American Goldfinches.

Description
4½–5½" (11.5–14 cm). In fall and winter, these small birds are olive-brown above with black wings and buff-white wing bars. There is a yellow wash about the head, and the flanks are brownish-buff. In spring, the males are bright yellow with a black forehead and a black cap that looks as though it is tipped forward. The wings and tail are black; the wing has thin, white wing bars and feather edges; the rump is white. Females are dull olive-yellow above, with yellow on the throat and breast. In adults, the shoulder is yellow; in first-year birds, it is olive-green. The undertail coverts and uppertail coverts are whitish. The tail has large white spots on the tips of the concealed inner webs of the feathers; these white spots are apparent in flight. The male in winter is olive-brown like the female, but tends to be brighter yellow on the throat and shows a tinge of yellow on the rump. The shoulder patch is mostly olive-green, not yellow. Both sexes are browner and more buff-colored below in winter. Juveniles have rich cinnamon-buff wing bars and upperparts, with brownish to blackish wings and tail; otherwise they resemble the female.

Voice
Call a *chi-dup, chi-dee-dup,* or *ti-dee-di-di;* given in flight, usually between wingbeats. Sometimes a sweeter, whining *chi-ee.* Song has jumbled, sweet, twittering quality similar to end of Lazuli Bunting's song.

Similar Species
See Lesser Goldfinch. Immature Indigo Bunting also rich cinnamon-buff, but browner and streaked below with thinner buff wing bars.

Range
Breeds across southern Canada and northern United States from southern British Columbia to southwestern Newfoundland, south to northern Baja, and central Nevada, east across southern Colorado and northeastern Texas; less commonly in northern parts of Gulf States and north to South Carolina. Winters over most of breeding range in east and west, mostly leaving interior; also south to northern Mexico, Gulf Coast, and Florida. *Louis R. Bevier*

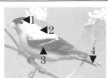

Breeding male
1. *Black forehead and cap.*
2. *Bright yellow back and underparts.*
3. *Black wings with white wing bars.*
4. *Black tail.*

   Shows white rump in flight.

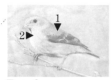

Female
1. *Dull yellow-olive upperparts.*
2. *Brighter yellow on throat and breast.*

Winter plumage
1. *Olive-brown back.*
2. *Yellow wash on head.*
3. *Black wings with buff-white wing bars.*
4. *Brownish-buff flanks.*

Evening Grosbeak

Coccothraustes vespertinus
The Evening Grosbeak is a gregarious, chunky, Starling-size finch with a short tail, enormous bill, and large white wing patches. In flight, its undulating movement, wing patches, and loud call notes are distinctive. This bird winters irregularly in the southern parts of its range, where it frequently visits sunflower-seed feeders. In northern areas during the winter, flocks of Evening Grosbeaks often congregate along roads. There, the birds feed on salt that has been put down to melt ice.

Description
7–8½″ (18–21.5 cm). The male Evening Grosbeak has a yellow forehead and eyebrow stripe; the rest of the head, the nape, upper back, and breast are rich brown, becoming yellow on the lower back, rump, and belly. The wings are black with a large white patch on the rear inner edge; the tail is black. The female is mostly gray, tinged below with yellow; its wing pattern is similar to that of the male. The large, cone-shaped bill is greenish-yellow.

Voice
Song a wandering, jerky warble. Call note a loud *cleep* or *cleer* like that of House Sparrow, or soft, clicking note given when perched and in flight.

Similar Species
American Goldfinch much smaller, with tiny bill and no white wing patches.

Range
Breeds from north-central British Columbia east through central Canada to northern Ontario, southern Quebec, southern Newfoundland, and Nova Scotia; south in western mountains to central California and southern Mexico. In East, breeds to northeastern Minnesota, central New York, and northern New England. Range expanding eastward and southward. Winters from southern Canada irregularly south to southern United States.
Wayne R. Petersen

Adult male

1. *Conical yellowish bill.*
2. *Yellow eyebrow.*
3. *Brown foreparts.*
4. *Yellow belly.*
5. *Yellow rump.*
6. *Large white wing patch.*

Female

1. *Conical yellowish bill.*
2. *Grayish upperparts.*
3. *Large white wing patch.*

Old World Sparrows

(Family Passeridae)
In North America this family is represented by only 2 species, both of which have been introduced from the Old World. The members of this family are finchlike, thick-billed, and short-legged; they are also robust and have relatively large heads. Some species are sexually dimorphic. Most members of the family are highly gregarious; their vocal repertoires are limited to various loud chirps. The House Sparrow has adapted tremendously to life on this continent in a very short time; it is an abundant resident throughout the region around human habitation, except in the far North. The Eurasian Tree Sparrow, in contrast, is very local, being found only in the area of St. Louis, Missouri. House Sparrows are one of the few species able to survive and reproduce prolifically in the midst of metropolitan America. (World: 37 species. North America: 2 species.)
Scott B. Terrill

House Sparrow

Passer domesticus
Found in almost every city in the United States and Canada, the House Sparrow is probably one of the first birds that most people learn to recognize. Male House Sparrows are more distinctively plumaged than either females or immatures, but in general this species is rather plain and nondescript; birds inhabiting urban areas tend to be dingier and dirtier looking than those in rural environments. Full of nervous energy, House Sparrows have an extremely aggressive and pugnacious disposition. They are quite sociable and sometimes travel in large flocks. These birds were first introduced into this country in 1850, primarily to help control cankerworms. In the following years, many more introductions took place, and the House Sparrow rapidly became common throughout the country. Contrary to what was originally thought, this species is mainly vegetarian and consequently has not been of much use in controlling crop pests; ironically, it has become something of a pest itself. In spring, House Sparrows can typically be found feasting on the tips of branches and on young, tender fruit buds. Flocking together in winter, these birds cluster around garbage and waste containers in cities and around barns and grain storage facilities in rural areas to find easy food supplies. In the 20th century, this species' population apparently declined in the East, possibly because the automobile has replaced the horse, greatly reducing the supply of food available to House Sparrows in cities.

Description
5½–6¼" (14–16 cm). The male in breeding plumage has a gray crown, chestnut nape, white or whitish cheek, black throat and breast, gray belly, and streaked back. The bill is black. Males in winter plumage have the black confined to the chin and have yellowish bills. Female and young are much plainer, with a streaked back, plain, dingy, light brown underside, and dull eyeline. Males that inhabit rural areas are usually whiter or cleaner in appearance .

Voice
Mixture of various twitters and chirps, nervous and sometimes garbled; certainly anything but musical.

Similar Species
Male distinctive and could be confused only at first glance. Plain

House Sparrow
Eurasian Tree Sparrow

Breeding male
1. *Black bill.*
2. *Black throat and upper breast.*
3. *Whitish cheek.*
4. *Gray crown.*
5. *Chestnut nape.*
6. *Streaked back.*
7. *Bold white wing bar.*

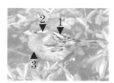

Female
1. *Streaked upperparts.*
2. *Pale eyebrow.*
3. *Plain, dingy underparts.*

female and young could be confused with several of 'plain' western sparrows, but habits, habitats, and voice separate true western sparrows from this weaver finch. See Eurasian Tree Sparrow and Dickcissel.

Range

Introduced; common throughout contiguous United States and into central Canada (north to limit of major cities and towns). Also introduced into South America, Australia, New Zealand, Hawaii, and elsewhere. Originally native to Eurasia and northern Africa.
Jack Van Benthuysen

Eurasian Tree Sparrow

Passer montanus
In the United States, this introduced member of the Old World sparrow family occurs only near St. Louis, Missouri. Far less aggressive than its pugnacious relative the House Sparrow, the Eurasian Tree Sparrow has nevertheless managed to hold its own and inhabits residential suburbs and farmlands, where it moves about nervously and energetically. In the winter, it is quite often found in flocks containing as many as 100 birds.

Description

5–5½" (12.5–14 cm). The sexes look alike, and both are somewhat similar to the male House Sparrow; however, they are slightly smaller and thinner. The 2 species are often found together; the Eurasian Tree Sparrow can be distinguished by its white cheek with a black patch on the ear covert, a black chin patch that is narrower and smaller than the House Sparrow's, and a chocolate, rather than gray, crown. There are 2 white wing bars, the lower one narrower and much less conspicuous.

Voice

Eurasian Tree Sparrow has slightly higher-pitched voice than that of House Sparrow, but both chirp and have little other song. Both tend to mix twittering with notes that are not quite musical. Chirping and chattering soon become monotonous.

Similar Species

House Sparrow has similar habits but is decidedly shabbier in comparison.

Range

Introduced and found sporadically within a 50-mile radius of St. Louis, Missouri. Range has jutted northeast into Illinois as far as 100 miles. Native to most of Eurasia.   *Jack Van Benthuysen*

Winter male
Yellowish bill.
Black chin.

Adult
Chocolate-brown
crown.
White cheek with
black patch on ear
coverts.

Adult
Black chin.
Two narrow white
wing bars.

Thinner build than
House Sparrow.

Part Three

Accidental Species

Accidental species are those that have strayed from their normal ranges and have been recorded only a handful of times on the North American continent.

Middendorff's Grasshopper-Warbler

Locustella ochotensis. 6¼″ (16 cm). Unlike any other North American passerine. A drab skulker, olive-brown above, creamy-white below. Long, graduated tail feathers have black spots near base and white tips. Shows prominent whitish eyebrow and pale bill. Extremely difficult to see because it usually skulks in the thickest vegetation. Utters a soft call note. Native to Asia. Casual in fall, accidental in spring to western Alaska.   *Theodore G. Tobish Jr.*

Wood Warbler
Phylloscopus sibilatrix. 5″ (12.5 cm). Has more yellow than most members of the genus, including Arctic Warbler: yellow on breast, throat, and eyebrow, olive-green on back. Nearest breeding area over 2000 miles away in south-central Asia. Accidental in western Aleutian Islands, Alaska.   *Theodore G. Tobish Jr.*

Dusky Warbler
Phylloscopus fuscatus. 4½″ (11.5 cm). A tiny Old World leaf-warbler. Plain olive-brown above, dusky white below; lacks wing bars. Has pale buff-white eyebrow and short, thin, horn-colored bill. Call a distinctive *tchak-tchak*, like that given by Winter Wren. In Alaska, confused only with Arctic Warbler, which is larger, greener above, and has 1–2 pale wing bars. Breeds in northeastern Asia. Two records from Alaska in fall. Accidental at Farallon Islands, California, in fall.   *Theodore G. Tobish Jr.*

Red-breasted Flycatcher
Ficedula parva. 5¼″ (13.5 cm). A compact Old World flycatcher. Male has orange-red throat and sooty-gray face and chest; female paler buff above, mostly white below. Both sexes have black tail feathers with squarish white patches at base of outer pairs. Feeds on or near ground and flashes its tail open. Casual in spring to the western Aleutians and St. Lawrence Island, Alaska. *Theodore G. Tobish Jr.*

Siberian Flycatcher
Muscicapa sibirica. 5½″ (14 cm). Very similar to Gray-spotted Flycatcher. Dull sooty-brown above. Adults have white throat and sooty breastband of fused streaks and smudges and a subtle buff wing bar. Very small and short-tailed with a small dark bill. Native to northeastern Asia. Accidental in Alaska: 1 autumn immature with white-spotted back.   *Theodore G. Tobish Jr.*

Gray-spotted Flycatcher
Muscicapa griseisticta. 6″ (15 cm). Plumage closely resembles that of Siberian Flycatcher. In spring, has off-white lores, distinct dark streaks on underparts, and faint whitish wing bar. Can be distinguished from Siberian Flycatcher by larger size, larger culmen, longer tail, and pale lores. Native to northeastern Asia. Rare; probably annual spring migrant in western Aleutian Islands, Alaska.   *Theodore G. Tobish Jr.*

Dusky Thrush
Turdus naumanni. 10″ (25.5 cm). A large, boldly patterned *Turdus* thrush, with a prominent white eyebrow and rufous upperwing surfaces. Males of race *eunomus* have 2 black, scaly breastbands and black scales on belly and flanks. Rich brown upperparts, rufous wing linings, and bases of tail feathers also unique. Females duller and browner, with less black on underparts. Native to northeastern

Asia. Casual spring migrant in western Aleutian Islands, Alaska.   *Theodore G. Tobish Jr.*

Fieldfare
Turdus pilaris. 10″ (25.5 cm). The largest *Turdus* thrush occurring in North America. Gray head and rump contrast with rich red-brown back and wing coverts and black tail. Pale underparts have bold black chevrons across buff breast and flanks. Short white eyebrow, black legs, and yellowish bill also unique. Flashes silvery wing linings. Native to Eurasia. Casual in northeastern Canada and Atlantic states. Accidental in Alaska.   *Theodore G. Tobish Jr.*

Redwing
Turdus iliacus. 8″ (20.5 cm). General *Turdus* shape; similar to American Robin but smaller, with shorter tail. Upperparts brownish. Bold whitish eyebrow and line under eye. Whitish throat curves up below auriculars and contrasts with blackish malar stripe. Underparts heavily streaked. Flanks and underwing coverts reddish. Call a high, penetrating double note. Native to Eurasia. Has occurred in Newfoundland during summer.   *Scott B. Terrill*

Aztec Thrush
Ridgwayia pinicola. 8½″ (21.5 cm). A boldly patterned, rotund thrush with thick, longish, slightly decurved bill and relatively short tail. Male has primarily blackish-brown upperparts, head, breast, and tail; these boldly contrast with white underparts, uppertail coverts, wing patches, and tail tip. Female similar, but dark areas more brownish, and appears very streaked overall. Native to high mountains of Mexico. Has occurred in summer in Texas at Big Bend; in spring and summer in southeastern Arizona.   *Scott B. Terrill*

Mimic-Thrushes

Bahama Mockingbird
Mimus gundlachii. 11″ (28 cm). Resembles Northern Mockingbird but larger, rather thrasherlike. Plumage more brownish, especially on upperparts, and with streaking on head, back, and flanks that is entirely absent in Northern. Lacks extensive white patches in wings of Northern. White in wings restricted to covert edgings. Native to West Indies. Accidental in Florida Keys.   *Scott B. Terrill*

Accentors

Siberian Accentor
Prunella montanella. 6″ (15 cm). This bird is a member of the family Prunellidae, a small group of Old World songbirds that are mostly found in alpine and barren habitats. They are sparrowlike in general appearance, but have slender, pointed bills. The Siberian Accentor is small and distinctive. Feathers on upperparts have black-brown centers and rich chestnut fringes. Distinctly masked, with black crown and cheeks. Rich orange-buff eyebrow, throat, and breast. Rusty flank streaks and gray collar. Native to northeastern Asia. Casual in fall on Bering Sea Islands of Alaska. One fall record from south-central Alaska mainland.   *Theodore G. Tobish Jr.*

Wagtails and Pipits

Gray Wagtail
Motacilla cinerea. 7½″ (19 cm). Reminiscent of Yellow Wagtail but with blue-gray upperparts, pale legs; size and proportions like those of White Wagtail. Male has black throat and white malar lines; female's throat duller white. In flight has bright white wing stripe and yellowish rump. Autumn immatures resemble females but dull brown above with white throat, buff-white underparts, and yellow undertail coverts. Call notes like those of Black-backed or White wagtails but clearer and more defined. Typically very wary. Native to Old World. Casual spring migrant on Bering Sea Islands of western Alaska.   *Theodore G. Tobish Jr.*

Brown Tree-Pipit
Anthus trivialis. 6″ (15 cm). Similar to Olive Tree-Pipit but has clear dark streaks on distinctly brown back and less boldly spotted breast.

Face much less patterned, closer to female and immature Red-throated or Pechora pipits. Upperparts lack the pale border streaks present on Pechora or Red-throated. Readily perches and roosts on vegetation. Native to Eurasia. One record from Wales, Alaska. *Theodore G. Tobish Jr.*

Pechora Pipit
Anthus gustavi. 6″ (15 cm). Brightly marked with rich rust-edged feathers on upperparts. Washed with warm yellow-buff on face and across dark-streaked breast and flanks. Two clear white streaks border the back. Dingy buff outer tail feathers visible in flight. Slightly larger than other North American pipits, with a larger bill. Usually silent and very inconspicuous. Call a loud dry *pwet*, often repeated. Native to northeastern Asia. Casual spring migrant to Bering Sea Islands of western Alaska.   *Theodore G. Tobish Jr.*

Brown Shrike   *Shrikes*
Lanius cristatus. 7¾″ (19.5 cm). Slightly smaller than Loggerhead Shrike with a rust-brown back and tail, clear white underparts, white eyebrow, and black eyeline. Wings unmarked. Immature dingier above and narrowly barred on back and sides of underparts. Native to Asia. Two records from western Alaska: 1 in spring, 1 immature in fall.   *Theodore G. Tobish Jr.*

Thick-billed Vireo   *Vireos*
Vireo crassirostris. 5¼″ (13.5 cm). Plumage and song closely resemble those of White-eyed Vireo. Entire underparts are pale yellowish, paling slightly or fading to whitish posteriorly. White-eyed has clear yellow sides and flanks that contrast clearly with white throat, upper breast, and central underparts. Iris never white as in adult White-eyed. Also slightly larger, thicker billed, and more sluggish than White-eyed. Native to West Indies. Four sight records from Florida, 3 in winter.   *Scott B. Terrill*

Gray-crowned Yellowthroat   *Wood Warblers*
Geothlypis poliocephala. 5½″ (14 cm). A long-tailed, thick-billed warbler usually seen close to the ground or on it. Male has olive-green upperparts, yellow underparts, and a gray head. Forehead and lores black. Broken white eye-ring. Female similar, but paler, lacking gray head and black lores. Common Yellowthroat smaller, with smaller bill, and has white on underparts. Native from Mexico south to Panama. Formerly resident in southern Texas; quite rare in this century.   *Scott B. Terrill*

Slate-throated Redstart
Myioborus miniatus. 5″ (12.5 cm). Resembles Painted Redstart in plumage and behavior, but lacks white in wing; upperparts more gray, underparts more orange than black and red of Painted Redstart. Native to Neotropics and West Indies; common in mountains of northwest Mexico. Two records: 1 from New Mexico and 1 from Arizona, both in mid-April.   *Scott B. Terrill*

Fan-tailed Warbler
Euthlypis lachrymosa. 6″ (15 cm). Unique among North American warblers. An active bird with long, rounded tail. Tail flipping and spreading reminiscent of American Redstart. Upperparts, sides of head, and tail blackish-gray; tail feathers tipped with white. White spot on lores and eyelids. Underparts bright yellow with brownish-orange wash on breast. Native to Mexico. Has occurred twice in Arizona.   *Scott B. Terrill*

Golden-crowned Warbler
Basileuterus culicivorus. 4½–5″ (11.5–12.5 cm). Greenish-gray on upperparts, yellow on underparts, tinged with greenish on sides and flanks. No other North American warbler has this bird's unique

combination of conspicuous yellow central crown stripe bordered by black, with paler yellowish eye-ring and eyebrow and dark eyeline. Does not have wing bars or tail spots. Has occurred in extreme southern Texas. Widespread throughout New World tropics. *Scott B. Terrill*

Cardinals and Their Allies

Yellow Grosbeak
Pheucticus chrysopeplus. 9″ (23 cm). Unmistakable. A large grosbeak with a huge, deep bill. Adult male solid lemon yellow; black wings and tail boldly patterned with white. Female similar but duller, with streaked upperparts. Native to western Mexico. Straggler to Arizona in summer.   *Scott B. Terrill*

Blue Bunting
Cyanocompsa parellina. 5″ (12.5 cm). A stocky bunting with a large, deep bill. Indigo Bunting has much smaller bill. Adult male very dark blue, appearing largely black with brilliant light blue on forehead, whisker area, rump, and bend of wing; male Indigo Bunting much lighter blue overall. Female Blue Bunting very dark, rich, rusty brown; female Indigo duller. Native from Mexico to Central America. Casual in southern Texas. Accidental in Louisiana.   *Scott B. Terrill*

New World Sparrows and Their Allies

Black-faced Grassquit
Tiaris bicolor. 4½″ (11.5 cm). Adult male unique in North America: small and finchlike, with dark, dull green upperparts and black on sides of head, neck, and breast. Female much more difficult to identify: a nondescript olive-brown (paler on underparts) bunting-like bird. Female Painted Bunting greener; female Indigo Bunting browner. Native to West Indies. Accidental in Florida. *Scott B. Terrill*

Little Bunting
Emberiza pusilla. 5″ (12.5 cm). Size of Savannah Sparrow, with boldly patterned head. Spring males have rich chestnut eyebrow, cheeks, and median crown stripe, all with thin black outline. Remaining upperparts streaked with warm buff and dark brown; underparts white and finely streaked with dark brown. Females and immatures also have chestnut shading but head pattern duller. Female and young Rustic Bunting have rusty rumps and rust streaks on underparts. Native to northern Eurasia. Accidental in fall in western Alaska.   *Theodore G. Tobish Jr.*

Gray Bunting
Emberiza variabilis. 6½″ (16.5 cm). One of the largest and heaviest-billed Old World buntings. Males unique, with sooty-gray plumage. Females considerably paler; dingy white and streaked below, gray-brown with dark streaks above. Rump outlined with rufous. Plain dingy face shows an off-white eyebrow. Both sexes lack white in tail feathers and have pinkish legs and bill. First spring males gray like adult but back, rump, and wings outlined with rusty brown. Recorded twice in spring in western Aleutian Islands, Alaska. *Theodore G. Tobish Jr.*

Pallas' Reed-Bunting
Emberiza pallasi. 5½″ (14 cm). Very similar to the larger Common Reed-Bunting but back paler and more grayish-brown with a grayish rump. Lacks any rusty tones, including lesser wing coverts, which are rusty in Common Reed-Bunting. Black head pattern basically identical to that of Common Reed-Bunting. Females also difficult to identify but paler, more sandy-colored above with a paler rump and nape. Bill smaller and stubbier but shaped like that of Common Reed-Bunting. Breeds mostly in interior northeastern Asia. Two spring records from northwestern Alaska. *Theodore G. Tobish Jr.*

Common Reed-Bunting
Emberiza schoeniclus. 6" (15 cm). Most closely resembles the smaller
Pallas' Reed-Bunting. Characteristically warm rust above with no
grayish tones, and very large-billed. Female usually shows a more
patterned face and throat than Pallas', with more rusty streaks on
the underparts and a warm buff rump. Native to Eurasia. Three
spring records from western Aleutians, Alaska.
Theodore G. Tobish Jr.

Tawny-shouldered Blackbird
Agelaius humeralis. 7½–8½" (19–21.5 cm). Very similar to Red-
winged Blackbird but usually smaller. In general, sexes are similar.
Both have buff-orange shoulder patches outlined with buff; patch
often reduced in females. Red-winged can show extreme variation in
shade of epaulette and thus can appear very similar in coloration.
Native to West Indies. Accidental in Florida.   *Scott B. Terrill*

*New World
Blackbirds and
Orioles*

Black-vented Oriole
Icterus wagleri. 9" (23 cm). Adult has solid black head, upper back,
throat, upper breast, wings, tail, and crissum; these contrast starkly
with bright orange at bend of wing and on lower breast, belly, and
rump. Other similar North American orioles with black head and
back have orange or yellow patches in tail. Strays from western
Mexico into Texas (Big Bend and San Ignacio). Native to Mexico
and West Indies. One sight record for Chiricahua Mountains,
Arizona.   *Scott B. Terrill*

Common Rosefinch
Carpodacus erythrinus. 5¾" (14.5 cm). Size and pattern like those of
Purple or Cassin's finch. Male has greater amount of rich red on
mostly unstreaked head and breast; red often extends onto back and
rump. Female dull brown with indistinct back streaks and 2 faint
buff wing bars. Black eye conspicuous on plain face. Female Purple,
Cassin's, and House finches have more pattern on face and are more
streaked above. Native to Eurasia. Casual in spring, accidental in
fall in western Alaska.   *Theodore G. Tobish Jr.*

Finches

Oriental Greenfinch
Carduelis sinica. 5½" (14 cm). Slightly larger and more plump than
Common Redpoll, with a larger pale bill. Gray-green head and
green-brown back with bright yellow patches in wing and at tail
base quickly identify this finch. Wing linings and undertail coverts
also yellowish. Females and immatures more uniform green-brown.
Native to northeastern Asia. Casual in spring, accidental in fall in
western Aleutians, Alaska.   *Theodore G. Tobish Jr.*

Eurasian Bullfinch
Pyrrhula pyrrhula. 6" (15 cm). A small black-capped finch with a
white rump and a very short, stubby black bill. Plumage combines
soft gray back, black tail, and rich rosy-pink throat and breast.
Large white wing bar also distinctive. Females browner above and
pinkish below, with a gray nape. Utters soft call note. Native to
Eurasia. Casual in spring and fall in Bering Sea region of Alaska;
4 winter mainland records from Alaska.   *Theodore G. Tobish Jr.*

Hawfinch
Coccothraustes coccothraustes. 7" (18 cm). Slightly smaller than
Evening Grosbeak, with a similar large bill. Thick-necked as
Eurasian Bullfinch, with several subtle pastel feather patterns, 2
white wing bars in flight, and short white-tipped tail. Male shows
gray nape and rich brownish head and bluish bill. Female more
uniformly cool brown with paler bill. Two-syllable flight call a zippy
metallic *chizick.* Native to Eurasia. Casual spring migrant in
western Aleutians; rare on Bering Sea Islands to north. Accidental
in fall.   *Theodore G. Tobish Jr.*

Glossary

This glossary was prepared by Peter F. Cannell.

Accidental A species that has appeared in a given area a very few times only and whose normal range is in another area.

Allopatric Occupying separate, nonoverlapping geographic ranges. *Cf.* Sympatric.

Alula A small, feathered projection attached to a bird's wrist and extending outward along the leading edge of the wing; the alula can be moved independently and used to affect air flow over the wing during flight.

Anterior Toward the head.

Auriculars *See* Ear coverts.

Axillars The long, innermost feathers of the underwing, covering the area where the wing joins the body. *Cf.* Scapulars.

Back The portion of the upperparts located behind the nape and between the wings.

Barred Having stripes across the feathers.

Basal Toward or at the base of a structure. *Cf.* Distal.

Belly The portion of the underparts between the breast and the undertail coverts.

Bib An area of contrasting color on the chin, throat, upper breast, or all three of these.

Boreal Northern, specifically referring to the tundra and coniferous forest habitats.

Breast The area of the underparts between the foreneck and the belly.

Breastband A band of contrasting color that runs across the breast.

Breeding plumage A coat of feathers worn by an adult bird during the breeding season, usually acquired by partial spring molt, feather wear, or both; the male's breeding plumage is often more brightly colored than its winter plumage or than the adult female's breeding plumage.

Breeding range The geographic area in which a species nests.

Call A brief vocalization with a relatively simple acoustical structure, usually given year-round by both sexes. *Cf.* Song.

Cap An area of contrasting color on the top of the head.

Carpal joint *See* Wrist.

Casual Occurring infrequently in a given geographic area but more often than an accidental.

Cere A bare, fleshy area at the base of the upper mandible that surrounds the nostrils; swollen and distinctively colored in some birds.

Cheek The side of the face.

Chin The area immediately below the base of the lower mandible.

Collar A band of contrasting color that runs across the foreneck, hindneck, or both.

Colonial Nesting in groups or colonies rather than in isolated pairs.

Color morph or Color phase One of two or more distinct color types within a species, occurring independently of age, sex, or season.

Conspecific Belonging to the same species.

Cosmopolitan Occurring on all continents except Antarctica; worldwide.

Coverts Small feathers that cover the bases of other, usually larger, feathers and provide a smooth, aerodynamic surface.

Crepuscular Active at twilight.

Crest A group of elongated feathers on the top of a bird's head.

Crissum The undertail coverts, especially when these are distinctively colored.

Crown The upper surface of the head, between the eyebrows.

Cryptic Serving to conceal by camouflage, either by coloring or by form.

Culmen The midline ridge along the top of a bird's upper mandible.

Dimorphic Having two distinct forms within a population, differing in size, form, or color.

Distal Away from the center of the body. *Cf.* Proximal, Basal.

Diurnal Active during the day.

Dorsal Pertaining to the upper surface of the body.

Ear coverts Small, loose-webbed feathers on the side of the face behind and below the eye, covering the ear region.

Ear patch An area of contrasting color on the ear coverts.

Ear tuft A group of elongated feathers above the eyes that resemble ears; characteristic of some owl and grebe species, and the Horned Lark.

Escape A bird that has escaped from captivity rather than arriving in an area by natural means.

Exotic Not native to an area, and coming from outside North America.

Eyebrow A stripe on the side of the head immediately above the eye.

Eyeline A straight, thin, horizontal stripe on the side of the face, running through the eye.

Eye plate A small, horny plate adjacent to the eye.

Eye-ring A fleshy or feathered ring around the eye, often distinctively colored.

Eye stripe A stripe that runs horizontally from the base of the bill through the eye; usually broader than an eyeline.

Face The front of the head, generally including the cheeks, forehead, and lores, and sometimes the chin or crown.

Facial disk The feathers that encircle the eyes of some birds, especially owls.

Facial frame A color pattern that borders or encircles the face, as in many owls.

Field mark A characteristic of color, pattern, or structure useful in identifying a species in the field.

Filoplume A hairlike or bristlelike feather that consists of a shaft, few side branches, and no vanes.

Flank The rear portion of the side of a bird's body.

Flight feathers The long, firm feathers of the wings and tail used during flight. The flight feathers of the wings are the primaries, secondaries, and tertials; those of the tail are called rectrices.

Forecrown The portion of the crown just behind the forehead.

Forehead The area of the head just above the base of the upper mandible.

Foreneck	The front or underside of the neck.
Frontal shield	A fleshy, featherless, and often brightly colored area on the forehead.
Gape	The angle between the upper and lower mandibles when the bill is open; the opening between the upper and lower mandibles.
Gonys	The prominent midline ridge along the lower surface of the lower mandible.
Gorget	In hummingbirds, a throat patch composed of iridescent feathers.
Greater wing coverts	A row of short feathers that covers the bases of the secondaries; also called greater secondary coverts.
Hallux	The innermost toe of a bird's foot; it usually extends backward, is sometimes reduced or absent, and sometimes raised above the level of other toes.
Hindcrown	The rear portion of the crown.
Hindneck	The rear or upper surface of the neck; the nape.
Hind toe	*See* Hallux.
Hood	A distinctively colored area usually covering most or all of the head.
Hybrid	The offspring of a pair made up of two different species. In certain cases (*e.g.*, Brewster's and Lawrence's warblers), hybrids may have their own names.
Immature	A bird that has not yet begun to breed, and often has not yet acquired adult plumage.
Inner wing	The part of the wing between the body and the wrist.
Introduced	Established by humans in an area outside the natural range.
Irruption	A large-scale movement into an area by a species that does not regularly occur there.
Juvenal plumage	The first covering of true feathers, usually of a somewhat looser texture than later plumages; the juvenal plumage, often brown and streaked, is usually replaced during the bird's first summer or fall.
Juvenile	A bird in juvenal plumage.
Lateral	Toward or at the side of the body.
Leading edge	The forward edge of the wing, composed of the lesser coverts, the alula, and the edge of the outermost primary; in flight, the surface that first meets the air.
Lesser wing coverts	The short feathers on the shoulder of the wing that are arranged in several irregular rows and cover the base of the median wing coverts.
Local	Of restricted occurrence within a larger, discontinuous range; birds with local distributions are often dependent on some uncommon habitat type.
Lore	The area between the eye and the base of the bill; sometimes distinctively colored.
Lower mandible	The lower of the two parts of a bird's bill.
Malar streak	*See* Mustache.
Mantle	The upper back and occasionally the scapulars and upperwing coverts when these are the same color as the upper back.
Mask	An area of contrasting color on the front of the face and around the eyes.

Maxilla	*See* Upper mandible.
Median	Situated in the middle or on the central axis.
Median crown stripe	A stripe of contrasting color along the center of the crown.
Median wing coverts	The row of short feathers that covers the bases of the greater wing coverts.
Melanistic	Having an excess of black pigment; melanistic birds are usually rare, but certain species have a high percentage of dark-phase individuals. *See* Color morph.
Migrant	A bird in the process of migrating between its breeding area and its winter range.
Migration	A regular, periodic movement between two regions, usually a breeding area and a wintering area.
Mirror	A translucent area on the extended wing of some birds, usually at the base of the primaries; in gulls, small white spots at or near the tips of the dark primaries.
Molt	The periodic loss and replacement of feathers; most species have regular patterns and schedules of molt.
Morph	*See* Color morph.
Morphology	The form and structure of an animal or plant.
Mustache	A colored streak running from the base of the bill back along the side of the throat.
Nape	The back of the head, including the hindneck.
Nares	The external nostrils; usually located near the base of the upper mandible; singular, naris.
Necklace	A band of spots or streaks across the breast or around the neck.
Neck ruff	Feathers of the neck that are enlarged or otherwise modified for display.
Nocturnal	Active during the night.
Outer wing	The part of the wing between the wrist and the tip.
Patagium	A membrane extending from the body to the wrist along the front of the wing, supporting many of the wing coverts.
Pectinate	Having short, narrow projections, like those of a comb.
Pelagic	Of or inhabiting the open ocean.
Permanent resident	A bird that remains in one area throughout the year; nonmigratory.
Phase	*See* Color morph.
Pinnae	*See* Ear tuft.
Plumage	Generally, the feathers worn by a bird at any given time. Specifically, all the feathers grown during a single molt; in this sense, a bird may have elements of more than one plumage at a time.
Plume	An elongated, ornamental feather, often used in displays.
Polyandrous	Mating with more than one male.
Polymorphic	Having two or more distinct types within a population, usually differing in size, form, or color.
Posterior	Toward the tail.
Postocular stripe	A stripe extending back from the eye, above the ear coverts and below the eyebrow.

Preen	To clean and smooth the plumage with the bill.
Primaries	The outermost and longest flight feathers on a bird's wing, forming the wing tip and part of the outer trailing edge; there are usually nine to twelve primaries on each wing, attached to the wing distal to the wrist.
Primary coverts	The small feathers of the wing that overlie the bases of the primaries.
Proximal	Toward the body. *Cf.* Distal.
Race	*See* Subspecies.
Rectrices	The long flight feathers of the tail; singular, rectrix.
Resident	Remaining in one place all year; nonmigratory.
Riparian	Pertaining to the banks of streams, rivers, ponds, lakes, or moist bottomlands.
Rump	The lower back just above the tail; may also include the uppertail coverts.
Scaly	Finely barred; the bars often formed by feather edgings of a different color.
Scapulars	The feathers of the upperparts at the side of the back that cover the area where the wing joins the body.
Secondaries	The large flight feathers of the inner wing, attached to the inner wing proximal to the wrist.
Sexual dimorphism	A difference between the sexes in size, form, or color.
Shaft	The stiff central axis of a feather.
Shoulder	The bend of the wing, or wrist, including the lesser wing coverts.
Side	The lateral part of the breast and belly.
Song	A specific and often complex pattern of notes, usually given only by the male during the breeding season. *Cf.* Call.
Spatulate	Spoon-shaped or shovel-shaped.
Spectacles	A color pattern formed by the lores and eye-rings.
Spishing	A squeaking or swishing noise made by some birders to attract birds into view.
Stray	A migrant found outside of its normal range.
Streaked	Having a pattern of vertical or longitudinal stripes, as opposed to horizontal bars; often formed by feather shafts that contrast with the rest of the feathers.
Subadult	A bird that has not yet acquired adult plumage.
Subspecies	A geographical subdivision of a species differing from other subdivisions in size, form, color, song, or several of these in combination; also called a race.
Subterminal	Before or short of the end or tip.
Summer resident	A bird that remains in an area during the summer but winters elsewhere.
Sympatric	Having overlapping ranges. *Cf.* Allopatric.
Talon	One of the long, sharp, curved claws of a bird of prey.
Tarsus	The lower, usually featherless, part of a bird's leg, often called simply the "leg."
Terminal	At the end or tip.

Territory	An area defended against other members of the same species, and usually containing a nest or food resource or both.
Tertials	The innermost secondaries (usually three), often with a different shape, pattern, and molt schedule from the other secondaries, and sometimes considered distinct from them; also called tertiaries.
Throat	The area of the underparts between the chin and the breast.
Trailing edge	The posterior edge of the extended wing, consisting of the tips of the primaries and secondaries.
Transient	A bird that occurs at a location only during migration between its winter and breeding ranges.
Underparts	The lower surface of the body, including the chin, throat, breast, belly, sides and flanks, and undertail coverts, and sometimes including the underwing surface and the under surface of the tail.
Undertail coverts	The small feathers that lie beneath and cover the bases of the tail feathers; sometimes referred to as the crissum.
Upper mandible	The uppermost of the two parts of a bird's bill; also called the maxilla.
Upperparts	The upper surface of the body, including the crown, nape, back, scapulars, rump, and uppertail coverts, and sometimes including the upperwing surface and the upper surface of the tail.
Uppertail coverts	The small feathers that lie over the bases of the tail feathers.
Vagrant	A bird occurring outside of its normal range, usually during or following migration.
Vane	One of the two broad, thin, flexible portions of a feather, separated by the shaft and composed of a row of barbs that are connected along the shaft; also called a web.
Ventral	Pertaining to the lower surface of the body.
Vermiculated	Marked by fine lines.
Web	The fleshy membrane that unites the toes of some water birds. *See also* Vane.
Window	A translucent area on the wing of certain birds that is visible from below on a bird in flight.
Wing bar	A stripe or bar of contrasting color on the upper surface of the wing, formed by the tips of one of the rows of wing coverts.
Wing lining	A collective term for the coverts of the underwing.
Wing stripe	A conspicuous lengthwise stripe on the upper surface of the extended wing, often formed by the pale bases of the primaries and secondaries.
Winter plumage	The plumage worn by a bird during the nonbreeding season; often duller than the breeding plumage and usually acquired by a complete molt in the fall.
Winter range	The geographic area occupied by a species during the winter or nonbreeding season.
Wrist	The forward-projecting angle or bend of the wing; also called the carpal joint.

The Authors

Davis W. Finch and Paul Lehman each reviewed some or all of the species accounts; Paul Lehman also read and commented on some of the special essays.

Henry T. Armistead,
a Philadelphia librarian, became interested in birds in 1949 when he was nine. He is a regional editor of *American Birds*, book review editor of *Birding*, and compiles the Cape Charles, Virginia, Christmas bird count. His special interests include birds of the Delmarva Peninsula, colonial water birds of the Chesapeake Bay, mist-netting fall land birds, May birding marathons, and collecting books. On his family's farm in Bellevue, Maryland, Armistead has seen 240 species of birds.

Larry R. Ballard
has served as a consultant for a variety of publications on the identification and distribution of western birds, including *Birding* and *American Birds*. He has also acted as consultant to the Santa Barbara Museum of Natural History, Santa Barbara City College, and the University of California. Currently working as a communications expediter in Santa Barbara, he spends about four hours a day in the field.

George F. Barrowclough
has done biochemical and population genetic research on problems of geographic variation and speciation of juncos, wood warblers, and other groups of birds. His studies have entailed extensive field work in the western United States and Canada. Barrowclough is currently assistant curator of ornithology at the American Museum of Natural History in New York City.

Louis R. Bevier
has been actively watching birds in California for 14 years. During the past five years, he has served as a field assistant and consultant for various research projects, environmental impact reports, and publications about birds. Currently, he is an undergraduate in environmental biology at the University of California at Santa Barbara.

Peter F. Cannell
graduated from Bowdoin College in 1977. After working at the Manomet Bird Observatory, he enrolled in a doctoral program at the American Museum of Natural History and the City University of New York. Cannell's doctorate work has concentrated on the systematics of the "pre-passerines," based on the anatomy of the syrinx. During 1979 and 1980, he served as acting director of Bowdoin's Kent Island ornithological research station in the Bay of Fundy. Cannell's field research has included such topics as molt, migration, seabirds, and the genera *Corvus* and *Empidonax*.

David F. DeSante
is the Landbird Biologist for the Point Reyes Bird Observatory. His current research interests include the population dynamics of California coastal scrub land birds, the stability of Sierran subalpine bird communities, and the occurrence of land birds on the Farallon Islands, a location renowned for the large number of vagrant birds it attracts. DeSante's doctoral work dealt with mirror-image misorientation in vagrant wood warblers.

Kim R. Eckert
lives in Duluth, Minnesota, where he has done extensive field work. The author of numerous articles for *The Loon, Birding*, and *American Birds*, he has also written *A Birder's Guide to Minnesota*.

Eckert has been a regional editor of *American Birds* magazine, and is currently a member of the Minnesota Ornithological Records Committee, and a naturalist of the Hawk Ridge Nature Reserve in Duluth. In addition, he has led bird tours in Minnesota and the Dakotas and taught bird identification classes.

John Farrand, Jr.,
is natural science editor at Chanticleer Press and an associate in the department of ornithology at the American Museum of Natural History. Co-author of *The Audubon Society Field Guide to North American Birds (Eastern Region)* and a past president of the Linnaean Society of New York, he has watched birds in most of North America, as well as in Central and South America, Europe, and East Africa. Farrand lives in New York City, and makes frequent forays into the surrounding countryside.

Davis W. Finch
lives in East Kingston, New Hampshire. Interested in birds since childhood, he has studied them in virtually all parts of North America including the Arctic, as well as in Europe and Central and South America. He is a founder and director of WINGS, Inc., a company that conducts bird-watching tours in many parts of the world.

Kimball L. Garrett
is currently an ornithologist with the Los Angeles County Museum of Natural History. He has had extensive field experience throughout western North America, and has led ornithological tours in California, Arizona, Texas, and Mexico. In addition, he teaches regular bird identification workshops for the extension program of the University of California at Los Angeles. With Jon Dunn, he has written numerous papers on bird identification for the Los Angeles Audubon Society newsletter, *The Western Tanager,* as well as *Birds of Southern California: Status and Distribution.*

Daniel D. Gibson
works at the University of Alaska Museum in Fairbanks, Alaska. He has studied the status and distribution of Alaska's birds for almost 20 years. Gibson's particular interests are the Palearctic and Aleutian components of Alaska's avifauna, their routes of migration, and their geographic variation.

Richard E. Johnson
is director of the Charles R. Conner Vertebrate Museum at Washington State University, where he is also an associate professor of zoology. A former editor of *The Murrelet,* he is a specialist on the systematics of Rosy Finches and the ecology and distribution of alpine birds and plants in western North America.

Kenn Kaufman
spent his teens birding throughout North America and Mexico. Now living in Tucson, Arizona, he continues to travel extensively as a leader of birding tours. He has served as editor of *Continental Birdlife,* and has been a regional editor for *American Birds* and a field identification consultant for *Birding.*

Ben King
is the world's foremost authority on the identification of Asian birds. The author of *A Field Guide to the Birds of South-East Asia,* he is currently writing *A Field Identification Handbook to the Birds of the Indian Region.* He has observed over 1,700 species of birds in Asia—more than anyone else—and has a North American life list that exceeds 700. In recognition of his birding exploration in Asia, King has been elected a corresponding member of the Explorer's Club and a fellow of the Royal Geographic Society.

Wesley E. Lanyon
has been on the staff of the American Museum of Natural History
for 26 years, where he is now Lamont Curator of Birds. He is a
recipient of the Brewster Memorial Award from the American
Ornithologists' Union and has served as president of that society.
He specializes in a museum and field approach to the identification
and specific limits of "problem birds"; his studies of meadowlarks
and tyrant-flycatchers have taken him throughout the Americas.

Paul Lehman
is a resident of Santa Barbara, California. His major interests are
bird distribution and field identification. He received a master's
degree in physical geography in 1982, and is currently a part-time
instructor of geography and environmental studies. He also teaches
bird classes to adults. Lehman spends most of his time birding.

Dennis J. Martin
received his bachelor's degree from Illinois State University and did
graduate research at the University of New Mexico before obtaining
his doctorate from Utah State University. His early research
concentrated on owl behavior; over the past decade he has studied
general behavioral ecology and vocal behavior, focusing primarily on
the Fox Sparrow. Martin recently retired as editor of *The Murrelet*,
and is currently an associate professor of biology at Pacific Lutheran
University in Takoma, Washington.

Harold F. Mayfield
is a retired businessman who has pursued a lifelong interest in birds.
He has published more than 100 articles in ornithological journals
and is the author of a comprehensive report on Kirtland's Warbler.
His field work has taken him on numerous trips to the tropics; in
addition, he has a special interest in birds of the Arctic region.
Mayfield lives in Waterville, Ohio.

Kenneth C. Parkes
is Curator of Birds at the Carnegie Museum of Natural History in
Pittsburgh. He formerly lived in New York City and in Ithaca, New
York. Parkes has traveled extensively in North America on birding
trips; his field work has also taken him to the West Indies, Trinidad,
Ecuador, Argentina, the Galapagos, and the Canary Islands,
western Europe, Kenya, the Seychelles, and the Philippines. His
research interests include taxonomy, molts, and plumages, with a
special focus on plumage characteristics used in determining the age
and sex of birds.

Roger F. Pasquier
works at the Smithsonian Institution as executive assistant to the
president of the International Council for Bird Preservation. He was
formerly with the department of ornithology at the American
Museum of Natural History in New York City. Pasquier has
contributed articles on birds and their conservation to numerous
magazines, and is the author of *Watching Birds: An Introduction to
Ornithology*.

Wayne R. Petersen,
a resident of Massachusetts, has been an avid ornithologist for more
than 25 years. His travels have taken him from Arctic Canada to
South America and the West Indies. An active bird bander,
Petersen is affiliated with the Manomet Bird Observatory and has
worked in James Bay with the Canadian Wildlife Service, and as an
Earthwatch investigator in Belize. In addition to his biology classes,
he teaches bird identification courses, lectures extensively, and has
published many papers on various aspects of ornithology. Petersen
has served on the Council of the Northeastern Bird-Banding
Association and as president of the Nuttall Ornithological Club.

H. Douglas Pratt
is a freelance wildlife artist and a research associate at the Museum of Zoology at Louisiana State University. For his master's thesis, he studied grackles in southwest Louisiana, and for his doctoral dissertation in zoology he researched the systematics of birds native to Hawaii. He has studied birds throughout Polynesia and Micronesia, as well as Hawaii, and is preparing a field guide to birds of that region. His work has been widely published in both technical and popular periodicals.

J. V. Remsen, Jr.,
received his doctorate in zoology from the University of California at Berkeley in 1978. Since then he has been employed at Louisiana State University as an associate professor of zoology and as curator of birds for its Museum of Zoology. Although his primary area of research is Neotropical ornithology, among his more than 40 publications are nine that address field identification and distribution problems in North American birds.

David Stirling
is a natural history specialist for the Parks of British Columbia, and is interested in the identification, population dynamics, and worldwide preservation problems of birds. An avid birder, he has led nature tours and made bird-watching trips to 35 countries. Recently, he has been involved in field work with the Northwestern Crow and Crested Myna.

Paul W. Sykes, Jr.,
is a wildlife research biologist with the Patuxent Wildlife Research Center of the U.S. Fish and Wildlife Service in Maryland. Involved in various national and state ornithological societies, Sykes is a regional Christmas count editor for *American Birds* and a member of the American Birding Association checklist committee. He is also a cooperator for three U.S. Fish and Wildlife Service Cooperative Breeding Bird Survey routes in Florida, and serves as a technical and scientific consultant to federal agencies and several conservation organizations. He has seen 746 species to date in North America north of Mexico.

Scott B. Terrill
has been birding since he was ten years old. While working on his bachelor's degree in zoology at Arizona State University, he, along with others, pioneered systematic vagrant hunting and investigated the distribution of the birds of Arizona. In addition, he became involved in ecological research and environmental impact studies while completing his master's degree in zoology. Currently, Terrill is enrolled in the doctoral program at the State University of New York at Albany. His research concerns the behavioral and ecological factors involved in bird migration. He shares his birding enthusiasm with his wife, Linda, with whom he has made birding trips as far south as the Guatemalan border.

Theodore G. Tobish Jr.
was born and raised in eastern Pennsylvania. He has had a lifelong interest in birds. Since 1973, he has lived in Alaska, where he received a bachelor's degree in biology from the University of Alaska. He has spent several field seasons in the Aleutian Islands and throughout Alaska, working for the U.S. Fish and Wildlife Service and leading bird tours. Tobish currently lives in Anchorage.

Jack Van Benthuysen
is president of an electrical engineering consulting company in St. Louis, Missouri. He is also president of the St. Louis Audubon Society and a regular contributor to *American Birds*. An amateur birder for more than 40 years, Van Benthuysen has kept a watchful

and concerned eye on the status of the Eurasian Tree Sparrow, an introduced species that offers a good opportunity for the study of the two contrasting members of the Old World sparrow family.

Peter D. Vickery
is on the staff of the Natural History Tour Services of the Massachusetts Audubon Society, and has traveled extensively throughout North America, Mexico, and Costa Rica. For six years, he was regional editor of the northeastern Maritime region for *American Birds*. Vickery is the author of the *Annotated Checklist of Maine Birds* and is now conducting further investigations into Maine's avifauna.

Richard Webster,
a lifelong resident of southern California, has been an avid birder since childhood. He has traveled extensively throughout the United States and has visited Mexico, Honduras, Colombia, Venezuela, Ecuador, Australia, and New Zealand on bird-watching and photography trips. Webster is co-author of *The Birds of Santa Barbara and Ventura Counties, California*.

Claudia Wilds
is a research collaborator in the division of birds at the National Museum of Natural History; she is also the field identification editor of *Birding* magazine. Wilds lives in Washington, D.C., and has recently published a guide to finding birds in and around the nation's capital. Most of her field work during the past decade has been at Chincoteague National Wildlife Refuge on the Virginia coast, where she has made an intensive study of shorebird migration.

The Artists

As art editor, Al Gilbert selected the artists who were called upon to provide color portraits and black-and-white illustrations. After assigning the pictures, he supervised their accuracy and production until completion.
Guy Tudor served as art consultant, making his knowledge of bird art and photographic sources available to the artists.

James E. Coe
has exhibited his bird paintings at the Leigh Yawkey Woodson Art Museum in Wausau, Wisconsin, and at the Cleveland Museum of Natural History in Ohio. His drawings have appeared in *The Living Bird* ànd *American Birds* magazines. Coe majored in biology at Harvard University, and is currently a graduate student in painting at Parsons School of Design in New York. His field work has been concentrated in New York and southern New England, with occasional forays into the Neotropics. Most recently, he completed illustrations for a guide to the birds of New Guinea.

Michael DiGiorgio
is a freelance artist living in Potsdam, New York. He enjoys field sketching and painting from life. His illustrations have been published by the National Wildlife Federation, the New York State *Conservationist*, the Cornell Laboratory of Ornithology, the Massachusetts Audubon Society, and the Nature Conservancy. He also illustrated the book *A Life Outdoors*.

Al Gilbert
began drawing birds and animals when he was a child. In his teens, he received advice and guidance from George M. Sutton and Don Eckelberry, who helped launch his career as a wildlife artist. Working closely with Dean Amadon of the American Museum of Natural History in New York City, he has illustrated many books, among them *Eagles, Hawks and Falcons of the World* and *Currassows and Related Birds*. His field work has taken him to Africa, Madagascar, Mexico, and South America. In 1978, Gilbert won the Federal Duck Stamp Competition. His paintings have been exhibited in museums and galleries throughout the United States, and he is currently president of the Society of Animal Artists.

Robert Gillmor
is a British freelance artist who received his training at the Fine Art Department of Reading University in England. He is currently chairman of the Society of Wildlife Artists, which he helped to found. His illustrations have appeared in 70 books, as well as numerous journals, and he has exhibited work in the United States, Kenya, France, and the United Kingdom. Gillmor is art editor of *Birds of the Western Palaearctic*, and a vice president of the British Ornithologists' Union. His travels have taken him to Spitsbergen, Iceland, the United States, and East Africa.

H. Jon Janosik
attended Oberlin College, where he studied zoology and anatomy. His ornithological illustrations have appeared in such publications as the *Encyclopaedia Britannica* and the *Florida Naturalist*. In addition, he has worked for the National Geographic Society, the Carnegie Museum in Pittsburgh, and the Saunders Company in Philadelphia. Janosik's work has been exhibited at numerous institutions, including the British Museum in London and the Los Angeles County Museum. His special interests lie in North American warblers and sea and shore birds.

Lawrence B. McQueen
first became interested in birds in his native town in central

Pennsylvania. He received his bachelor's degree in wildlife studies from Idaho State University in 1961, and went on to conduct field work on the birds of Idaho. He later attended art school at the University of Oregon, Eugene, where he now lives and specializes in ornithological paintings. His work has been exhibited at the Smithsonian Institution, and in England and Scotland. Currently he is doing field work in Peru.

John P. O'Neill
is a professional ornithologist and artist with a special interest in Neotropical birds. He served as the director of the Louisiana State University Museum of Natural Science from 1978 to 1982, and is currently acting as the university's coordinator of field studies. O'Neill lives in Baton Rouge, Louisiana, where he continues to research and paint birds.

Paul Singer
is a graphic designer who lives in Brooklyn. A graduate of the Philadelphia College of Art, he has designed exhibits for the Bronx Zoo, the New York Aquarium, the Franklin Park Zoo, the American Numismatic Society, and the Little League Baseball Museum. His work appears in more than 30 books, including the *Audubon Society Encyclopedia of North American Birds*.

Guy Tudor
is a resident of Forest Hills, New York, and has been a freelance wildlife illustrator for 25 years. With extensive field experience in 11 Neotropical countries, he has contributed illustrations to guides on the birds of Venezuela and Colombia. He is currently co-authoring a *Field Guide to South American Birds: Passerines*. His work has appeared in a variety of publications and has been exhibited at the Chicago Field Museum and the National Collection of Fine Arts. Tudor has co-authored articles for *American Birds, Birding,* and the *Wilson Bulletin,* and currently serves as a trustee of R.A.R.E., Inc., and as an elective member of the American Ornithologists' Union and the American Birding Association.

John C. Yrizarry
is a lifelong resident of Brooklyn, New York. He is a graduate of the Yale School of Fine Arts and a member of the Society of Animal Artists. His work appears in private collections and has been published in numerous books and magazines, including many nature guides. Yrizarry is an enthusiastic leader of birding tours in the United States, Central America, and the Caribbean.

Dale A. Zimmerman
teaches ornithology at Western New Mexico University in Silver City and serves as an elective member of the American Ornithologists' Union and as a fellow of the Explorers' Club. He travels frequently to his favorite African haunts, and has made birding visits to tropical Asia, Australasia, and the Neotropics. A former student of the late George M. Sutton, Zimmerman is chief artist and co-author of a forthcoming field guide to New Guinea birds. He is currently illustrating Ben King's comprehensive handbook to the birds of the Indian region.

Credits

Photo Credits
The letter immediately following each page number refers to the positions of the color photographs on the page; A represents the picture at the top, B, the middle, and C, the bottom.

Ardea London: J. B. Bottomley, 349B; G. K. Brown, 79A; S. Roberts, 35C; R. T. Smith, 351C; Richard Vaughan, 43C, 95A; Wolfgang Wagner, 351A.
Ron Austing: 39B, 47B, 97B, 103A, 105B, 135A, 157A, 163C, 169C, 195C, 209A, 295A.
Stephen F. Bailey: 73B.
David E. Baker: 143B, 179B, 179C.
William J. Bolte: 189B.
S. R. Cannings: 331C.
Ken Carmichael: 111B, 113A, 153C, 289B.
Robert P. Carr: 231C.
Roger B. Clapp: 93C.
Herbert Clarke: 47C, 55A, 71B, 99A, 119B, 119C, 137B, 141B, 141C, 175B, 183C, 185C, 197C, 207B, 209B, 223C, 237A, 239C, 249A, 251C, 265B, 265C, 269B, 273C, 297A, 297B, 311B, 321A.
Bruce Coleman, Inc.: E. Duscher, 351B; Edgar T. Jones, 173B, 173C, 175A, 255C; John Shaw, 67A.
Cornell Laboratory of Ornithology: 205B; Betty Darling Cottrille, 151B; John S. Dunning, 107C, 165A, 167B, 211A, 213C; Bill Dyer, 151C, 241C; Michael Hopiak, 55C, 103B, 143C, 167A; Chandler S. Robbins, 173A; M. and B. Schwarzschild, 235A; Gary Shackelford, 99B, 215A; Mary Tremaine, 253B; Frederick K. Truslow, 163B; J. Weissinger, 105C.
Betty Darling Cottrille: 159B, 159C, 171C.
Kent and Donna Dannen: 271C, 325A, 327A.
Harry N. Darrow: 79C, 85B, 247C, 285B, 337C, 339A.
Thomas H. Davis: 301B.
J. H. Dick: 109C.
Adrian J. Dignan: 37A, 133B.
Larry R. Ditto: 59B.
Georges Dremeaux: 137A, 163A, 281C.
DRK Photo: Stephen J. Krasemann, 347B; Wayne Lankinen, 243A, 273A, 303C, 307C, 331A, 335A, 335C, 345A.
Jacob Faust: 165B.
Kenneth W. Fink: 45A, 49C, 51A, 59C, 69B, 233B, 279C, 299B, 299C, 301A, 319A, 319B, 331B, 333C.
Jeff Foott: 155A, 223B.
N. R. French: 325C.
John Gerlach: 289C.
James M. Greaves: 39A, 103C, 141A, 179A, 293B.
William D. Griffin: 273B.
Joseph A. Grzybowski: 241A.
James Hawkings: 89B, 347A.
F. Eugene Hester: 267C.
Michael Hopiak: 37B, 107A.
Warren Jacobi: 263B, 349C.
Gord James: 47A, 115C, 127C.
Joseph R. Jehl, Jr.: 281B, 307A.
Isidor Jeklin: 67B, 115B, 129B, 129C, 177C, 211B, 345B.
R. Y. Kaufman/Yogi, Inc.: 301C, 333B.
Steven C. Kaufman: 75B.
G. C. Kelley: 213B, 217B, 315B.
E. F. Knights: 65B, 227A, 227B, 275B.
Wayne Lankinen: 85A, 231B, 267B, 269C, 327B, 327C, 335B, 337A, 339C.

Linnea Associates: Bud Lehnhausen, 279A.
Thomas W. Martin: 93B, 125C, 131C, 135B, 147A, 151A, 153B, 155B, 157B, 157C, 161B, 197A, 203A, 205A, 205C, 211C, 215B, 215C, 219C, 233A, 235B, 237C, 253A, 271A, 271B, 291A, 291B, 291C, 293C, 297C, 309B, 317A, 317B, 317C, 329B, 329C.
Virginia Mayfield: 221A, 261B.
Joe McDonald: 201C.
Anthony Mercieca: 41A, 49A, 55B, 61B, 69A, 69C, 139C, 195B, 199A, 199B, 201B, 207A, 209C, 233C, 243B, 341B, 341C.
Minnesota Ornithologists' Union: Betty Darling Cottrille, 171B; Warren Nelson, 337B, 339B.
C. Allan Morgan: 195A.
National Audubon Society Collection/Photo Researchers, Inc.: Bob and Elsie Boggs, 175C, 183B; John Bova, 249B; Townsend P. Dickinson, 303A; John S. Dunning, 113B, 167C; Bill Dyer, 125B, 181C; H. F. Flanders, 305C; David O. Hill, 325B; Thomas W. Martin, 133A; Karl H. Maslowski, 169A; Charles Ott, 87C; Kirtley Perkins, 207C; O. S. Pettingill, Jr., 277A; Sandy Sprunt, 189C; Dan Sudia, 309A; Patricia B. Witherspoon, 247B.
J. Oldenettel: 79B, 87B.
Arthur Panzer: 315C.
James F. Parnell: 153A, 257B, 259B.
Wayne R. Petersen: 251A.
John C. Pitcher: 263C.
Rod Planck: 53A, 165C, 345C.
Betty Randall: 321C.
James Rathert: 225C, 257C.
J. Van Remsen: 245C.
David G. Roseneau: 287A.
Leonard Lee Rue, III: 341A.
John Shaw: 303B.
Ervio Sian: 61A, 81A, 95C, 161C, 245B, 281A, 287B.
Perry D. Slocum: 193C, 313C.
Arnold Small: 81B, 81C, 91B, 101C, 117C, 119A, 127B, 135C, 137C, 139A, 147B, 181A, 181B, 203B, 203C, 223A, 249C, 261C, 265A, 279B, 293A, 295C, 307B, 309C, 311A, 329A, 343B, 343C.
Alvin E. Staffan: 63B, 161A, 169B, 171A, 177B, 183A, 267A.
Paul W. Sykes, Jr.: 259C.
Alice K. Taylor: 67C.
John Trott: 53B, 115A, 117A, 121A, 131B, 145C, 155C, 197B.
Rob Tucher: 131A.
Sandy Upson: 229A.
R. Van Nostrand: 63C, 333A.
VIREO (Academy of Natural Sciences of Philadelphia): K. Brink, 45B, 45C, 285C; Allan Cruickshank, 283B; Helen Cruickshank, 229C, 269A, 299A.
Wardene Weisser: 39C, 65A, 221B, 241B, 243C, 295B, 305B, 319C, 321B.
Larry West: 133C.
Burdette E. White: 49B, 91A.
Jack Wilburn: 71A, 83B, 89C, 123C, 255A.
Ron Willocks: 53C, 117B.
Dick Wood: 263A.
Dale and Marian Zimmerman: 37C, 51B, 121B, 177A, 193B, 219B, 221C, 237B, 275A, 275C.

Black-and-white Drawings
The letter immediately following each page number refers to the position of an illustration: A represents the drawing or portrait at the top of a page, B, the middle, and C, the bottom.

James E. Coe: 62B, 90A, 92B, 218A, 240A.

Michael DiGiorgio: 44A, 86B, 246A, 246B, 272A, 276A, 278A, 280A, 280B, 292A.
H. Jon Janosik: 108B, 162A, 166A, 168A, 170A, 172A, 174A.
Lawrence B. McQueen: 38A, 38B, 40A.
Paul Singer: 34A, 62A, 74A, 82A, 86A, 88A, 92A, 96A, 108A, 188A, 190A, 200A, 216A, 288A, 322A, 348A.

Color Portraits

The letter immediately following each page number refers to the position of an illustration: A represents the drawing or portrait at the top of a page, B, the middle, and C, the bottom.

James E. Coe: 73A, 75C, 83C, 97C, 101A, 101B, 107B, 239A, 261A, 283A, 305A, 313B, 343A.
Al Gilbert: 113C, 143A, 145B, 147C, 149C, 187A.
Robert Gillmor: 77A, 77B, 77C, 283C, 285A, 323B, 323C.
H. Jon Janosik: 51C, 111A, 111C, 121C, 123A, 123B, 125A, 129A, 139B, 145A, 149A, 149B, 159A, 185A, 185B, 187B, 187C, 219A.
Lawrence B. McQueen: 41B, 41C, 57A, 57B, 57C, 59A, 105A, 227C, 235C, 245A, 253C, 255B, 257A, 277B, 277C, 315A.
John P. O'Neill: 191B, 191C, 193A.
John C. Yrizarry: 65C, 127A, 225A, 225B, 247A, 259A, 311C, 313A.
Dale A. Zimmerman: 43A, 43B, 95B, 213A, 229B, 231A, 239B, 251B.

Comprehensive Index

In this index, the names of orders are preceded by red dots; family and subfamily names are preceded by blue dots. The volume in which an entry appears is indicated by parentheses.

Ruby-throated, (II) 204
Rufous, (II) 212
Violet-crowned, (II) 198
White-eared, (II) 196

Hydrobates pelagicus, (I) 417

• Hydrobatidae, (I) 70

Hylocharis leucotis, (II) 196

Hylocichla mustelina, (III) 54

I

Ibis
Glossy, (I) 124
Scarlet, (I) 418
White, (I) 122
White-faced, (I) 124

Icteria virens, (III) 184

• Icterinae, (III) 288

Icterus
cucullatus, (III) 308
galbula bullockii, (III) 318
galbula galbula, (III) 316
graduacauda, (III) 314
gularis, (III) 314
parisorum, (III) 320
pectoralis, (III) 312
pustulatus, (III) 310
spurius, (III) 308
wagleri, (III) 358

Ictinia mississippiensis, (I) 222

Ixobrychus exilis, (I) 108

Ixoreus naevius, (III) 60

J

Jabiru, (I) 418

Jabiru mycteria, (I) 418

Jacana, Northern, (I) 340

Jacana spinosa, (I) 340

• Jacanidae, (I) 340

Jaeger
Long-tailed, (II) 38
Parasitic, (II) 38
Pomarine, (II) 36

Jay
Blue, (II) 310
Brown, (II) 312
Gray, (II) 308
Gray-breasted, (II) 314
Green, (II) 312
Pinyon, (II) 314
Scrub, (II) 314
Steller's, (II) 310

Junco
Dark-eyed, (III) 272
"Gray-headed," (III) 272
"Oregon," (III) 272
"Pink-sided," (III) 272
"Slate-colored," (III) 272
"White-winged," (III) 272
Yellow-eyed, (III) 274

Junco
hyemalis, (III) 272
phaeonotus, (III) 274

Jynx torquilla, (II) 363

K

Kestrel
American, (I) 256
Eurasian, (I) 420

Killdeer, (I) 328

Kingbird
Cassin's, (II) 284
Couch's, (II) 284
Eastern, (II) 288
Gray, (II) 288
Loggerhead, (II) 364
Thick-billed, (II) 286
Tropical, (II) 282
Western, (II) 286

Kingfisher
Belted, (II) 216
Green, (II) 218
Ringed, (II) 216

Kinglet
Golden-crowned, (III) 36
Ruby-crowned, (III) 36

Kiskadee, Great, (II) 280

Kite
American Swallow-tailed, (I) 218
Black-shouldered, (I) 220
Hook-billed, (I) 218
Mississippi, (I) 222
Snail, (I) 220

Kittiwake
Black-legged, (II) 76
Red-legged, (II) 78

Knot
Great, (I) 422
Red, (I) 372

L

Lagopus
lagopus, (I) 276
leucurus, (I) 280
mutus, (I) 278

Lampornis clemenciae, (II) 200

• Laniidae, (III) 88

Lanius
cristatus, (III) 356
excubitor, (III) 88
ludovicianus, (III) 90

Lapwing, Northern, (I) 316

• Laridae, (II) 36

Lark, Horned, (II) 296

Larus
argentatus, (II) 58
atricilla, (II) 42
californicus, (II) 56
canus, (II) 52

Index

In this index, the names of orders are preceded by red dots; family
and subfamily names are preceded by blue dots.

Chanticleer Staff

Publisher: Paul Steiner
Editor-in-Chief: Gudrun Buettner
Managing Editor: Susan Costello
Natural Science Editor: John Farrand, Jr.
Project Editor: Ann Whitman
Senior Editor: Mary Beth Brewer
Editorial Assistants: Karel Birnbaum, Katherine Booz
Production: Helga Lose, Amy Roche
Art Director: Carol Nehring
Art Assistants: Ayn Svoboda, Karen Wollman
Picture Library: Edward Douglas, Dana Pomfret
Range Maps: Paul Singer
Design: Massimo Vignelli